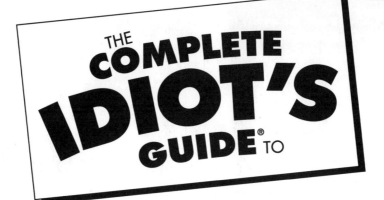

Winning
Customer Loyalty

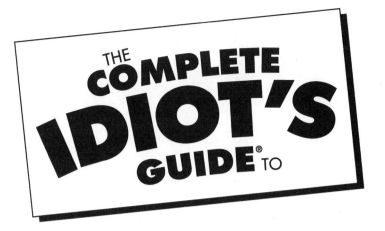

Winning
Customer Loyalty

by Murray Raphel, Neil Raphel,
and Janis S. Raye

ALPHA

A member of Penguin Group (USA) Inc.

To Ruth Raphel
Wife, Mother, Mother-in-Law, editor, and friend.

ALPHA BOOKS

Published by the Penguin Group

Penguin Group (USA) Inc., 375 Hudson Street, New York, New York 10014, U.S.A.

Penguin Group (Canada), 10 Alcorn Avenue, Toronto, Ontario, Canada M4V 3B2 (a division of Pearson Penguin Canada Inc.)

Penguin Books Ltd, 80 Strand, London WC2R 0RL, England

Penguin Ireland, 25 St Stephen's Green, Dublin 2, Ireland (a division of Penguin Books Ltd)

Penguin Group (Australia), 250 Camberwell Road, Camberwell, Victoria 3124, Australia (a division of Pearson Australia Group Pty Ltd)

Penguin Books India Pvt Ltd, 11 Community Centre, Panchsheel Park, New Delhi—110 017, India

Penguin Group (NZ), cnr Airborne and Rosedale Roads, Albany, Auckland 1310, New Zealand (a division of Pearson New Zealand Ltd)

Penguin Books (South Africa) (Pty) Ltd, 24 Sturdee Avenue, Rosebank, Johannesburg 2196, South Africa

Penguin Books Ltd, Registered Offices: 80 Strand, London WC2R 0RL, England

International Standard Book Number: 1-59257-383-5
Library of Congress Catalog Card Number: 2005925280

07 06 05   8 7 6 5 4 3 2 1

Interpretation of the printing code: The rightmost number of the first series of numbers is the year of the book's printing; the rightmost number of the second series of numbers is the number of the book's printing. For example, a printing code of 05-1 shows that the first printing occurred in 2005.

Printed in the United States of America

Note: This publication contains the opinions and ideas of its authors. It is intended to provide helpful and informative material on the subject matter covered. It is sold with the understanding that the authors and publisher are not engaged in rendering professional services in the book. If the reader requires personal assistance or advice, a competent professional should be consulted.

The authors and publisher specifically disclaim any responsibility for any liability, loss, or risk, personal or otherwise, which is incurred as a consequence, directly or indirectly, of the use and application of any of the contents of this book.

Most Alpha books are available at special quantity discounts for bulk purchases for sales promotions, premiums, fund-raising, or educational use. Special books, or book excerpts, can also be created to fit specific needs.

For details, write: Special Markets, Alpha Books, 375 Hudson Street, New York, NY 10014.

Publisher: *Marie Butler-Knight*
Product Manager: *Phil Kitchel*
Senior Managing Editor: *Jennifer Bowles*
Senior Acquisitions Editor: *Mike Sanders*
Development Editor: *Nancy D. Lewis*
Senior Production Editor: *Billy Fields*
Copy Editor: *Jan Zoya*
Cartoonist: *Richard King*
Cover/Book Designer: *Trina Wurst*
Indexer: *Brad Herriman*
Layout: *Ayanna Lacey*
Proofreading: *Mary Hunt*

Contents at a Glance

Contents

Appendixes

Foreword

Our mission at IGA is a simple one: we must win the loyalty of each of our customers every day we are in business. That is what makes *The Complete Idiot's Guide to Winning Customer Loyalty* such an important book for our company and for every business-person.

This book presents the philosophy and techniques of customer loyalty. It shows you how to bring your customers to the top of the "loyalty ladder." It also explains the database techniques many businesses use in their loyalty programs to motivate their customers to return. And last, but not least, I am glad that it stresses the importance of employees, who I strongly believe are a business' first line of creating customer loyalty.

At IGA, we consider ourselves to be a family made up of our stores, our employees, our suppliers, and our customers. We use the phrase "Hometown Proud" to describe our company, and we encourage each of our independent retailers to become involved in their community: by supporting local charities and community events, by hiring and promoting local personnel, by buying and featuring local produce as well as national brands from our supplier partners. We believe the family metaphor best describes our business: everyone working together for a common goal.

The authors of *The Complete Idiot's Guide to Winning Customer Loyalty* are also a family. The co-authors of the book are Murray Raphel, Neil Raphel, and Janis Raye. Neil is Murray's son and Neil is married to Janis.

The Raphel family has strong connections to the IGA family. Murray was the keynote speaker at our annual IGA conferences for many years. In addition, the Raphels have helped IGA in many marketing projects. They remain valuable advisors because they never moved far from their own experience as retailers in earlier years. They are authentic, not theorists.

In *The Complete Idiot's Guide to Winning Customer Loyalty*, Murray, Neil, and Janis show how small businesses can succeed through developing customer loyalty. They give practical advice, anecdotes, and statistics to show the best loyalty marketing strategy for your business.

When the Raphels give a seminar on loyalty marketing, they always tell the audience, "Find out what customers want and give it to them." They stress that you must find, capture and, most importantly, keep your customers. They believe that your current customers are far more valuable to you than potential new customers. They give you ideas, through detailed examples, on how to create a business where the customer always comes first.

If you can make your business one in which the care of your customers is your number one priority, you are on your way to success. So follow the precepts of customer loyalty in the book. The Raphels will applaud your efforts. Your customers will applaud the results!

Dr. Thomas Haggai
Chairman and CEO, IGA Supermarkets

Introduction

A huge granite stone greets visitors to Stew Leonard's supermarket in Greenwich, Connecticut. This store, according to the Guinness Book of World Records, does more business per square foot than any other retail store in the world.

On the granite stone are inscribed two rules:

Rule #1: The Customer Is Always Right.

Rule #2: If the Customer Is Wrong, Re-read Rule #1.

This way of thinking about your customers was given a slight twist by Don Gallegos, once the president of King Soopers Supermarket and now a consultant, author, and speaker. "The customer," says Gallegos, "is not always right, but she is always your customer."

We believe that. No matter how many complaints a customer may have, no matter how unreasonable a customer may seem, she is your customer and it is your task to please her.

Every day, every business must strive to find, capture, and keep customers.

You *find* customers by advertising your products and services to your market area.

You *capture* customers by having great products, services, and selection.

You *keep* customers by communicating with all your customers and rewarding your best customers.

Having a customer-centric philosophy will help your business to succeed.

Most businesses spend five times as much money on trying to find new customers as they spend on keeping the customers they have. Yet, study after study has shown that keeping your existing customer base happy and coming back again and again is far less costly and more rewarding than looking for new customers.

This book will give you the techniques necessary to win your customers' loyalty. We hope that your business will profit when you include new ways to build loyalty.

Here is a quick overview of what you will learn in this book:

Part 1, "How Your Business Prospers by Winning Customer Loyalty," focuses on the basics of customer loyalty. It explains why customers leave your business, and it gives you techniques for making sure your best customers come back. It also introduces the type of advertising strategies that will help you win customer loyalty.

Part 2, "Profiting from the Loyalty Ladder," uses an image of customers climbing a "loyalty ladder" to detail the progression of customer attitudes toward your business. All customers start on the bottom rung of the loyalty ladder as prospects—people who have heard about your business but have never bought anything from you. At the top of the loyalty ladder are advocates—people who tell everybody they meet how wonderful your business is. This section shows you how to move prospects all the way up the loyalty ladder until they become advocates for your business.

Part 3, "Making Loyalty Marketing Work Every Day," gives you techniques to use in your own business. It starts with making sure your employees are happy. You cannot win customer loyalty unless your employees are committed to your business and your customers. Then you have to listen to your customers to sell them the products or services they need. You will also learn how to brand your business to create a positive identity in the minds of your customers.

Part 4, "Putting Together a Loyalty Program for Your Customers," explains how to use customer information to create a loyalty program that enhances your business. There are many examples of loyalty programs currently being used and a discussion of the benefits and potential risks of the programs. You will see how and why loyalty programs can help you keep your very best customers.

Part 5, "Putting It All Together," helps you plan the future of your loyalty-marketing efforts. This section discusses potential problems inherent in loyalty programs, including privacy concerns of customers. You will see how large and small businesses win their customers' loyalty and how you can partner with other businesses in a loyalty program. You will learn how the Internet is helping businesses attract customers and use customer information in unique ways. Finally, you will understand how to develop a specific strategy for implementing loyalty marketing in your business.

Extras

The following sidebars will help you as you work your way through the book:

Loyalty Lingo

Definitions of some common words and phrases used by business people with customer-loyalty programs.

Significant Stats

Facts and figures to help you understand the importance of loyalty marketing.

People Power

Advice and information from people who have thought about what it takes to be successful at loyalty marketing.

True Tales

These show you how other businesses have handled some of the loyalty-marketing issues discussed in the book.

Acknowledgments

Many wise and successful businesspeople have helped us learn more about customer loyalty. They include the following:

Stan Golomb, who knew how to make business fun for customers;

Ken Erdman, who wrote a book with us about the benefits of direct mail;

Brian Woolf, who gave us insight into the mathematics of loyalty marketing;

Joe Sugarman, for showing us the power of advertising;

Stew Leonard, for his ideas and enthusiasm for creating excitement in his stores;

Feargal Quinn, who defied his accountants and showed the long-term benefits of customer loyalty;

John Stanton and Rich George, who showed us the joys of delighting customers; and

Tom Haggai, who taught us how your first and best customers are your employees.

These are a few of the many people who have helped us appreciate the value of our customers.

> We want to especially thank Ruth Raphel, for all her valuable research and editing of our book.
>
> We'd like to thank our Development Editor, Nancy Lewis, for all her help and valuable suggestions.
>
> Finally, thanks to our agent, Marilyn Allen, and our editor, Mike Sanders, for choosing us to write this book.

Trademarks

Part 1

How Your Business Prospers by Winning Customer Loyalty

All businesses—from a small-town dentist office to an international hotel chain, from a large discount store to a garage band—need the same thing: customer loyalty.

Your first priority as a business owner or employee is to take care of your customers. In this part of the book, we will explain what customer loyalty is and how you can win it.

You will see the importance of your current customers and how to overcome their reluctance to buy from you. You will hear about the importance of developing information about your customers and how that information can save you advertising costs and increase your sales.

Why Your Business Needs Customer Loyalty

In This Chapter

- Why your customers say "No!"
- The reasons why your customers leave
- Bringing your customers back
- Developing a niche
- Protecting your brand

Here is some good news for you: Your business will succeed if you develop customer loyalty. And you will learn how to create that customer loyalty in this book.

But here's a warning: The opposite of customer loyalty is not customer disloyalty. It is customer apathy. The customer who has a complaint or runs to another store to take advantage of a sale is not your greatest threat. You should worry more about all your one-time customers who just do not care about you any more.

One of my relatives worked for a very successful clothing company headquartered in Baltimore, Maryland, called Merry-Go-Round. For many years, this company had the hottest clothing, the coolest displays, the sexiest music, the salespeople with the most piercings. But when the company failed to excite their customers one buying season, sales plummeted. Within two years, this once-thriving clothing company was bankrupt.

Merry-Go-Round was trying its best to come up with new designs and new trends. But when it failed to meet the ever-changing cycle of what teenagers and young adults like in their clothing, it quickly slid off their customers' radar. More important, since Merry-Go-Round did not have information on its customers, it had no way to try to make contact with those disappearing customers and lure them back into the store.

This chapter examines why businesses lose customers, why once-prosperous companies are no longer in business, and what you can do to avoid the mistakes other businesses have made. It all starts with the attitude your customers have about your business.

The Five Reasons Why People Do Not Buy

If you want to run a positive business, you have to eliminate customer negativity. Here are some reasons people give when asked why they do not spend money at a business:

- No need
- No money
- No hurry
- No desire
- No trust

By overcoming these five objections your customers might have to buying from you, you will dramatically increase your sales. Let's take these reasons one at a time and see if we can overcome these no-no-no-no-no's.

No Need

You have to give people a reason to buy what you have to sell. If they see no need, they won't spend their money.

Joe Sugarman is one of the best promoters I have ever met. He developed JS&A catalogues featuring new products that were the predecessor catalogs to Sharper Image and Brookstone. His main success in selling stemmed from his ability to convince customers in words and pictures that they really needed the products he was trying to sell.

One day Joe tried on a pair of sunglasses that blocked out blue light. He loved the fact that everything he looked at appeared bright. He did some research and found out that blue light focuses in front of the retina. By eliminating the blue light, objects appear sharper, clearer, and more defined.

Before Joe started selling the sunglasses (which he called BluBlockers,) Americans did not realize they had a need to block out blue light. But by describing the benefits of the product, Sugarman created the need. And his sales skyrocketed when Sugarman developed infomercials that showed consumers reacting very positively when they tried on a pair of the BluBlockers. Consumers realized that they, too, needed a pair of these new sunglasses. Sugarman offered his readers and viewers a need. And he filled it.

No Money

Have you ever heard this from a potential customer: "I really like your product (or service), but I can't afford it right now."

As a business owner, you must figure out a way that potential customer can afford your product. There are many ways you can achieve that goal. You can reduce the price, extend the payments, accept credit cards, or issue store credit. You can lease the product or offer a layaway, where the customer is able to use the product after paying a percentage of the product price over time. It is a proven fact that the more ways you give a customer to purchase what you are trying to sell, the more often the customer will buy.

> **True Tales**
>
> Before the widespread use of credit and debit cards, we often heard from customers of our clothing store that they couldn't afford our clothes right away. We wanted to help our customers out so they could pay for our clothes over time. So, in addition to running a retail clothing store, we visited our customers and sold clothing door-to-door. When customers told us they wanted to buy but had no money in that week's budget, we said, "No problem. Just give us a dollar a week on your bill when we see you every week."
>
> This doubled our sales the first year. Soon we not only collected just the $1.00 every week, we also sold them new merchandise.

> **Loyalty Lingo**
>
> A **limited edition** is a guarantee from a business that only a limited number of items will be produced. In the art world, a limited edition print is often signed by the artist and numbered (e.g., Number 1 of 100). The plate used to make the prints is destroyed when the last one of the limited edition is created.

No Hurry

You should always make your customers feel as though they will gain benefits by ordering right away. That is why stores run limited-time sales and why direct mail offers have expiration dates. Having a *limited edition* is another way to ensure that customers will feel the urgency to buy a product.

For example, the Franklin Mint offered a limited number of reproductions of classic books bound in leather and numbered. When that number was reached, the customers ordering too late received their money back with a "Sorry, you didn't order in time." Now, will customers who didn't get the book they wanted order faster next time? Of course.

No Desire

Dr. Ernst Dichter, of the Institute of Motivational Research, said that when people come to a restaurant, they are hungrier for recognition than they are for food. When writing to a customer, include her name in the letter. This recognition increases the chances she will read the letter, and then buy your product.

Another way to create desire is to appeal to someone's city, country, or favorite sporting team. Any kind of tie-in generates increased bottom-line results. That is why credit card companies bombard you with offers to sign up for credit cards from your college, from your favorite sports team, or from your favorite charity.

> **People Power** _____
>
> Consultant Robert Ringer says the best-selling headline he ever wrote was to promote Douglas Casey's best-selling book, *Crisis Investing: Opportunities and Profits in the Coming Great Depression* (Harpercollins, 1980). His headline was "Why You Will Probably Lose Everything in the Coming Depression." The headline created a desire for people to find out how their financial well-being was at stake. The book sold 400,000 copies and was on The New York Times best-seller list for 15 weeks.

No Trust

Writer and consultant Robert Ringer tells of the most unsuccessful headline he ever wrote. Here it is: "An Open Letter to Howard Hughes." But the product had absolutely nothing to do with Howard Hughes. It was just a gimmick to have someone read the ad. They did read the ad, but found nothing about Howard Hughes. They stopped reading, and stopped trusting the product.

A nationwide survey asked customers, "Why do you buy where you buy?" The number-one answer was NOT price. The number-one answer WAS "confidence." If people have confidence in you, then they not only will buy from you but will also tell their friends to buy from you.

Why Do Customers Leave?

Do you ever wonder about one of your customers, and think, "Whatever happened to (fill in the name) and how come she doesn't shop with us any more?" Losing customers is one of the main reasons why businesses fail.

Several surveys asking this same question were taken over the years by the American Society for Quality Control, the *Harvard Business Review, U.S. News & World Report*, and even the Swedish Post Office in a survey titled "Satsa pa kunden" ("Focus on the Customer").

Each survey came up with the following similar results:

◆ 14 percent of customers left because of complaints that weren't taken care of.

◆ 9 percent left and became customers of the competition.

- ♦ 9 percent moved out of town.

- ♦ 68 percent said they left for "no special reason."

In other words, almost seven out of ten people who were "steady" customers said that they left for "no special reason."

I don't believe that. I think there was a reason.

I think the reason was that the business did not keep in touch with their customers. They took them for granted. And when people are taken for granted, they don't feel important and are susceptible to the next mating cry.

When customers come back to you, your business succeeds. Here's why:

> *It is far, far easier to sell more to the customer you have than to sell to a new customer.*

And yet the average business spends five times as much time and money searching for a new customer than they do on the customers they already have. If they keep following that path, they'll soon discover that the customers they thought they had locked up, committed, and loyal have disappeared.

Significant Stats

The national average of customers who stop frequenting your business every year is about 20 percent. That's one out of five of your current customers! If that trend continues for a few years, you will be out of business if you don't either find a way to obtain 20 percent new customers or—better yet—recapture some of the ones that left.

A study by Bain & Company, a large marketing consulting firm with offices around the world, said that if you can cut the number of customers who leave you every year in half, then you can double your bottom-line profit! Why is that? Because …

- ♦ Of the money you spent to secure them the first time.

- ♦ Their income typically increases.

- ♦ They will spend more as the years go by.

- ♦ Their family (or business) grows larger.

- ♦ They tell others to buy from you.

The longer you keep a customer, the more money you make. An auto service company said that their expected profit from a customer who stayed with them for four years was more than triple the profit the same customer generated in the first year.

How do you know when a customer is about to leave? New computer programs can track your customers' behaviors past and present. When their buying pattern shows fewer sales, smaller sales, less contacts, you should hear warning bells. It is time to contact that customer and ask if everything's all right.

People Power

John Romero, the premier direct marketer in the casino industry, tells of the time a senior executive came to his office and said, "We need new business." John's answer was, "What's wrong with old business?" His point was this: Businesses overlook the once-productive customers they still have hidden away in the company's database.

His question was, "Why would you spend years developing a customer, but then ignore him because he stops coming? There's pure gold in that file of names waiting for you to dig it out. It's the best 'new' business you can find."

The Boomerang Theory

Most businesses concentrate on getting new customers to come to their operation. But this eagerness to have new customers come in is not often matched by an eagerness to please customers once they show up.

Several years ago, Feargal Quinn wrote a book called *Crowning the Customer* (Raphel Marketing, 2001). Feargal, an Irish supermarket owner and now an Irish Senator, focused his book on how his business had prospered through outstanding customer service. Feargal called the driving force in his business the "boomerang theory." He based the theory on experiences he had as a child, working in his parents' summer camp.

The camp worked on a prepaid basis. Customers paid for the summer vacation in advance (meals included) and did not have to pay for anything once they arrived. Yet Feargal's parents worked extremely hard all summer to make sure that their guests had a wonderful time.

Feargal once asked his father why he worked so hard if the customers had already paid and he had no hope of getting any more money from them.

"Son," his father said, "It's easy to get people to come once. The trick is to get them to come back again."

Feargal remembered this lesson all his life, and when he opened his business he tried to instill the boomerang theory in all his employees.

People Power

Feargal Quinn tells a great story about the time he was bagging groceries (yes, the owner of the supermarket chain does bag groceries at least once a week), and a customer told him she would feel "guilty" if she ever stopped shopping at his store.

When he asked why, she told him that one day when she was checking out, she realized she had forgotten her wallet. The cashier told her to take the groceries home and to pay the next time she came in.

The amazing part of the story was that this incident had occurred 10 years earlier. The one act of kindness from a cashier had so impressed the customer that she would still feel "guilty" if she ever stopped shopping at Feargal's supermarket.

Here are some of the innovations Feargal Quinn made in his supermarket to encourage people to be boomerangs and come back to his store:

- He eliminated candy in the checkout aisles, because of complaints from mothers with young children, even though the candy purchases were quite profitable.

- He put in playhouses for young children, even though his accountants yelled at him for taking up valuable space.

- He sold bread and other fresh products only on the day they were made. Anything left over was given to charity.

- He accepted recyclables at his store even though he had to operate at a loss. He realized the alternative was to send shoppers to one of his competitors who did accept recyclables.

- His customer loyalty program enabled him to identify his customers' birthdays and give them a small cake (with their name on it) when they shopped on their birthdays.

Feargal says that when faced with any business decision, business owners should get in the habit of asking, "What will this do to help bring the customer back again?"

Developing a Niche

One of the keys to winning customer loyalty is to develop a following of customers who go out of their way to shop with you. A way you can develop that group of customers is by focusing on a market niche.

In the small town of Littleton, New Hampshire, there is a store called Chutters. They carry candy, candles, gifts, gourmet food, and collectibles. But their primary claim to fame is having the "World's longest candy counter"—111 feet, 11 inches long. Chutters is listed in the Guinness Book of World Records and recently received an award from the state's Small Business Administration as Retailer of the Year. Whenever our children go to Littleton, they beg us to stop at Chutters, because they want to look at that world record candy counter.

In my first few years in business as a small children's clothing shop, I looked for a reason for people to shop with us. We had very limited resources, so I decided to promote the store as having "The World's Largest Selection of Children's Gloves, Hats, and Mittens." These items, at the time, sold for one dollar or less, so we could stock them in large quantities. Customers came from miles away to choose from this large selection and, while they were shopping, might also buy a child's snowsuit that sold for 20 times more than the just-purchased hat, scarf, gloves, or mittens.

Promoting special products works because it is an example of a successful marketing concept first introduced by advertising Hall-of-Famer Rosser Reeves.

Reeves was Chairman of the Board of the Ted Bates Advertising Agency in the 1960s, and he introduced a marketing technique to sell products he defined as the product's Unique Selling Proposition, or USP.

The concept of a Unique Selling Proposition works as a selling tool for most businesses. Are there rules you can follow to create your own USP? Yes. The sections that follow provide a few.

Make Your Business Interesting—Not the Ad

How many times have you watched a TV commercial that grabbed your attention, made you laugh (or wince), but if you were asked a minute or two later, "What was advertised?" you could not remember?

The oft-repeated TV ad of an automobile (any automobile) speeding through the countryside passing other cars may be exciting to watch, but what makes the car different than any other car?

If the car has special safety features, tell your customers about them. If your car handles better than the competition, explain the difference. Showing a pretty country scene with cars driving by will not be as effective as showing you customers why your car is special.

Reeves called these "distraction techniques." They entice you to watch the ad, but your interest is with the pretty girl, the sudden accident, the humorous moment, but, uh, what was the product again?

Think of advertising as a conversation with your customers. You want to show the consumer benefits of your product in an interesting way.

People Power

In 1954 two men named Charles White and John MacNamara walked into Reeves' office. MacNamara was president of M&M Candies. He said that their advertising wasn't successful. They talked for a few minutes and Reeves quickly saw that the best advertising idea was inherent in the product itself.

M&Ms were the only candy in America that had chocolate surrounded by a sugar shell. This meant that the candy would not melt in your hand. This was the candy's USP and led to his slogan: "M&M candies melt in your mouth, not in your hand." That slogan is still used by M&M candies today, more than 50 years after it was developed.

Have an Easy-to-Remember Slogan

A few years ago, I was walking through the aisles at the food industry's annual convention and met Michael Copps, CEO of the Copps Supermarket chain in Wisconsin. He said he was interested in having someone work with his company as an advertising consultant. His immediate need was a slogan for their planned expansion. He wanted something that would alert customers in new areas that his supermarkets would soon arrive. He asked me to think about it and to call him later that week.

Remembering Rosser Reeve's USP, I asked, "If I give you the slogan now, will you hire me as your consultant?"

He said, "Sure. What's the slogan?"

I said, "The Copps Are Coming!"

This slogan, which was a play on a popular expression, told customers clearly that a new store was coming to town.

"You're hired," he said. His advertising agency quickly picked up this USP theme by creating animal cartoon characters, each representing a different area of the supermarket, wearing Keystone Cops costumes. The campaign won many advertising awards and each opening drew great crowds. They wisely followed up their arrival with the slightly changed phrase: "The Copps Are Here!"—an extended USP.

Repeat It!

More often than not you'll discover there are certain ideas, techniques, and concepts that are reproduced in the most successful campaigns. If it works, repeat it. Again. And again. And again.

For example, I wanted to increase our Saturday business at our "Gordon's Alley" shopping center. I started running ads with the theme, "If it's Saturday, it must be Gordon's Alley."

What did that mean?

Really … nothing.

But the implication was, if you did NOT shop our stores on Saturday, then you were missing something special. An example of a Saturday enticement would be a woman who would set up a stand with home-baked pies. (Our ad would say: "The Pie Lady's here today! If it's Saturday, it must be Gordon's Alley.")

Other Saturday's would feature interesting attractions such as a chess match inside our store or a farmer's market on our parking lot. Saturday quickly became our biggest business day and we used this same theme for 12 years.

Image and Branding Mistakes

Once you have developed an image that a consumer can recognize, then you are well on your way to developing winning customer loyalty. Now make sure you don't dilute the image you have created by going too many directions at once.

One of the biggest mistakes companies make is to associate their *brand* with other products that fail to share the original brand's strengths.

> **Loyalty Lingo**
>
> A **brand** is something that exists in the minds and actions of customers. A relationship between a customer and a product or firm.

For instance, do you remember Bic perfume?

Bic aftershave?

Life Savers gum?

Failed.

Failed.

Failed.

Levis decided that since they were selling jeans, they could branch out and sell men's suits. But the customer wondered if the suits were made out of denim. It failed.

Pepsi-Cola introduced clear, see-through Crystal Pepsi, and the consumer wondered how it could be "clear" if it was "cola." "Clear" was 7-Up. So, what did 7-Up do? They introduced a cola-colored product they called 7-Up Gold. And the consumer asked how could it be 7-Up if it was cola-colored? This was the same company that *gained* market share saying they were the "UNcola." They *lost* $70 million on that one, plus they lost sales of traditional 7-Up.

True Tales

When you think of replacing an old ad with something new and different, remember the Pepsi-Cola story, told to us by our newspaper advertising salesman.

Many years ago, a senior executive of Pepsi told his ad agency he thought it was time for the agency to replace the current ad. He asked, "How many people do you have working on my account?"

"Fifty-seven," replied the ad director.

"Fifty-seven?" asked the CEO. "What do they all do?"

"Well, one comes up with new ideas and the other fifty-six make sure we don't change what's working now."

"Wrongly" Extending Your Market

Not all new products are successful. Large pharmaceutical companies spend millions to develop new products that have harmful side effects and have to be withdrawn from the market.

According to Nancy Smith, Ph.D., vice president and food industry consultant at Arthur D. Little, over 90 percent of new food products introduced every year fail. She estimates that the cost of these failed products is over $20 billion per year.

Does this mean that the big guys are not always right? That they make mistakes? That you do not hear about the mistakes but only their successes?

Yes. Yes. And yes.

But what does that tell us? This: When you vary from what you are, consumers become confused, undecided, and switch to the more familiar because they understand what it is and what it does.

Kodak is a classic example of wrongly trying to extend the market for a widely recognized brand name. In 1932 Kodak had 75 percent of the world market in photographic equipment. The competition kept on eroding Kodak's share. Their answer was, "Let's create a lower-priced product and call it (would you believe?) Kodak!

The customer was confused. They were accustomed to paying the Kodak price for the Kodak quality. But look, there on the shelves was a lower-priced product with the same name. After all, if it walks like a package of film in a yellow box and it talks like a package of film in a yellow box, then it must be ….

Professor Susan Fornier, assistant professor of business administration at Harvard Business School said, "The consumer needs to build a relationship with the product, and the product needs to have an identity. When you weaken a brand, you weaken brand loyalty."

True Tales

One time I was in Finland buying clothing for our shops. I found high-quality winter ski jackets manufactured by Lhuta, worn by Finnish ski patrols and Olympic winners. As wages increased in Finland the company thought they might be pricing themselves out of the market. They went to lower-waged Portugal to make the jackets for a lower price. The name they put on these jackets? Lhuta.

"Wait!" I cried, "How do we tell the customer the difference between your higher-quality jackets made in Finland and the lower-priced styles made in Portugal if they both are named Lhuta?" Their answer: A shrug of the shoulders. If we were confused, how about our customers? They, too, were confused and sought another label instead. Sales fell dramatically.

Advertising guru Brian Courtenay says that businesses should consider their brand like a trusted friend whom they invite into their homes. Our customers slammed the door when Lhuta came to visit because they no longer knew who they were.

Successful Brand Characteristics

Marketing guru Tom Peters said it well, "Branding is more—not less—important than ever if you want to stand out in the crowded marketplace."

Howard Draft, chairman CEO Draft Worldwide, agrees, saying, "The object of marketing is to build a relationship with the consumer."

Here are four characteristics of a successful brand:

- Building image: making your business part of your community.
- Market segmentation: emphasizing merchandise or services where you excel.
- Innovative merchandising: working with manufacturers for in-store displays, contests, and so on.
- Creative advertising: using your logo for instant identification.

And here are some additional points to remember:

- The big guys are not always right. They are often wrong. They DO have the luxury (read "big bucks") to afford mistakes while waiting for the one sure-fire, can't-miss, finally-profitable product that comes along and wipes out the losses.
- Remember that success happens gradually through evolution, not revolution.
- Remember what made you successful when you first opened your store. Always emphasize, market, promote, and advertise your special relationship, not only with your customer but also the community where you live and work.

As Andrea Mayer, a colleague of Tom Peters, said, "I figured out why the little businesses work. They've got to."

The Least You Need to Know

- It's easy to have customers visit you once. The trick is to have them come back again and again.
- People leave your business for a reason: You didn't give them enough attention or rewards.
- Develop a special niche for your business, and customers will flock to your door.
- Your brand is the core of your business; don't dilute your brand by trying to extend it to noncore products or services.

Chapter 2

The Importance of Current Customers

In This Chapter

- ◆ Your customers' favorite radio station
- ◆ The three ways to increase your business
- ◆ Where 80 percent of your business comes from
- ◆ Knowing the value of your customers
- ◆ Finding new business in your own backyard
- ◆ Asking your loyal customers what you are doing wrong

Here's a surprising but true statistic. The top 10 percent of all your customers spend 50 times more than the bottom 10 percent of your customers do. And not only do they spend more, the top 10 percent of your customers are your most profitable.

In fact, for most businesses, the bottom 10 percent of the shoppers is unprofitable. Your business probably loses money every time these customers do business with you. How could that be? Well, the bottom 10 percent are the cherry pickers, the ones who frequently return items, the unhappy customers who are just waiting for an excuse to leave.

Ignore the bottom 10 percent of your customers. But pay attention to the top 10 percent. The top rung of your customers is responsible for most of your business and all of your profits. In this chapter, you will learn why it is so important to cultivate your very best customers. So let's learn how to go fishing where the fish are.

WII-FM

If you want to reach out to your customers, and if you want to increase your business, you have to enter the minds of your customers. You have to figure out what your customers are thinking about.

It turns out that your customers are thinking about themselves. They really only care about your business to the extent that it helps them achieve their goals.

Every day, every one of your customers is listening to the same radio station, the most popular station in America. This radio station is located in every city in every state. Its call letters are WII-FM. Those letters stand for "What's In It For Me?"

When customers hear your message on their personal radio station, they ask, "What's In It For Me?" What do they gain?

What value do they receive? What benefit will they have? If the gain, value, or benefit is not enough, they'll take your commercial off the air.

The most important lesson you can learn about customer loyalty is the simplest one. Your customers will not be loyal to you. You have to be loyal to your customers.

It should not be surprising to you if your customers shop somewhere else because of lower prices. Customers you have been very nice to will drive 20 miles to buy the same goods or services that they can get around the corner from you. Customers do not have to be loyal to you. Remember: They are listening to station WII-FM, and if your competitor weighs in with a special offer, they may drop you like a hot potato and go running to the next special deal or offer.

> **Loyalty Lingo**
>
> **Advocates** are loyal customers who tell anyone who will listen how great your business is.

What customer loyalty is all about is your being loyal to your customers. Winning customer loyalty is about what you can do each and every day to gather more information about your customers, make your business a better enterprise, and eventually turn your customers into *advocates*.

Three Ways to Increase Sales

Despite the fact that customers listen to WII-FM, you must focus on your customers because they are the most critical element of your business. In fact, there are only three ways for you to increase your sales. Here they are:

- Have more customers.

- Have customers come into your business more often.

- Have customers spend more money when they arrive.

The sections that follow contain some guidelines on how to use these techniques in your business.

Have More Customers

The average business loses 20 percent of their customers every year because some customers die, some move, and some go to the competition. In order to maintain the same amount of business, you have to replace 20 percent of your customer base every year.

What can you do to attract new customers? Here are some ideas you might want to try:

- Run a contest or sweepstakes. This also gives you the person's name and address for future direct mailings.

- Offer an outstanding value to first-time shoppers. "You receive the first three issues of our magazine for free. We're that sure you'll enjoy it enough that you'll want to subscribe …."

- Ask to speak at a local civic club. They're always looking for speakers at their weekly luncheons. Talk about a subject that involves your business but is not an outright commercial for your business. If you are a dentist, you might give away free toothbrushes and toothpaste. If you're an accountant, you might begin with, "Up until the end of March every year, all your salary goes to pay your taxes. Is there a way you can save on taxes and put more money in your pocket? The answer is 'Yes.' Here's how …."

If you own a retail business, remember to give the audience gift certificates with a very special value to redeem within the next two weeks.

Try a new move-in program. You send a postcard or letter with an offer to people who have just moved to your town. Response rates are as high as 40 percent. Once the customer is in the store, arrange for a store tour and a special gift for the customer's "next visit." Refer to Appendix C for a sample Direct Mail Postcard Mailing (New Move-In Promotion).

True Tales
Businesses that have customers who come in regularly will often do very well with programs geared for new arrivals in town. These types of businesses include supermarkets, dry cleaners, pizza parlors and other restaurants, beauty salons, and auto dealers that offer tune-ups. Once customers establish a pattern of visiting a business, they become valuable repeat customers.

Have Customers Come to Your Business More Often

When a customer visits your store twice as often as she used to, you will definitely do more business. Sometimes, the extra visit will only be "window shopping," but other times she will make a purchase while she is there.

There are many ways to encourage customers to visit you more often. Here are some ideas:

◆ A coffee shop or convenience store can give customers a card for a free cup of coffee after they buy 12 cups.

◆ You can advertise a contest that you sign up for only in the store (no purchase necessary—but once they're in, many will buy something).

◆ Offer a very special price on an item but limit how many a customer can buy at one time. Supermarkets often do this with butter or orange juice. If the customer wants to stock up, she'll visit the store several times that week—and certainly buy more each time she comes in.

◆ Put a notice in your monthly newsletter about a special promotion, or extended hours for shopping at holiday time. (What? You don't have a monthly newsletter? Quick, start one!) This way you're keeping in touch with your customers—all of whom have short memories.

♦ Think about developing a customer loyalty "KIT." KIT means "Keep in touch." KIT works because your customers WANT to hear from you. They shop with you. They spend their money with you. They trust you.

Find excuses for your customers to visit your store or buy from you more often.

True Tales
I had each staff member call four of their best customers every week. Our staff would tell these customers about just-arrived merchandise. (There was no labor cost since the calls were made during a slow time of the day.) The customer would usually thank the salesperson for thinking of her. When you call a customer you already have a relationship with, the phone call usually has a much more positive result than calling a total stranger. In the years we did this, we estimated that we increased our business two percent a year with almost no increased cost.

Have Them Spend More Money When They Arrive

If your customers spend more money with you every time they visit, then you'll do more business. That's what "merchandising" is all about—displaying your products in an attractive, easy-to-grab way that entices the customer to buy more when they see the displays. Supermarkets and packaged consumer-goods companies are the masters of this technique.

A recent survey said that people shopping in a supermarket make 60 percent of their buying decisions while in the supermarket. They are attracted to end-aisle displays or walls of specials or sampling of new products. Those "impulse purchases" add up to big profits.

Displays, sampling, bulk buys are all ways that supermarkets create additional purchases. Your business can use the same ideas to increase your share of the customer's wallet.

True Tales

Send your customer gift certificates to use for a limited time when they come to your store (Note: Do NOT send customers "coupons" unless you're a supermarket. "Gift Certificates" are more prestigious.)

Here's how to increase sales when you send out gift certificates. In our twice-a-year "sale" mailings of several thousand customers, we originally sent out gift certificates for the customers to use when they came to the sale.

One year we took the extra step and printed each customer's name on each certificate. Redemption tripled! Here's why: The certificate was not for anyone. It was for someone.

The 80/20 Formula

All customers are not created equal. That is why even though you have to treat all customers well, you do not have to treat all customers equally. You should lavish your best benefits on those special customers who are responsible for the great majority of your business.

An Italian economist named Pareto introduced the 80/20 formula in the late 1800s. His theory was that 80 percent of your sales are brought to you by only 20 percent of your customers.

This formulation is a good approximation, and works for all businesses of all sizes. It works for discount stores, it works for jewelers, it works for dry cleaners, and it works for clothing designers. Most of your business comes from a small percentage of your client base.

Meat packers and ice cream vendors know the 80/20 formula. They know that your stomach has only so much capacity—around 14 ounces. Their goal is for their ice cream or meat to fill as many of those ounces as possible.

The goal of your business is to capture as many of each customer's expendable dollars as possible. To make sure that your top 20 percent of customers shop with you, you have to meet their expectations.

The Lifetime Value of Your Customers

It's important to remember just how valuable every encounter you have with your customers is. If your customers are satisfied with how you treat them, they will tell five other people. If they have a problem, they will tell 13 other people. Try to have the odds on your side!

In addition to counting on customers to spread the good word about your business, you should focus on how much that individual customer is worth to you throughout her buying lifetime.

We visited Stew Leonard at his famous "Stew Leonard's" supermarket in Norwalk, Connecticut, and he explained why each customer is important: "The lifetime value of a customer in a supermarket is about $246,000. Every time a customer comes through our front door, I see, stamped on her forehead in big red letters: $246,000! I'm never going to make that person unhappy with me. Or lose her to the competition."

Stew told me about the event that created this philosophy.

A customer returned a quart of buttermilk she had bought at his store. She said it didn't "smell right." Stew smelled the carton and told her, "Smells right to me."

The woman disagreed. Stew and the woman then argued back and forth over who was right.

Finally, Stew gave the customer her money back.

The woman left. But not before she gave him this parting sentence: "I don't like the way you treat your customers. I'm never shopping here again."

Stew had done the right thing (he refunded the customer's money) but he had the wrong attitude. He lost $246,000 arguing over a quart of buttermilk.

Now Stew Leonard has a huge concrete block at the entrance of his supermarket in Norwalk, Connecticut. On the block are Stew's two rules of customer service:

> Rule #1: "The Customer Is Always Right"
>
> Rule #2: "If the Customer Is Wrong, Reread Rule #1"

Significant Stats

A survey from the Ernst & Young accounting firm said most businesses felt that the personal relationship with the customer was only 10 percent of the buying decision. When customers were asked, they said it was 70 percent!

Acres of Diamonds

If you buy into the philosophy that loyal customers must be developed and nurtured, you may be wondering where you should begin looking for customers. The answer may surprise you!

At the turn of the twentieth century, a minister by the name of Dr. Russell Conwell traveled throughout the United States and gave the same speech nearly 6,000 times. The effect was so powerful that wherever he went, audiences would pack the halls to hear him talk. He earned several million dollars and donated the proceeds to found Temple University in Philadelphia.

His speech was titled "Acres of Diamonds." He told the story of fortune seekers who spent many, many years wandering continents in search of the ever-elusive pot of gold. When they returned old and weary, they discovered that there were literally acres of diamonds in their own backyard.

His theme was this: "Diamonds are not in far-distant mountains or in yonder seas; they are in your own backyard, if you just dig for them."

The diamonds in your business, your future customers, are right in your own backyard. All you have to do is dig them up. Here are four sources of diamonds: new customer prospects, your current customers, customers you have lost, and your best customers.

New Prospects

Start with people who live around your store who match the *demographics* of your current customer.

> **Loyalty Lingo**
>
> **Demographics** are characteristics of people such as age and income or family size. You can use demographics to try to find new customers with characteristics similar to your existing customer base.

You can use voting lists or zip codes, or work with a list broker to try to find prospects for your businesses. A bank in suburban Dallas sent a mailing to over 60,000 customers, selected by both income and proximity to their businesses. The mailer included a personalized check redeemable for several different checking-account offers. They achieved a remarkable 20 percent response rate and customers started new accounts worth 100 times the cost of the mailing!

Current Customers

Your business probably already has a listing of your current customers either in a mailing file or in an accounting file. If you don't have a customer list, start one today! Use this list to encourage your current customers to spend more money with you.

We have a client who runs a birthday and anniversary club for their restaurants in Mississippi. Every month they send a postcard out inviting their customers to come by either for a monthly special or a birthday or anniversary treat. The response has been great. When they asked their customers what else they wanted, the customers replied, "More special offers!"

But be aware that nearly 20 percent of your customers move every year. At least once every six months, send out an inexpensive first-class postcard mailing to your mailing list. You'll receive notification of change of address and you can update your customer file.

Lost Customers

If you are keeping track of your customers and when they purchase, you will also know which customers are no longer shopping with you. These "lost customers" can often be encouraged to visit you again (remember, many customers leave you for "no reason at all").

You should make an effort to recover lost customers. Try sending them a good offer (such as X dollars off their next purchase). Those who take advantage of the offer might start shopping with you again. You can save yourself some money in postage by dropping customers who do not respond to your mailing list offers.

Best Customers

If you keep records of how much your customers spend (and you should!), then it is easy to sort your customer list by amount spent over a period of time. You can send your best customers a special offer that only goes to those customers. You can count on the fact that the return from a mailing to your best customers will yield far better results than a prospect mailing.

> ### True Tales
>
> Don't always think about giving your best customers a reduction in sale price or an offer that requires them to buy something. Try giving them tickets to a special event (art gallery opening, private party, baseball game) or giving them recognition (happy-birthday card).
>
> We send a big tin of popcorn to our best customers during the holiday season. It's just a pleasant way of saying, "We care about you."

Some casinos carry this idea of rewarding their best customers to great lengths. The casinos give every customer a loyalty card that can be inserted into slot machines or handed to pit bosses at casino games. The casinos then track the amount that the customer gambles and gives set rewards for certain levels of play. Credit cards also provide similar rewards that are usable for airlines tickets and hotel stays.

All of these examples can be used to increase sales from people who have already bought something from you. By looking in your own backyard, you will find that there are many diamond patches waiting to be mined.

Stealing the Competition

After you've gone to all the trouble to develop a customer base, you may start to worry about keeping your competitors away from your hard-earned customers.

> ### Significant Stats
>
> A recent survey asked 700 major companies the question, "Does your salesman care about you and your business?" 92 percent said, "No!"

Here are some suggestions for keeping your customers:

1. **Hire the right people**.

   Singapore Airlines employs less than two percent of all applicants. They carefully pre-screen applicants to make sure that their staff is customer-conscious.

2. **Train and motivate your employees, and give them authority.**

   The Hyatt Regency believes in their employees taking responsibility for their customers' problems. Their employees can solve customer complaints on their own without asking permission of higher-ranking supervisors (up to a specified dollar limit).

3. **Invest early and heavily in technology to support customer service.**

The Wal-Mart Corporation is known for their low prices and wide selection. But one of the major sources of their success is their heavy investment in customer technology, which was started by their founder, Sam Walton. Today, the headquarters in Bentonville, Arkansas, can monitor sales by item in all of their thousands of stores and then adjust inventories accordingly. The largest corporation in the world is also one of the most efficient technologically.

4. **Keep an eye on the competition.**

Yes, your competitors are watching you. But make sure you have one eye peeled on what your competitors are doing. If you do, you can take advantage of any of their failings.

One of the most effective kinds of all advertising is the comparison ad. A computer company recently showed two of their competitors' products and showed their own product, which had some striking advantages. It enclosed coupons so that the reader could request information from all three companies separately! The point is that when the customers did the comparison-shopping, they would pick the product of the computer company that ran the ad.

5. **Ask customers to rate your quality of service.**

Think of your customers as quality-control engineers. Your customers know your business at least as well as you do. Questionnaires, suggestion boxes, in-depth customer interviews, and *focus groups* are just some of the ways that progressive companies are having their customers help them improve their businesses.

> **Loyalty Lingo**
>
> A **focus group** is a small group of customers gathered together at a meeting where their opinions about a company or a product are solicited.

A better way to fight your competition is to increase your customer service and your loyalty to customers. If you do that, no matter how loudly your competitors yell, they will not steal your customers.

When Feargal Quinn starts off his weekly focus-group meeting in Ireland, he tells his customers, "Today I don't want to hear what is right about our company. Tell me what's wrong. Tell me the problems. That way, I can fix them."

The Least You Need to Know

- ◆ The most valuable asset of your business is your customers.

- ◆ Some of your customers are more valuable to you than other customers.

- ◆ Establish a program to keep track of your customers and their spending.

- ◆ Your best source of additional business is closer than you think.

- ◆ To keep your customers, encourage them with rewards.

Chapter 3

How to Use Advertising to Build Loyalty

In This Chapter

- ◆ Secrets of advertising success
- ◆ The value of direct marketing
- ◆ Why old customers are better than new ones
- ◆ How to brand your business

Your customers are bombarded every day with messages from advertisers. In this chapter, I show you how you can have your message pass through advertising clutter and make its way directly to your customers.

Do you know who hates junk advertising even more than the angry consumers who have to sort through a pile of spam on their computers and unwanted mail and dreadful television and radio advertising every day?

The answer is not that surprising if you think about it a little. The people who hate junk mail even more than the angry consumers are the advertisers who send the unopened, unread junk advertising! They are the ones whose companies foot the bill and have to face bosses who complain that advertising just doesn't work.

So if nobody likes junk advertising, how do we eliminate it?

Customer loyalty makes it possible! This explains the benefits of advertising. It also gives you ways to keep track of your customers so that you can reduce your advertising costs and at the same time increase your business and profits.

The Five Ways That Advertising Works

The patient wakes up in the hospital room after the operation. She looks around and asks, "Where am I?"

She does not ask, "How am I?" which you think would be her first question. The first words the patient utters shows that she wants to be in a familiar situation.

Being familiar is one of the basic messages that your business should convey. In fact, it is "one of the five ways that advertising works" as compiled more than 50 years ago by James Webb Young, a director of the J. Walter Thompson advertising agency and recognized as a dean of American advertising.

If you want to develop loyalty in your customers, you should check your advertising to make sure that it meets one—or more—of these criteria:

- Be familiar
- Be a reminder
- Be newsworthy
- Be action stimulating
- Be able to add value to the product

Let's look at these important advertising concepts one by one, and examine how they'll work to increase the loyalty of your customers.

True Tales

Advertising expert James Webb Young (who devised these five ways advertising works) tells of the time he ran a mail order color page in *LIFE* magazine. The ad received a "read most" rating of 20 percent of the circulation. But the response in orders was only one tenth of one percent of the circulation. On one level the ad was a success (great readership). But the ad was ultimately a failure (not enough orders).

Be Familiar

People want to be in a familiar setting and/or buy a familiar product. Once a customer begins buying, she is likely to continue to do business with you.

Most people go to restaurants they are familiar with, buy the same brand of car over again, and read the same paper every day. The old phrase "familiarity breeds contempt" is not true for most people. Familiarity is actually very comforting.

That's also the reason you see advertising that repeats the name of the product over and over in commercials. The advertiser wants to implant the name in your subconscious so that when you see it in the marketplace, you respond with, "Oh yes, that name IS familiar to me …."

Psychologists say that this repetition establishes a "degree of comfort" in a consumer. A customer does not have to make a decision based on whether or not your business is reliable, courteous, trustworthy—all the Boy Scout adjectives—because you have already passed the approval test.

Significant Stats
A readership survey revealed that people who owned or purchased a product were twice as apt to read an advertisement of the product than someone who never bought the product. And these "familiar" readers are even more likely to buy the product again. When you send your direct mailer to your present customers, the response rate can range from 5 to 20 times greater than when the same piece is mailed to people who never bought from you.

Be a Reminder

Much of today's advertising is not directed toward purchasing a product as much as to remind you that the product is waiting for you to come and buy. Here are a few examples:

- ◆ A few weeks before election, you are reminded to vote.
- ◆ Your church sends you a bulletin to remind you of what's happening at services on Sunday.

◆ Your shoe store sends notes to remind you that the time has arrived to purchase new shoes for your children.

◆ Your dentist, physician, optometrist, or (fill in the blank) mails you a reminder note to call for your next appointment.

Look at the calendar. Every month has several holidays. Most offer a reason for buying something! Valentine's Day, Halloween, Christmas/Hanukkah/Kwanzaa, as well as Mother's and Father's and Grandparent's Day. These days remind a customer that there is a gift to buy. Take advantage of these special days by running a sale and giving your customers another reason to buy a present.

What do you think is your customers' favorite holiday? Why, their birthday, of course. Consider starting a birthday program for your customers. If you don't already have a birthday list, consider running a sweepstakes or raffle with a sign-up card. Your customers will give you birthday information (just ask for month and day—not year of birth!). Then, at the appropriate time every year, you can send out a birthday greeting and/or present for them to pick up at your business.

Refer to Appendix C for a samples of a Direct Mail Reminder Postcard, Direct Mail Holiday Mailings, and a Direct Mail Postcard (Birthday Promotion).

Be Newsworthy

Notice how many times you see the word "new" atop packages of soap products and cereals. That's because "new" is "news." Here's a caution: Just because it is new does not mean that sales automatically increase. Only a tiny percentage of "new" products introduced every year succeed. This is because the product or service must not only be new, but must also supply a need or be an improvement over a comparable product already on the market.

Opening a new department in your store? Carrying a new item? Offering a "Frequent Buyer" promotion? Having an early opening or later closing hours? Running a special promotion or sale that you want your regular customers to know about before anyone else? All of these are reasons to contact your customers and offer them something "new."

Be Action Stimulating

The average newspaper has less than 100 editorial stories and two to three times as many ads. How do you motivate readers to pay attention to your advertising to the point where they pick up a pencil or phone or type their name, address, and credit card number into their computer?

The desire to act is there—deep inside the consumer. How do you overcome the reader's initial inertia? Listing impressive numbers ("Look how many we sold of this artist's previous limited edition print") are ho-hum. We must offer specific benefits.

Sometimes the choice of words can help. For example, life "insurance" is not sold in England or Australia, but life "assurance" is. That has a different sound. If insurance means that the company pays when I leave, does assurance means that I'm going to be around a while longer?

Ask yourself, "What am I doing today to sell my merchandise?" A speaker at a marketing seminar asked his audience, "What are you going to do tomorrow?"

The real estate agent said he was going to show some houses.

The insurance salesperson said he was going to line up some medical examinations for customers.

The gallery salesperson said he was going to display more art.

No one in the audience said, "I'm going to make a sale."

The bottom line of good advertising is not how many awards are won at annual ceremonies but how much money is put in the register. It is fine, commendable, and to-be-desired to give the customer reasons why they should buy. But nothing happens if no sale takes place.

Be Able to Add Value to the Product

See those boxes of baking soda in refrigerators all over America? The reason is to make the refrigerator smell nicer.

Wait a minute. Isn't baking soda supposed to be used for baking? Yes. But the company came up with an additional reason to buy the product. They practiced "line extension."

Arm and Hammer has extended the uses for baking soda even further, adding baking soda to toothpaste and bathroom and carpet cleanser.

If you own a share of the market with what you presently sell, how can you add a new reason to buy your product and capture additional business? The answer is this: Create Added Value.

Prestige is also "added value": The Polo horse on your shirt, the CM for Countess Mara on your tie, the robin's-egg-blue package from Tiffany's, the Movado watch, the Steuben glass, the Rosenthal china .... These products not only work well, the fact that these brands are recognized by other people as prestigious adds value to the products.

Direct Marketing vs. General Advertising

Writing a letter is the simplest form of direct mail, which is a form of direct marketing. Direct marketing is different from general advertising, which tries to promote brands to the general public. Direct marketing has a specific message for a specific consumer.

Loyalty Lingo

Direct Marketing is selling goods and services directly to consumers. Direct marketing usually has a response mechanism, some device in which the consumer can directly communicate with the seller of goods.

The best part of direct marketing is that it can be tested. When you put a commercial on television telling people how good your dry cleaning is, it is difficult to tell if you are actually increasing your business through that form of advertising.

With direct marketing, you can test an offer and see how many people respond. A simple form of direct marketing is a gift certificate inserted in a mailing piece. Simply count up the number of coupons returned, then compare them to the number of mailing pieces you sent out, and you have your response rate to the mailing. When you compare the amount of profit you made on the business from the mailing compared to the cost of the mailing, you can judge if this type of mailing is approved by your customers and is beneficial to you.

Direct Mail Tips

Direct mail is the medium that shows up your strong points: friendliness, reliability, service, and (most important) the amount of personal attention lavished on the customer.

Here is a list of 25 direct mail tips you should know about:

1. Dollar for dollar, nothing returns as much to your business as direct mail.

2. Half of your customers' names and addresses are inaccurate within three years unless updated.

3. Your customer list will return two to ten times as much as a rented list.

4. Sending the same offer to the same list the second time returns 50 percent of the first-time response.

5. Mail postcards first class. This cleans your list at NO cost.

6. Average delivery of third-class mail is seven to ten days.

7. Dimensional mailings (pop-ups) work! An example of a pop-up is a direct mail piece which unfolds to reveal a car or a vodka bottle. About 40 percent of recipients remember receiving this type of mailer six months later!

8. Mail ALL the names in your database at LEAST four times a year.

9. You'll receive 90 percent of the responses to your mailing within two weeks from the time you sent your mailing (three to four weeks for bulk mail).

10. The time you need to plan and send a direct-mail campaign is 10 to 14 weeks. It takes about six weeks to write the copy and prepare the illustrations and photographs. Plan on another six weeks to have your mailing printed and sent out.

11. Fulfill your customer's order within 48 hours of receipt.

12. Check with the post office BEFORE you send your mailing to see if it fits postal rules.

13. Send copies of mailers to post offices of key zip codes telling them to "be on the lookout for your mailing piece …."

14. What's read first in a letter? The headline.

15. What's read second in a letter? The P.S.

16. Offer "yes" and "no" options. The reason is that 25 percent of people who say "no" the first time will say "yes" the second time if you give them one more reason to buy.

17. Include a request to "Write names of people who would like to hear from us." Leave room for three names and addresses.

18. The more ways to buy or respond, the more response.

19. Prepare your order form before you make your offer. Your offer will flow naturally from the products you list on your order form.

20. Use surveys that can be completed in one minute.

21. The more you use the word "you," the greater the response.

22. Customers buy confidence: Put the number of years in business along with a big (BIG!) and easy-to-read guarantee.

23. More than half of your future business comes from your current customers.

24. Consider "piggy backing" with other noncompetitive businesses. This cuts printing and postage costs.

25. The most powerful word in the English language is "FREE!"

Direct mail shows your customers that you care, because you have taken the time to send your customers a personal message. No other form of advertising is as cost-effective as direct mail.

Spending Too Much on New Customers

You've all seen the big promotions on television and in newspapers that say, "Discount available to first-time users only." This type of advertisement is an example of one of the biggest marketing mistakes most businesses make: Relying totally on new customers to increase business. And this kind of advertising infuriates current customers.

Most businesses spend most or all of their advertising budgets to attract new customers. In fact, businesses, on average, spend five times as much money to attract new customers as they do to advertise their products or services to their existing customers. Business owners must think that their current customers will keep coming back and new customers will only add to the business' profitability.

Both assumptions are wrong. New customers are very fickle and very seldom become your best customers. Research by loyalty-marketing expert Brian Woolf has shown that only 1 percent of new customers become one of a business's best customers within one year. In fact, some stores reported losing more than 60 percent of all new customers within a year.

On the other hand, advertising to existing customers is very cost effective. Promotions aimed at existing customers are, on average, five times more productive than promotions aimed at people who have never shopped in your business. This makes sense. People who are familiar with your business, people who already have a relationship with you, are far more likely to want to visit you again than are people who have never shopped with you.

A certain percentage of people who don't shop with you don't come in because they have an existing relationship with a competitor. Others think your location is too far away. Still others have no need of your product or have heard bad things about you or have had an unpleasant experience at your business. These potential customers are not as likely to shop with you as an existing customer.

Try a "member get a member" promotion. You give an existing customer a discount or some other reward for bringing a new customer to your store. It's a great way of rewarding current customers and also gaining new business.

Branding Your Business

From 1779 to 1783, the Spanish tried to capture the Rock of Gibraltar from the British. They failed.

This strength, this invincibility, this unconquerable identification of the Rock of Gibraltar caused the Prudential Insurance Company in 1896 to use this symbol as their brand—symbolic of a defense from all obstacles. The Prudential use of the Rock of Gibraltar has become an important part of its advertising. It brands the company in the mind of its customers.

Why should you brand your business?

Here's why:

- Branding separates you from the competition.
- Branding creates trust, simplifies choice, and saves time and effort.
- Branding builds a bond between the product and the consumer.
- Branding is a unique business identity including (but not limited to) personality, quality, and likeability.

However, you don't have to be a major corporation to develop a brand. Small companies can create an image just as powerful as large corporations. Your business's "brand" should be explicit and easily define who you are and what you do.

Buy an Irish sweater hand-made in the Aran Islands and you'll see a little note attached to the sleeve from the weaver hoping that you'll enjoy what he or she made for you. THAT'S branding!

Here are some rules you should keep in mind while developing your brand image:

1. Branding says who you are and what you do.

2. Branding builds loyalty.

3. Branding relates to your total marketing package.

Branding Says Who You Are and What You Do

Your brand should "ring a bell" with customers. It should say what business you're in, what benefits you provide, and why you're better than the competition. Your business name reminds customers of your special brand.

If you own a dry-cleaning business, when someone just moves into your community and asks his or her neighbor, "Where's a good dry cleaner?" your name should be the brand that immediately comes to mind.

I'm always amazed when I suggest to new business owners they use their own name as their brand.

"Oh no, I can't do that," is a typical answer.

Why not?

"Well, I'd be uncomfortable."

Really? That feeling never occurred to folks like Saks Fifth Avenue, Macy's, or L.L. Bean. The list of successful companies that use their owner's name is almost endless.

> **True Tales**
>
> Stan Demski's name for his frame shop in Collingswood, New Jersey, says it all. His brand is "The Traveling Framer." That's who-he-is and what-he-does. He has a complete framing workshop in his van and travels to individual and company premises to do their framing on site. He is what he says he is: a traveling framer.

> **People Power**
>
> Stanley Marcus of the famous Neiman-Marcus specialty store agreed. He wrote, "Once you establish excellent service, you provide a safe harbor to which customers can always return."

Branding Builds Loyalty

When someone has a positive experience with your brand, they are more likely to buy that product or service again rather than a competing brand.

Carl Sewell, the world's largest-selling Cadillac dealer and author of "Customers for Life" says,

"We're trying to provide a warm, enjoyable experience like going to a fine hotel. You're willing to pay a little more because they treat you so nice, and there's that piece of chocolate on the pillow; and the shower is not two drops a minute, but comes out full force when you turn it on, and the towels are big and fluffy. Take care of your customers and they'll come back and bring their friends."

Branding Relates to Your Total Marketing Package

Your company's branding includes the colors you use in your logo, your bags, your slogan, and the special "look" of your advertising, marketing, and promotion.

I ran a small ad in our local paper in the same location every day. It had a very distinctive typeface with merchandise shown in a unique style created by a local artist. One day I ran a sale on men's lightweight jackets. Same location in the paper, same artist, same unique type faces. Good ad.

But the newspaper left off my store's name and address!

I called the paper complaining. They apologized and said they would run the ad—this time with our name and address—in their next issue at no charge.

Around noon that day, the manager of the store came to me and said, "Twelve!" I asked him what that meant. He said, "We've sold 12 of the sale jackets so far."

How could that be? The ad didn't have our name. How could a customer know where the jackets were on sale?

At the end of the day we sold 35 jackets. I took care of the last customer from a woman who wanted to buy one of our sale jackets for her grandson.

I brought her the jacket, wrote up the sales slip, rang up the sale, placed it in our store's bag, gave it to her and asked, "How did you know it was our store that had these jackets?"

"Why," she replied, "I saw your ad in the paper."

I quickly brought out that day's newspaper from behind my desk, showed her the ad and said, "Look—here's the ad. And it doesn't have our name or address."

She studied it carefully and then said to me, "In my paper at home, it has your name."

The customer was wrongly convinced our business name was on the ad because the typeface, copy, and illustrations were so similar to ads we had run in the past.

The Least You Need to Know

◆ Your advertising should create a personal relationship with your customers.

◆ Direct marketing is more cost productive than general advertising.

◆ Advertising to your current customers is more effective than acquiring new customers.

◆ Develop a brand identity that is distinctively yours alone.

Part 2

Profiting from the Loyalty Ladder

Here's how you can make your business grow: find, capture, and keep customers. The loyalty ladder is a metaphor for how customers become more and more committed to your business. When a customer has climbed to the top of the loyalty ladder, she cares almost as much about your business as you do.

You want all your prospects to become advocates. In this part of the book, you'll learn how to have your customers climb up to the top of the Loyalty Ladder.

Chapter 4

Prospects: Getting Them to Your Business

In This Chapter

- ◆ Prospecting potential customers
- ◆ Using newspaper advertising to reach new prospects
- ◆ Targeting your marketing
- ◆ Developing a signature product
- ◆ Outflanking larger competitors

As a business owner, prospects are all around you. They are people who may be interested in buying from you. They are the first rung on what we describe as the loyalty ladder. Your job is to get these prospects to buy something and to eventually turn them into loyal customers.

That's not an easy task.

The average consumer is hit with more than 5,000 advertising messages a day asking him to buy something somewhere. Linda Kapler Thaler, CEO & Chief Creative Officer of the Kapler Thaler Group (KTG), says, "It's hard to get your message heard in this noisy world."

Agreed. It's even harder to have prospects become loyal customers.

But you have to start somewhere as you try to have people climb your business's loyalty ladder. You have to start at the bottom rung and try to lure prospects into your business.

What's Your Yield Per Acre?

Farmers use the term "yield per acre" to measure their productivity. They look at how many bushels of corn or beans they harvest per acre. If the farmer is only getting 60 bushels per acre and the average is 100 bushels per acre, well, he knows he's doing something wrong.

> **Loyalty Lingo**
>
> **Market area** is the geographic region that most of your customers come from. For some businesses, this is very small (for example, most customers of convenience stores live within one mile of the store—that's why it's "convenient"). The average market area for the average single-location small business is within a five-mile radius of the store's location.

Your job is to calculate your own business's yield per acre and see if you measure up to the industry average or whether the competition is "farming the land" better than you.

Your "acres" are your *market area*. This is where 80 percent of your customers come from. For most small businesses, 80 percent of your customers live within a short distance of your store—three to five miles away. These are where your most likely prospects will come from, too.

If you know where the majority of your current customers come from, you'll know your market area for prospective customers as well. You can determine this from examining the addresses of a random sampling of your current customers.

Determining Market Area: Your Yield

Now, here's how to determine your "yield" in your market area, find out the following:

1. How many households are in your market area? Your postmaster can help you with this, if your area is local.

2. If you know the size of your customer base, you can compare it to the number of households in your market area.

3. How many families live in your market area?

4. What percentage of them does business with you? That's your "yield per acre."

This concept, although not an exact figure, will help you get a feel for how many more prospects are out there for you to do business with.

There are a lot of factors to take into consideration about your market area, including the …

◆ Geographic boundaries of your market

◆ Density of the market

◆ Income level of the market

◆ Type of work the people in the market perform

◆ Lifestyle of the market

◆ Ethnic characteristics of the market

◆ Median age of the market

◆ Amount of competition in the market

◆ Nature of the competition

If you learn about your market area and understand how these factors may affect your business, you will know how to communicate with new prospects.

Think of what farmers do to improve their yield per acre. They add water, they use fertilizer, they sprinkle insecticides. They hybridize their seeds. They plant, they cultivate, and they work at the job of getting as much of a profitable crop out of each acre as they can. What can you do in your business?

You have to live with some unchangeable elements. Consider them as givens. You can't change the economy of your area, or the density, or the geographical boundaries. You may or may not be able to change your location. You can't do much about how your competitors promote their business or charge for their products and services.

But you can respond to your specific market area. Understand if your area is higher or lower income, and offer the products and services people want at appropriate prices.

If your market includes area professionals, give talks at local service clubs. Run promotions to attract prospects who don't yet shop with you. Hold a contest or hire a celebrity (local celebs are great—and cheap!) to highlight your business. If your market area is full of young families, then sponsor a local children's sports team. Target your operation to reflect what your market area looks like.

And don't forget to improve the store's physical appearance. Four out of ten prospects, according to a survey by American Research Associates, decide whether to enter your business by what it looks like from the outside.

Improving Your Yield Per Acre Locally

One way to improve your yield per acre is to become involved with a local institution. Even though you may start small, your business can grow rapidly.

Years ago, my community had more than a dozen parochial schools. Each school had different uniforms. I approached the Mother Superior at the school closest to my clothing store and asked if we could supply the uniforms. She said that they were buying everything from an out-of-town firm who satisfied their needs.

I remained outside the school for a while looking at the boys and girls in their uniforms and noticed the boys did not have neckties.

I returned two weeks later for another appointment with Mother Superior. I said I noticed that the boys did not have ties. I then showed her ties with the embroidered school's logo I proposed to have available for all the boys.

She asked the price and I gave her the invoice. "You can have the ties for what we paid for them," I said. "And I will give you a couple dozen extras at no charge in case anyone forgets to bring his tie to school." She agreed.

The next year I suggested she consider our supplying pants for the boys. I would meet their existing price, do all the necessary alterations, and again supply extra pants for anyone who could not afford them. We were soon supplying the hundreds of children in the school with all their uniform needs.

In a short time, her "loyalty" to us had her recommending us to other schools as well. Within three years we were supplying the uniforms for more than a dozen parochial and private schools. All because of a necktie.

Attracting Prospects with the Newspaper

Prospects are people who have never shopped with you. So how do you attract them? For many businesses, newspaper ads are one effective way to cast your net wide across your market area.

Significant Stats
More ad dollars are spent in newspapers than any other advertising medium except direct mail—nearly $45 billion a year or about one half of the entire ad dollars spent for local advertising. Newspapers reach more than 120 million adults in the United States every day. Seven out of ten families subscribe, so when you advertise in newspapers, you are reaching a broad cross-section of your market. Newspapers are a guaranteed delivery to your prospects. You receive a more consistent audience with newspaper advertising than with radio or television.

About six out of ten subscribers say that they read every page of the newspaper. Nine out of ten read the general news. Nine out of ten men read the sports pages. Eight out ten women read the entertainment pages.

Because different segments of the audience read different sections of the newspaper, you can target a specific audience by advertising in a specific part of the paper. If you are selling products that mostly men buy, then advertise in the sports pages. If your audience is women, you might want to use the food section, the entertainment section, or the social pages.

Nowadays, newspaper advertising may not be the best way to reach the under-35-year-old market. If that is your audience, consider less newspaper advertising and more alternative media such as radio, cable television, and the Internet.

Creating Great Newspaper Headlines

When you advertise in newspapers, your competition is the other ads in the paper. You have to make your ads stand out from the crowd. To do this, you have to have a distinctive headline and text that your prospects will want to read. Let's start with the headline.

Ten rules for creating a great newspaper headline are as follows:

1. Your headline must either promise a benefit or provoke curiosity. If your product benefits senior citizens, then your headline might read, "An important message for senior citizens."

2. Stress the benefit of the product, not the product itself. If the shoes you are selling have crepe soles (the feature), then say that they are "shock absorbing" (the benefit).

3. Put the name of your product in the headline if possible. Place your business name on the bottom of the ad. Your name alone won't entice the potential prospect to read the ad. The provocative headline will.

4. There are certain words that really work well in headlines. They include (but are not limited to) new, free, how to, amazing, introducing, guarantee, now, you. A survey of the best-*pulling* and award-winning headlines found that the word "you" was used in almost all of them.

> **Loyalty Lingo**
>
> **Pull advertising** tries to have consumers buy your particular version of a product. *Push advertising* tries to increase consumer demand for a product.

> **People Power**
>
> The headline is the most important part of your newspaper ad. One of America's most famous advertisers, David Ogilvy, said that 75 percent of consumers read the headline of an ad. But only 25 percent keep on reading. When you have written the headline for your ad, you've spent 75 percent of the cost of the ad.

5. Include a local reference if possible. People tend to respond favorably to what they are familiar with.

6. Don't write your headline in capital letters. Putting it in upper and lower case INSTEAD OF WRITING IT LIKE THIS will increase readership.

7. Make it believable. You'll read an ad with the headline, "How to Lose Ten Pounds in Two Weeks." You'll skip over "How to Lose Ten Pounds in Two Hours." One is believable. One isn't.

8. Fulfill a dream. One of the classic newspaper headlines was used to sell a correspondence course on learning to play the piano. The headline was, "They Laughed When I Sat Down at the Piano." It broke sales records offering courses on learning to play the piano through mail instruction.

9. Try different headlines for the same product. Award-winning writer John Caples said that he tried different headlines for the exact same product, and one would pull as much as 20 times more business than the others. Doubleday Books ran this headline successfully for years: "Buy These Four Books for 99¢." But a slightly different headline worked much better: "Buy Three Books for 99¢— Get One Free!"

10. Offer excellent value. Don't waste your valuable advertising dollars on offers that are too minor to be interesting to prospects.

I've written more than 25,000 headlines over the past 40 years. A small fraction work almost all the time. Here's one that will work for you. Simply state the original price, sale price, and the item. "Would You Buy a $30.00 Shirt on Sale for $14.99?" It tells the original price and the sale price, and makes you want to keep reading to find out more.

Newspaper-Advertising Copy That Attracts Prospects

The relationship between newspaper headlines and copy is like the relationship between a movie poster and a movie trailer. The poster grabs a viewer's attention, but the trailer shows scenes from the movie and tells the viewer more. The trailer is designed to get the viewer to make the decision to spend his money to watch the whole film at the theater.

Only one out of ten readers of your newspaper ad will read the body copy in your ad. But if they're captured by your headline, they will read on. If you can get someone to read the first 50 words of what you've written, they'll probably read the next 250 words.

Ten rules for writing newspaper-advertisement copy:

1. Get to your main point fast! You should expand on the benefit promised in the headline.

2. Include the price. If it's on sale, tell me how much the original price was, how much the sale price is, and what I'm saving.

3. Don't exaggerate. Make sure that "the story isn't better than the store." Promise a lot but deliver more.

4. Be specific. People read ad copy both to be entertained and to get information. To quote Kipling: "I keep six honest serving men (they taught me all I knew); their names are What and Why and When and How and Where and Who."

5. Write as though you are talking with someone in the same room.

6. Write in the present tense. Avoid past tenses such as "has been" or "were done." Writing in the present tense implies immediacy.

7. Use testimonials. Other people who say nice things about your products makes your offers more believable than just when you say so.

8. The word "Free" is still the most powerful word in the English language. "Buy one for $10, get one free" pulls 40 percent better than "Half Price" or "50 Percent Off."

9. Anticipate questions. What would you ask yourself about the product or offer that you are advertising?

10. Remember the "rule of three":

   ◆ Say what you're going to say

   ◆ Say it

   ◆ Say what you said

And if writing is simply not your cup of tea, then spend the money to hire someone who can. Newspaper advertising is too valuable to your business to waste on poorly written, ungrammatical copy. Decide what the main points of your ad need to be, and then go over them with a professional writer to polish the ad. Remember, your ad is often a prospect's first impression of your business. You don't get a second chance to make a first impression!

Target Your Marketing to Specific Groups of Prospects

Many businesses make the mistake of saying, "I only advertise in the local newspaper. Everyone knows our business is here." WRONG!

Newspapers are great for reaching many prospects, but not everyone reads the paper. Go back to who your target customers are. You aren't likely to reach them with a newspaper ad if …

   ◆ They are under 35 years old.

   ◆ They are out-of-towners or visitors to your area.

   ◆ They speak another language and don't read the local English-language news-paper.

Since prospects are just potential shoppers hanging out there somewhere, you have to find out where they are and advertise in those places.

New Residents

Every year, 20 percent of the population in the U.S. moves. New residents who have just moved into your market area are a huge source of prospects for your business. A direct-mail postcard or letter to these new movers, telling them about your business with a special offer to use on their first purchase, can be very effective in turning a "prospect" into a "shopper."

You can do this kind of mailing yourself if the number of new residents in your area is small. A local realtor may be willing to supply you with names and addresses, and you can send a card to that list. If you would rather have someone else handle this, there are marketing companies that will send out your mailings to lists of new residents in your area every month. Businesses for products and services that most people use regularly find new-mover marketing especially effective (supermarkets, dry cleaners, pizza parlors, beauty salons, dentists, etc.).

Advertise in Other Media

If the under-35 set doesn't read newspapers, what do they do? Many listen to the radio—an under-utilized but extremely effective medium for advertising to this group. In Chapter 5, you'll find more detail on how to use radio and television to attract prospects and shoppers to your business.

Use the Internet

We've reached the point where a big segment of the population goes straight for their computer when they want to know where to buy something. You don't want to miss out on this market—most of them are young, with money to spend.

Our advice on Internet marketing is this: Get some professional help here. It's not like the newspaper, which can help you set up your ads, or radio and television that have personnel and facilities to produce your spots. A home-grown website will usually look like just that—amateurish. A website can be simple but it should reflect the "look" of your business. To do that, you probably need a website developer.

Work with the developer to create a website that describes your business and perhaps make it possible for people to purchase directly from the website. Then be sure that your developer knows how to get your website seen in the various "search engines"—Google, Yahoo, America Online (AOL), etc. That's how prospects will look for your business and find you on the web.

Be Known for Something

One effective way to attract potential prospects is to offer something exclusive. If you have a unique product, potential customers will want to visit you just to see what everybody is talking about.

What you want to do is develop a "signature" product, one that will generate publicity and keep your business at the front of people's minds.

Here are some examples:

♦ Clothing stores strive to develop products such as the Burberry raincoat and the L.L. Bean boot.

♦ Dorothy Lane Supermarkets in Dayton, Ohio, has developed a line of "killer brownies" that are one of their foremost attractions. The brownies have gained such acclaim that they are sold to people all over the world on the Internet.

♦ The Apple iPod not only created a new category for listening to music (replacing the former signature product, the Sony Walkman), it also became so ubiquitous that Apple redesigned its new computers to look like iPods!

True Tales

When Ben Sears retired from the circus, he opened a small restaurant in San Francisco. But aren't all restaurants alike? Don't they all sell food?

Ben remembered his favorite meal to start the day: Swedish pancakes. The recipe was handed down through generations of his wife Hilbur's Swedish family. Because they were small in size, Ben offered 18 for a breakfast at a low price. They were an instant success.

Today the Sears Restaurant has people standing outside as early as 6 A.M. waiting for the restaurant to open so that they can order the "world-famous Swedish pancakes." Sears Restaurant now makes 11,000 pancakes a day and sells the mix to customers from around the world.

Competing With the Giants

How do you gather new prospects in a retail landscape increasingly dominated by the retail giants? There are now large discounters/department stores like Wal-Mart and Target, *category killers* like Barnes and Noble and PetsMart, and the ever-increasing challenge of Internet sites like Amazon and eBay.

How can a retailer compete with a store like Wal-Mart, which often can sell items for less than a retailer can buy them from its distributor? Obviously not on price.

Loyalty Lingo

Category killer is a store that specializes in one type of product and has a tremendous selection of that product. Examples include Borders for books, Toys 'R' Us for toys, and Circuit City for electronics. A **big-box store** is a large discount store built in a nondescript rectangular building which resembles a big box.

But there are ways retailers and other businesses can distinguish themselves from their much larger competitors. A smaller business can entice prospects by using some of the following tactics:

◆ Offer knowledgeable employees who understand your products and services and can help customers decide which particular products or services to buy. One of the failings of the *big-box stores* is that often their employees are not familiar with the products in the store.

◆ Have enough help. Often, super-sized stores are short on staff. During off-peak hours customers sometimes have to search wide and far just to find someone to take their money.

◆ Make sure complaints are handled speedily. Employees should be empowered to make decisions, especially when a customer has a complaint. This is the perfect opportunity to turn a prospect into a true believer in your business.

◆ Promote, promote, and promote some more. The presence of competition should make you want to tighten your cost structure, but don't make the mistake of eliminating your advertising. The surest path to the bankruptcy court is to neglect your marketing.

◆ Find out what your competitors are doing—and do something else. The more you can make your business unique, the less fear you should have of competitors. If your competitors are cornering the market on low-priced soap, try to find high-quality brands that are unique in your marketplace. You may have to shift the focus of your store to items the big-box stores do not carry.

If you can have friendly and helpful employees, if you can carve a niche different from your competitors, and if you can have interesting products and services, then you have a chance to succeed in a big-box environment. You have to supplement everything you are doing right with a marketing campaign that emphasizes the benefits to prospects of checking out your business. It also helps to add some excitement and promotion and fun.

If you do all that, your business will survive and grow, when others are running their "out of business" final sales.

The Least You Need to Know

- ◆ Look closely at your market area to determine your business's potential sales.
- ◆ Newspaper advertising is important for helping prospects pick out your business from a crowded marketplace.
- ◆ Not all prospects read the newspaper, so advertise in the appropriate media for your market.
- ◆ Develop a "signature" product, and prospects will line up outside your door.
- ◆ Compete with the giants on service and unique selection, not on price.

Shoppers: Getting People to Buy from You

In This Chapter

- ◆ If at first they do not buy … try, try again
- ◆ Making the first purchase—FREE
- ◆ Spreading your enthusiasm around
- ◆ Getting on the radio
- ◆ Giving shoppers reasons to come back to you again

Okay, you've gotten your prospect up to the second rung of the loyalty ladder—she's actually shopping for goods with you. She's in your store, online at your website, on the phone with your customer-service people, reading your catalog … whatever. She's a shopper! She has been convinced to try your business and to see if what you have to offer matches what she wants to buy.

Now your job is to sell something to her—to move her up the loyalty ladder again to become a customer. How are you going to do it? That's what this chapter is all about.

Perseverance

It's not easy converting a shopper to a customer. Shoppers are checking you out, looking at your merchandise, evaluating your operation. Often they're not ready to buy.

Persevere. Your patience will be tried with shoppers, but if you keep at it, the rewards can be great.

A McGraw-Hill survey said that it takes four consecutive calls to convert a shopper into a customer. So don't become discouraged after a first, second, or third try. If you do, your business competitor will come in and make the sale you should have made if you just persevered one more time.

> **People Power**
>
> President Calvin Coolidge (a man not known for wordiness) alleged, "Nothing in the world can take the place of persistence. Talent will not; nothing is more common than unsuccessful men with talent. Genius will not; the world is full of educated derelicts. Persistence and determination alone are omnipotent."

Make sure that your employees understand how to handle shoppers. All the rules of how to treat customers apply to shoppers, too. Remember the old caricature of the shoe salesman who brings out 25 pairs of shoes to the woman who, in the end, doesn't buy any of them. Maybe the next time she comes in, she will buy. That's the attitude your employees must have when working with a shopper. "She didn't buy today, but she will the next time she comes in."

Owners of antique shops know this well. Customers often like to see an item several times, take measurements, see if that item fits in her home, and check with her spouse, all before making a final purchase commitment.

Giveaways

A great way to encourage a shopper to buy from you is to give the first purchase free.

Wait! Aren't I in business to make money?

Yes—and sometimes this can be the best way to encourage a shopper to come back to you and buy. If you're in business for the long haul, you're interested in the lifetime value of the customer, not just today's purchase. How much will that shopper—soon to be a customer—spend with you over the course of the next 20 years? Is that total worth an investment of a few dollars?

This is the psychology behind the move toward "sampling" at supermarkets and specialty food stores. Give a shopper a taste of the product for free. If it's good, she will be back to buy more.

Diaper companies provide "sample packs" for hospitals to give away to new parents. Pharmaceutical companies provide sample sizes of their prescription drugs for physicians to give you the first time it is prescribed. Many publishers allow you to download the first chapter of a book from the Internet. In all of these cases, they are hoping you'll buy-after-you-try.

Your giveaway doesn't have to be a complete handout. Many times a "free gift" is contingent on another purchase. For example, cosmetic companies often give away "free samples" of their products when you buy a certain dollar's worth of products. We mail thousands of New Move-In offers each month for different supermarkets across the country that give away $5 in free groceries when the customer buys at least $25. And most stores report that the customers who redeem the free $5 will spend at least $50 in that visit.

On a big scale, giving a product away can be a major marketing coup. Duke University decided to "give away" an Apple iPod to every student in its freshman class starting in the fall of 2005. They said that new educational uses for the iPod had been developed and they wanted to encourage their students to take advantage of the product. The cost of the $300 item is minimal, compared to the annual cost of enrolling at Duke—about $40,000. But what publicity did that announcement get!

Enthusiasm Triumphs

One of the first things shoppers notice about your business is the ambiance. Are the employees happy and spreading their enthusiasm to customers? Is the business fun and cheery or dreary and drab? Shoppers will want to come back if employees seem friendly and eager to help.

Enthusiasm can help counteract "tough times." When your customers see the joy and vigor with which you greet the world, they want to be around you and do business with you.

People Power

Enthusiasm emanates from the motivational speaker Charlie "Tremendous" Jones (when people ask Charlie how he feels, he roars back, "Tremendous!"). Charlie greets everyone with a giant bear hug and a cheery "I want you to remember how glad I am to see you!" What a way to start the day!

Enthusiasm is habit forming. People who feel better, act better. Stimulate positive feelings within yourself and those feelings start bouncing back from the people who work with you every day.

Enthusiasm is contagious. According to Dale Carnegie, "Enthusiasm can't be taught. It must be caught."

We once ran a seminar on customer service with a panel of experts. When I asked for questions at the end of the discussion, a lady in the audience asked, "Is it more important to make customers happy or employees?"

I knew the answer to that one and quickly answered, "Of course, the customers."

To my amazement, every one of the panel members disagreed. The consensus was that there is no way customers will be happy without first having happy associates.

After thinking about it, I agreed.

Employees need to be looked at as an investment, not a cost. Then making a commitment to creating a pleasant work place and ongoing training makes sense.

When you have accomplished making your associates happy, you can then ask the following questions:

To the clerks: Since you see the name of shoppers when they write a check or give you a credit card, do you say to them, "Thank you (and their name)" because you see it printed on the check or card?

> **True Tales**
>
> A recent New Yorker cartoon showed a wife answering the phone in her home. She turns to her husband and says, "It's the waiter we had at the restaurant this evening. He wants to know if everything was all right."

To the manager: Do you ask shoppers, before they leave, if they were satisfied? (And really want to know the answer? Not like the time when we visited a new restaurant for the first time. Most of the meal was good, but one of the dishes was not to our liking. We told the manager on the way out. Her answer: "Well, at least you'll know what not to order next time." But "next time" never happened.)

To build enthusiasm in your associates, you should check your own "enthusiasm temperature."

From our Australian friend Tony Ingleton: "About eight or nine months ago, I had a lot of financial pressure. It really started to get me down. Then I realized that besides being responsible for the payroll each week, I was in charge of company enthusiasm. If the head person is giving out bad vibes, that isn't going to do anyone any good.

"I decided to adopt a new attitude. Despite problems, when I picked up the phone or greeted an associate or a customer, I sounded happy, positive. That attitude changed me and gave confidence to my employees, and I was eventually able to save my company."

As prominent investor advisor Charles Schwab said, "A man can succeed at almost anything for which he has unlimited enthusiasm." Make sure your enthusiasm is catching—it will be healthy for your business if you spread it around!

People Power

Businessman Ross Perot says people don't need to be managed. They need to be led. How you act, react, perform is closely watched by the people who work with you. They imitate.

Confidence

A shopper makes the decision to purchase based on many factors. But the number-one reason why people buy where they buy is confidence. Confidence in the store, in the people, and in the product. This was confirmed by a recent nationwide survey. (The other reasons to buy, in order, were quality, selection, service, and price.)

People want to shop where they feel they will be taken care of. Where the quality of the product is consistent. Where what you promise is what you deliver.

Showing confidence in your products is why mail-order companies have guarantees in their catalogues. But most retailers don't offer a guarantee.

Why not? Won't you stand behind your products or services? Won't you do everything you can to make sure your customers are satisfied with their transactions? Why not tell your shoppers, loud and clear? A printed guarantee engenders great confidence in shoppers, showing them clearly that this business is trustworthy.

I received a catalog of supplies for my store. One page had big illustrations of store-policy signs available. They read as follows:

- ◆ "No refund. Exchange ONLY."
- ◆ "No refund or exchange on sale merchandise."
- ◆ "NO REFUND OR EXCHANGE."
- ◆ "No Refund after 7 days on regularly priced merchandise."

Every sign began with the word "NO."

What an exciting, marvelous, constructive way to inspire confidence in your store. Wherever the customers look, they see big gold and black signs saying "NO!"

I want signs that say "YES!"

- "Yes, we will refund and exchange anything anytime."

- "Yes, we will make you happy."

- "Yes, we will make you satisfied."

That's confidence!

Significant Stats

Some interesting statistics about shoppers:
- Shoppers decide in the first eight seconds if they are comfortable in a store;
- Eight out of ten shoppers dislike a dirty parking lot or storefront;
- Three out of four shoppers visit a business first because of a "sale";
- Four out of ten shoppers judge a salesperson by his or her professional "look";
- Eight out of ten shoppers think that all ads for any particular business look alike.

It's important to convert a prospect into a shopper. But we can't stop on this rung of the loyalty ladder. In any business, you have to give shoppers reasons to come back.

Do you give your shoppers a coupon, a certificate, a smile, a "something" that encourages them to come back at least one more time? If they come back and buy, then you have advanced your shopper to a customer.

Loyalty Lingo

Niche marketing is advertising to specific audiences, rather than to the general public. When you know what "niche," or segment of the general population, that your business appeals to, then you can focus your marketing efforts to that group.

Radio Advertising Will Attract Shoppers to Your Business

Radio is a valuable marketing tool for your business. It informs and educates, and it is flexible, targetable, and intrusive. Radio works as a *niche marketer*.

Your customers often choose one format of radio programming and listen to that format every time they listen to the radio. The 10 most popular formats in the United States are (in order):

1. Country

2. News/Talk

3. Oldies

4. Adult Contemporary

5. Hispanic

6. Adult Standards

7. Top 40

8. Sports

9. Classic Rock

10. Hot Adult Contemporary

(Source: Radio Advertising Bureau)

The top two make up almost one third of all the radio stations—country is 19.4 percent, and news/talk is 11.3 percent.

What you're doing when you choose the station where you advertise is customizing your message for your shoppers. The average American listens to radio 20 hours a week. Find out what stations your shoppers listen to, and when they listen. Then you'll be well on your way to an effective radio marketing strategy.

So what radio stations should you use? That's easy. The ones your shoppers listen to. And you can find that out by asking them. Survey the shoppers in your store once a year to find out what media they read, listen to, and watch.

Radio works very effectively when used in one of two ways:

◆ Institutional advertising. Telling the listener who you are, what you do, and why shoppers should shop with you. This kind of radio ad runs for weeks and months.

◆ Saturation advertising. This is when you can "own" a radio station with a flurry of radio commercials just before the big sale in your store. You buy a month's worth of commercials and use them up in one to three days. They run every hour of the day because somewhere, sometime, someone is listening to radio.

There are some businesses that use radio advertising frequently. They include food products, drug products, automobiles, internet services, long-distance services, health and beauty aids, and beer. Those categories provide nearly 60 percent of radio's advertising dollars. If your business is one of those, you should probably consider radio advertising, because so many of your competitors have figured out that it works for them.

> **Significant Stats**
>
> Nine out of ten people listen to the radio in the car; six out of ten people listen to the radio at work; there are over 11,000 commercial radio stations on the air in the United States—about 4,800 stations on AM radio and 6,200 on FM radio.

Businesses that use radio the least are sporting goods, toys, jewelry, and photo shops. That doesn't mean you can't if you're in any of those categories. It just means others aren't using it. Maybe that could be a plus for your business to stand out on the radio.

The following is a list of frequently asked questions (and their answers) about radio advertising:

Q: Does radio have any clear advantage over other media?

A: Yes. Speed. If pushed (and you have a cooperative radio station), you can put a message on radio in a few hours. Or less. It takes a much longer time to prepare a newspaper ad, direct-mail piece, or television commercial.

Q: Is radio expensive?

A: Yes, but ... you can always find a "deal" in radio. Buy X amount of spots in the best time spot and they will often throw in extra spots in the wee hours of the morning. You can often barter more easily with radio than with any other advertising medium. I've had a radio salesperson say to me: "If you give us ten $25 gift certificates from your business, we'll give you $250 worth of radio advertising if you also buy 10 hours worth of regular advertising." The radio station uses your gift certificates for promotions. These types of deals are common in radio advertising.

Q: Every station that comes into my business tells me that they're number one in the ratings, and show me their Nielsen or Arbitron charts to prove it. How can they all be number one?

A: Believe it or not, they can be—but in different time sequences and different age brackets. One station might be number one in listenership in early-morning drive time. Another station is number one for the adult population ages 34 to 50. Another station is number one for late-night programming. The rating services rate by different age groups and different time slots. It's difficult for a station NOT to be number one for something. Your job is to select the number-one slot for the audience you want to reach for your business. Ask to see the actual ratings and find out how the station's rating fits into your potential audience.

Q: Is there a technique for writing a radio script that works most of the time?

A: Here's one four-step technique that I know works: First, identify your brand or the name of your business early in the commercial. Second, identify it often (mention your firm's name again and again and again). Third, promise the listener a benefit early in the commercial. Fourth, repeat the benefit (again and again and again).

Significant Stats

There is no set point you should stop running a radio commercial. I think one way to test whether or not a commercial is effective is to offer some benefit to the customer to come into your place of business when she hears the radio ad. If no one mentions your ad, you know the ad is no longer effective (or that you are running it on the wrong station).

Q: How often should I change my commercial?

A: Not as often as you might think. You will become tired, bored, and anxious with your present radio ad much more quickly than the listeners, many of whom will hear it for the first time the next time it runs.

Q: How many products can I sell in one ad?

A: One. Imagine a furniture store listing 15 items with the original price and the sale price in a one-minute radio ad. The audience will remember … nothing! Advertise a storewide sale. Advertise a newly arrived product. Advertise a specific brand. That's it.

Q: How about music in my radio commercial?

A: Be afraid … be very afraid. Music is good when it works, but very bad when it doesn't. Be wary of jingles. The good ones are very expensive. Amateur jingles sound just that: amateur. Another problem with jingles (including the professional ones) is that you can't understand many of the words. People don't concentrate on listening to the radio—they just listen to the radio. David Ogilvy, author of *Ogilvy on Advertising* (Vintage, 1985), had a great thought about singing commercials: "Would you go into a store and expect the sales person to start singing at you?"

Q: Should I use well-known radio personalities?

A: Sure. You might have to pay an extra "talent fee," but the cost is worth it because the audience identifies with the individual. Give the person an outline of what you want him or her to say. Often just the product and the price are enough, and then tell the person to say whatever he or she wants to say. The ad will be far better because it will sound off-the-cuff, extemporaneous, and "believable."

Q: Who writes the script?

A: The radio station has full-time staff to do just that—they write what you want to sell. Insist that the salesperson bring the finished script for you to review and the finished cassette of the ad BEFORE it goes on the air. Then bring in some other folks in your business to listen to the finished advertisement. You always want to have other people preview your ads before they go out to the public.

Q: Should I alternate the times when my ad runs?

A: Yes. Running your ad at different times on different days makes the customer feel that they hear the ad many more times than it actually runs. But there are exceptions. If a certain time slot works for you (for example, adjacent to the news, if your shoppers listen to that), then keep on using it. Or if a special time ties in with a special characteristic of your business, then use it. We remember a great tie-in for a radio ad: "Good morning. It's 9:13. And today's news is brought to you by the Boardwalk National Bank at 913 Atlantic Avenue …." Clever. And memorable.

Q: Can I do only radio advertising?

A: No. Radio is strictly complementary to your other advertising. It targets certain markets and can reach those well. It reinforces, re-emphasizes, and repeats the message that you tell in other media. But never forget that it is the cumulative effect of all your advertising—all carrying the same message at the same time— that makes your advertising work for you.

Radio is an efficient day-in and day-out advertising medium. It is relatively inexpensive to advertise on radio and the production costs are very low. By picking the right radio stations, you can target your message to the customers you want to reach.

True Tales

In our area there are 12 radio stations. We did most of our advertising on the station we listened to. After all, if we liked it, our customers would like it, right? Wrong. When we surveyed our shoppers, we discovered 67 percent of them were listening to one station. But it wasn't the station we were advertising on. We switched our advertising dollars to that station, of course!

More Techniques to Turn Shoppers into Customers

When someone is checking out your business, that's your opportunity to bring him up to the next rung of the Loyalty Ladder. In every business, there are tried-and-true things you can do.

Mailing List, Mailing List, Mailing List

Can we say it enough? Your business is nothing without customers. Get their names and communicate with them.

When a shopper comes to your store, calls you for information, or visits your website, GET HER NAME AND ADDRESS. Only then can you contact her again to follow up on her question, to let her know when something she was looking at is going on sale, to tell her that the new shipment is in. And you can use that information for future direct-mail campaigns to entice her to shop with you in the future. Whether e-mail or snail mail, GET HER NAME AND ADDRESS.

Here are some ways to do this:

♦ Ask the shopper if she would like to sign up for your mailing list, to be notified about future offers and sales.

♦ Hold a contest or sweepstakes that doesn't require a purchase to enter (that's how most contests have to be run, to comply with state law). If you have a small sweepstakes every few months, you'll always have an excuse to collect shoppers' names and addresses. The prizes don't have to be huge for a sweepstakes to be exciting. Refer to Appendix C for a Direct Mail Sweepstakes sample.

Taking the Suggestion

Suggestion boxes may seem simple, but they are a very effective way to get feedback from people who shop with you. Many people love to give their opinions, and the best thing for them is when you ask.

Put the Suggestion Box up front where it can be seen (or make it a prominent "button" on your website). Make sure there are plenty of pencils and forms for the shoppers to use. Then, answer each suggestion—the next day if possible. Answer them with a personal letter or e-mail for each suggestion in the box, not a form letter that isn't responsive to the suggestion. In your response, include a gift certificate from your business that they can use the next time they shop with you, as a "thank you" for suggesting the idea.

Doing Shopper Surveys

Another way to get feedback from your shoppers is to survey them. Ask them what they want. This can be especially helpful if you are contemplating a move or a major change.

Furr's Market in Albuquerque, NM, was considering remodeling one of their stores. Before they finalized their plans, they surveyed over 2,000 shoppers and asked, "What do want to see in our new store?" People requested a scratch bakery up front, a deli near the entrance, and more seafood. Furr's included them all and doubled their volume.

Hey, it never hurts to ask!

Selling 'Em One at a Time

Some days, all those window shoppers and "I'm just looking" shoppers who come through your store can make you wonder how you'll ever sell enough for your business to be profitable. That's a BIG nut to crack! Be patient. Those window shoppers of today can easily turn into the big sales of tomorrow.

I once gave a seminar to the World Hockey Association. A team owner came up after the program and said, "I've got one basic question you haven't answered here today. How do I sell 10,000 tickets?

My answer: "One at a time."

It's difficult to focus on 10,000 tickets. It's easy to sell one ticket.

The Least You Need to Know

- Most shoppers will visit your business more than once before they buy. Don't give up on them.

- Radio advertising works well to target shoppers.

- Make your guarantees explicit to show shoppers how much you believe in your products and services.

- Excitement in a business comes from the top and radiates throughout the organization.

- Your shoppers can give you a lot of information if you just ask.

Chapter **6**

Customers: Getting People to Buy Your Products or Services

In This Chapter

- The reasons why customers buy
- Customers never forget a bad experience
- Focusing on your customers
- Remembering to say "Thanks"
- Using direct mail—a powerful marketing tool

If you can have your prospects actually come visit your business, you have created a shopper. If that shopper actually buys something from you, you now have a customer.

No matter why someone visits you, when that customer buys from you, you have started a pattern. Get that same customer to buy from you on four distinct shopping trips and you have created a loyal customer. (See the next chapter on "clients.")

This chapter will explore the reasons why customers make that first buying decision and why they decide to come back. By catering to your customers, you are well on your way to winning customer loyalty.

Why People Buy

There are only two reasons people buy:

◆ Good feelings

◆ Solutions to problems

Satisfy either of these needs and you make a sale. You now have a customer.

True Tales
Feargal Quinn, CEO of Super-quinn in Ireland, learned in a focus group how tiring it was for seniors to navigate his large supermarkets. Feargal listened and acted. Now seniors enjoy chairs strategically placed around his markets to ensure their rest and "good feelings."

Good Feelings

A woman goes to the beauty parlor or buys new clothes. She's buying good feelings.

A man buys life insurance to guarantee an income for his family if he's no longer here. He has bought good feelings.

A man and or a woman go to a restaurant for an enjoyable evening. They spent their money on good feelings.

True Tales
"Solutions to a problem" is a very important concept in selling and advertising. Many sales peo-ple and advertisers list the "fea-tures" of a product when in fact they should concentrate on the "benefits." Take decaffeinated coffee, as an example: feature = no caffeine; benefit = lets you sleep (solution to a problem).

Solutions to Problems

Your feet are tired at the end of the day. You buy cushion innersoles for extra comfort. A solution to a problem.

You have to drive several miles and then wait in line to buy postage stamps. You find out how to buy the stamps on the web. A solution to a problem.

A senior citizen is housebound after an injury. She finds out that she can buy her groceries at a local supermarket that will deliver them to her home. A solution to a problem.

Think of the products or services you have in your business. Promote them by appealing to one of the two reasons why people buy.

When the Negative Outweighs the Positive

When you have somebody buy something from you, you are on your way to creating a loyal customer. However, there are several pitfalls on the way up the loyalty ladder. Customers say that they will tolerate only two negative experiences before they take their business elsewhere, according to a customer service survey from Amdocs, a creator of business software. In addition …

◆ Three out of four people in this survey said that they would hang up on a call after waiting on hold for longer than five minutes.

◆ Eight out of ten people said that they'd rather visit the dentist, pay a tax bill, or sit in a traffic jam than deal with an unhelpful customer-service representative.

Remember the scene in the movie "Network" in which the TV announcer Howard Beale leaned out his window and yelled, "Get up. Open your windows. Stick your head out and yell, 'I'm mad as hell and I'm not going to take this anymore.'"

Customers increasingly hold companies accountable for poor customer service, saying that they "will not take it any more" and will change providers if given anything but good service. And, most people will tell their friends and family about negative service experiences.

Here's an example of how a business lost $50,000 worth of business from me. It began when I went to a local photography shop where I spent several thousand dollars a year for film developing.

I had received a mail offer from Kodak for a free 8 x 10 photograph if I sent the negative to them before the end of the month. Since my camera shop was a Kodak dealer, I brought them the negative to handle the free offer.

"But you're one day late," said the woman behind the counter. I looked at the offer and she was right.

"But I've been out of town for a few weeks and didn't realize I was late."

"Well, you are."

I asked for the owner of the store. He came out and I explained about the Kodak offer. "But you're a day late."

I assured him that Kodak would want a good customer to be given a day's grace. "Sorry," he said, "I have to say 'no.'"

And so did I. "No" to any future business with him.

By not giving me the free 8 x 10 picture, he lost, conservatively, over the next five years, $50,000 in business. (If he understood the value of a customer, he would have said, "Hey, the free picture is on me. Let this be my reward to you for all your business.")

No wonder there's an empty store today where his business used to be.

The Different Kinds of Customers

Customers are not all alike. Period.

Once you attract a customer to your business, you will want to sell to that customer again and again. But to do that effectively, you have to realize that there are many different kinds of customers. One of your tasks as a business owner is to differentiate among your customers and figure out which marketing approach is right for each group.

Customers Who Buy According to Brand

This is where having information about your customers in a loyalty program is really helpful. You can have the computer track repetitive product or brand buying by your profitable customers to make sure that those brands are kept in stock and new items are added. Then communicate, communicate, communicate!

Customers Who Come in Seasonally or to Stock Up

These customers can be heavy hitters even if they shop infrequently. You can identify the profitable ones with a loyalty card.

They may need a more patient and knowledgeable clerk to help them with their longer list. Maybe a gift certificate for a lunch nearby so that they can leave, and then come back and shop some more. How about delivering their purchases to their homes? (That offer promotes both "good feelings" and a "solution to a problem.")

True Tales

Customers who come in during the Christmas season may not be your most frequent shoppers, but they may be important customers because they spend so much money during the holiday season.

During the Christmas holiday season I saw many customers that I did not see during the rest of the year, including many grandparents. Also, I saw people who considered our merchandise too high end for regular shopping but loved to have their gifts come from our store.

We treated all of our customers very well. But those occasional shoppers with long lists received royal service. For example, we gave them our best foil gift-wrapping with matching bows for free, free gift cards, a free lunch, and free delivery. Sometimes we even told our customers, "You don't have to wait to have each gift wrapped. We will take the information, wrap them later, and deliver all your packages to you gift-wrapped."

Customers Who Only Shop Sales

Why are business owners upset when a customer comes to their business only for a sale?

I loved sale customers. I made sure they were treated with respect. They buy. And they shop often. They are also providing us with a valuable service. They were reducing our inventory of items that we no longer wanted to carry. One way I kept them coming back was to have a special sale section in the store at all times. Items were added daily. Items that didn't sell were reduced further and further until they landed on our famous $1 rack.

All customers should be treated with the same measure of respect. That maxim was not observed when I went to an airline counter with an upgrade certificate (tantamount to a "sale" offer) for a free trip to Hawaii. The agent looked at the coupon and said, disparagingly, "Oh, you've got one of these ...."

"Yes," I admitted, "and 'one of these' means I am a very good customer of your airline."

"Well," she sighed, "I guess I have to fill out the paperwork."

And she did. But not without making me feel like I was an unwanted customer, when, on the contrary, I was a very loyal and frequent customer (up until that point).

Focus on Focus Groups

Focus groups are the perfect opportunity to expand your future direction by simply asking advice from the people who know what works in your business—your customers.

Loyalty Lingo

A **focus group** is a meeting to bring together a cross-section of your customers to discuss your business. This definition is from Forbes magazine: "Six people around a table eating pizza is a party. Six people around a table talking about eating pizza is a focus group."

So how do you gather the people around a table to talk about YOUR business? Start with your customers.

The following are 10 steps to running a focus group:

1. Ask your customers to participate in your focus group. Tell them all about the focus group: how it works, what they have to do. Recruit them with a notice on your bulletin board, or with stuffers in their shopping bags. Or, as Giant Supermarkets did in Washington, D.C., use a full-page newspaper ad asking people if they'd like to sign up.

2. Get their basic information. Their name, address, phone number, e-mail, age, gender, and whatever other information you can gather.

3. Limit each focus group to eight to ten people. In each group, try to have a cross-section of your stores' customers, if possible. Make sure you include men and women, young and old shoppers, and some shoppers who only shop seasonally.

4. Decide what subjects you want to cover in the focus group and develop an agenda. The agenda is a starting point and a way to give structure to the meeting. Don't try to cover too much ground; the conversation will naturally move from topic to topic. Mail the agenda. Let focus group members know what's on the program before they arrive.

5. Begin the meeting with having them say who they are. Members should introduce themselves and say a few words about their jobs, families, and how long they've shopped with you.

6. Hire a professional moderator. Don't run the meeting yourself because your emotions get in the way. Your local college can recommend one of the professors from their business department to moderate. This will free customers to be more honest with feedback than if you were running the session.

7. Have staff attend. Not many; just a few each time. Their job is not to offer excuses or give reasons why things cannot be done as suggested. They are there to listen.

8. Keep it short. Two hours is maximum. If it's longer, people tire or start to repeat their comments.

9. Tape it. You need a record of the meeting. Otherwise you find yourself saying, "What did they say about …" or "Who remembers the solution to …" Even better is someone making a transcript of the group's conversation. Look for a good stenographer or court reporter.

10. Give gifts. Not money. Gift certificates are good (for example, a $20 gift certificate as a "thank you").

Plus one more:

11. Have some food at the focus group. Not a meal—munchies and something to drink are fine. M&Ms are the traditional focus-group snack.

Okay, everyone's assembled. Memorize these do's and don'ts for your focus group. They are as follows:

- Do give everyone a chance to talk. Your moderator will encourage the quiet ones to speak, asking questions like, "What's your opinion of this, Jack?" Or, "Do you agree with Margaret?" That's the moderator's job—to get everyone involved.

- Do meet every two or three months. More often it becomes a chore. Less, it becomes unimportant to the business and you will soon find excuses not to have them.

- Do have staff attend. Divide them by department heads, direct interface employees, and back-office staff. Distribute the key points of the meeting to those who did not attend. But make sure that the staff are there as observers only. Otherwise they will stop the conversation flat, and negate anything useful you could have learned from the focus group.

- Don't assume that it's scientific. It's not. It is simply a cross-section of your customers telling you what they don't like about your business. The most successful focus groups often start with, "Don't tell us what you like about our business. Tell us what you DON'T like…"

◆ Don't steer the conversation. Don't ask only what you want to ask. Listen to what they want to say.

◆ Don't have any customers attend more than four focus groups. If they do, they regard themselves as fixtures and lose their fresh objective. Give them dates in advance so that they can schedule the focus groups on their calendars, and have someone telephone a day in advance to remind them.

What do you gain from the results of a focus group? You'll learn how your business is perceived by your own customers. This is a valuable piece of information for any business. You'll often solicit complaints that you haven't heard about before, but just as often you'll find out what's going really well at your business. You'll learn something about your competition, too, since your customers are probably also their customers (or used to be).

Another extremely valuable outcome from focus groups is the intangible feeling that customers get from having their opinions sought and listened to. Let all your customers know that you run focus groups. This tells them that you are truly interested in what they have to say.

Make sure that you publicize what changes you make based on the focus-group information, too. That will be worth its weight in gold to establish your credibility as a business where customer input is valued.

A recent article in *The New York Times* quoted authorities who said that the most successful transactions are when people enter into a buyer-seller relationship in a cooperative, not competitive, frame of mind.

Whatever Happened To "Thank You?"

In the past year I bought a car, a refrigerator, an air conditioner, and a pair of shoes. I never heard from any of the businesses or the salespeople after the sale—except for the shoe salesman. He wrote a thank-you note and told me to call him if I had any problems. And the shoes were much less expensive than any of the other items!

Dorothy Lane Markets in Dayton, Ohio, calls every person that spends $100 or more in their store the same day to say, "Thanks for shopping with us."

What a simple, easy-to-do, and extremely profitable return on the investment of a little time for a phone call, letter, or e-mail.

People Power

Stanley Marcus, the guiding force behind the success of the Neiman-Marcus specialty-store chain, once wrote about young executives: "Many have not learned the rules of politeness, such as standing up when a visitor comes to the office or walking the guest to the door when he leaves. Schools have not taught that a letter of inquiry is due a prompt response, a letter of complaint an immediate one. All telephone messages should be answered the day of receipt."

His message was that "a 'thank you' may not be remembered, but a failure to say 'thanks' can be stored in a memory for a decade."

"Thank-you's" help your business by encouraging current customers to come back. In addition …

◆ Customers generate more profits every year that they stay with you.

◆ Customers give you free advertising.

◆ Continuous improvement in service (including the easy-to-do "thank you" to acknowledge the customer) is not a cost, but an investment.

I called the salesmen who sold me the automobile, refrigerator, and air conditioner and asked why they didn't send me a thank-you message.

Here were their answers:

"I know I should do it, but I don't have the time."

"We started that a few years back but somehow we stopped."

"Great idea. I'll bring it up at the next sales meeting."

My answer was this:

Don't have the time? Just stopped? Bring it up at the next meeting?

It seems to me it's not a difficult task. All each had to do was memorize and write two words: "Thank you."

> ### True Tales
>
> Ira Hayes, motivational speaker and salesman with NCR, said he always carried thank-you cards with postage stamps on the envelopes. Whenever he made a sale, he immediately filled out the card with a personal message thanking the customer for the order, and mailed it that day. He retired from NCR as an award-winning salesman.

The Importance of Direct Mail

When you've got customers and you know their names and addresses, you are ready to start marketing by direct mail. Direct mail is specific. It's a rifle shot compared to the shotgun approach of broadcast or newspaper advertising.

A direct-mail piece often includes a letter, a brochure, and a reply device. The key part is the letter, especially if it is personalized. A letter can be a one-on-one relationship between you and your customer. Refer to Appendix C for samples of Direct Mail Letter Promotion and Direct Mail Brochure.

True Tales

The First National Bank of Winnetka, Illinois, sent a letter to their depositors describing new bank services.

A few days later, a customer called the bank manager saying she received the envelope but there was nothing inside. What were they writing her about? (People are often nervous about receiving a letter from a bank, even if there's nothing inside.)

The manager explained it was only a listing of services the bank offered and apologized for someone forgetting to put this information in the envelope. The customer was not satisfied. "When will you send me what was supposed to be in the envelope?"

The manager said it was on its way.

The sections that follow highlight seven important rules for writing a successful direct-mail letter.

Rule 1: Promise a Benefit Up-Front

My nephew opened a small deli. He ran out of money for opening-day advertising. I suggested he write a letter to 200 executives who worked within a 10-block radius of his deli. These people worked within a 10-minute walk from their offices to the restaurant.

This was the opening sentence: "Whoever said there's no such thing as a free lunch didn't know about this letter."

The letter offered them their first lunch free and included his menu. About 125 people accepted. Of the 125, 100 became steady customers. He built on this customer base with future letters and new offers. For a budget of less than $50 he built a successful business.

Rule 2: Enlarge the Benefit

Give more information explaining your opening sentence. The Deli letter explained how the program worked, and, as an added benefit, each person receiving a free lunch became a member of his "Taster's Club." This free membership gave a list of advantages including another free-lunch "bonus" after they bought 10 lunches.

Rule 3: Be Specific

Write to your customers with their name. I received a membership application in the mail from the Direct Marketing Creative Guild in New York City. I filled out the form and mailed it back. I received an acknowledgement of my letter with a greeting that began, "To whom it may concern." That's not me. I resigned.

People Power _____

John Romero is the "father" of writing direct-mail letters in the casino industry. No casino had a direct-mail executive when he started doing letters for them in 1985.

The Lady Luck Casino in downtown Las Vegas hired him as a consultant. He asked for their database. He was given a dusty shoebox filled with 3 x 5 file cards. He gave them some dramatic advice that they followed, changing almost all their advertising budget to direct mail.

Within five years the property grew from 120 rooms to 840, added two skyscrapers, three new restaurants, a showroom, and expanded the casino to an entire city block. Sending letters to customers created a relationship that sent the casino's repeat business soaring.

Copywriter Ed McLean wrote *Newsweek* magazine's most successful subscription letter. It was used as a "control" against all other letters for 17 years and out-pulled them all. One reason for the success was the number of times the word "you" was used. More than 20 times just on the first page! That's specific.

"You" is a close runner-up to "free" as the most important word to use in your letter.

Rule 4: Give Proof

If you send a sale-mailing piece, don't simply say "sale" or "half-price sale" Tell me the specific savings on the selected items you offer. Many businesses advertise that they're having a "half-price sale" but they don't give examples.

There are three parts to proving the value of the sale item: the original price, the sale price, and the amount of savings. Show all three.

Do you ever wonder who won the "Free Trip To Hawaii" on those contests you see advertised in supermarkets and in magazines?

If you have a sweepstakes or a lucky drawing during your sale, tell who won in your next ad. No last names and no addresses because the winners will receive unwanted calls. Simply say, "Mary in Atlanta won the free trip to Hawaii."

Another effective "proof" is listing testimonials from people who came and bought at your last sale and said that you had great values. Testimonials are easy to obtain. You know the customers to contact. Ask them for a simple sentence or two on why they believe your sales are great. Show each customer his or her testimonial for approval BEFORE it is printed.

Rule 5: What Happens If They Don't Act

One of our most successful headlines for our famous New Year's Day Sale was "A Sale So Great It Only Happens Once Every 365 Days." The direct-mail piece implied that if customers didn't come to the sale, they wasted a whole year.

Rule 6: Repeat

If you are writing about a single service or product, repeat the offer in the beginning, middle, and end of your mailing piece. If you can think of a clever way to include your offer in the P.S., do it! (The P.S. is the second-most-read part of the letter, after the opening.)

Rule 7: Ask for the Order

Direct-mail gurus often suggest that you do a two-part mailing for new customers. You tell the benefits of your product and include a card that says, "If you would like more information, please fill out this card."

Many people see these cards, tear them up, and throw them away. One award-winning campaign from an Australian retailer enclosed two cards. One was torn in half. The letter explained, "We have already torn up the card you were going to tear up, so you can fill out the other one and mail it to us."

To learn how to write a good "ask for the order" letter, save the best letters you receive from nonprofit groups and study them. The people who put these campaigns together are experts. Use ideas that can be translated to your business.

True Tales

Reese Palley, an Atlantic City art dealer, acquired a group of lithographs signed by Salvador Dali. Each lithograph was of the face side of playing cards: jack, king, queen, and ace in hearts, diamonds, clubs, and spades. A hundred of each one—a total of 1,600 lithographs. Palley bought them for $100 each.

He wrote a letter for his "Palley-Dali Paris Birthday Party" to his basic mailing list of 2,500. It said, "I'm going to celebrate my fiftieth birthday in Paris. I'd like you to come with me. At no charge. All you have to do is buy a Dali lithograph from me for $650 and I will give you a trip for two to Paris for a weekend at no cost."

The letter went on: "As we fly to Paris in the 747, I'll have a large art collection in the upstairs cabin. If you buy any piece of art going over, you'll save 10 percent. Buy anything coming back and you'll pay 20 percent more."

Within 72 hours he sold out a 747 plane. Within a month he sold out another 747 and became the only businessman to ever lease two 747s.

He made over a million dollars on this direct-mail campaign. All because of a letter that—creatively—"asked for the order."

The Least You Need to Know

◆ "Good feelings" and "solutions to problems" are the only reasons why people buy.

◆ There are many different kinds of customers, but they are all important to your business.

◆ Focus groups give you invaluable information about what you are doing wrong in your business.

◆ "Thank you" is a secret weapon to keep customers returning.

◆ Direct mail is an important way to reach your current customers with offers they want.

Chapter 7

Your Clients

In This Chapter

- ◆ The little extras that create new clients
- ◆ Unexpected rewards
- ◆ What works better than customer service?
- ◆ How to prosper with a loyalty program

The first rung on the loyalty ladder is a prospect, someone who has heard about your business but has never come in. The next step up the loyalty ladder is a shopper, someone who has come into your place of business. That shopper becomes a customer when he buys a product or service from you.

One step up from a customer is a client. A client is a very valuable customer who buys everything that you have to sell that she could possibly use. These types of customers are the backbone of your business. This chapter shows how to create and nourish a client.

Servicing Your Clients

Question: If a client is someone who buys everything that you have to sell that he or she could possibly use, then how do clients know what ELSE they should have in addition to what they came to buy? Answer: You have to tell them.

When a client comes to your business and asks for an item or service, and you or your staff sells them only that item or service and stops there, then they are only a clerk. Not a salesperson. Not a consultant. Not a trusted advisor. In fact, you have done your clients a disservice. You have not completed the sale. You have not shown them or had them consider other items that would be beneficial or give more value to what they asked for initially. And you have to ASK FOR THE ORDER.

When someone bought a suit in my store and I suggested a shirt, tie, and socks, they bought these items more often than not, and were pleased that I made the suggestion. Consider the alternative: The customer goes home and discovers that he does not have the right shirt or right tie or right socks. Is he happy that you did not suggest these items? Or is he mad?

True Tales

Sid Friedman was featured in *Forbes Magazine* as one of America's top salesmen. He managed his Philadelphia-based insurance firm's 200 employees, operated three other companies, was an international speaker, and directed the Philadelphia chapter of the Children's Make-a-Wish Foundation.

He specialized in million-dollar-plus estate insurance. One time he put together a new program for one of his customers who had bought other insurance policies from him. But he couldn't secure an appointment to sit down and give him the two hours needed to complete a very big sale.

"I'm just too busy, Sid." said the customer, "Every minute of the day is taken." Sid asked, "What are you doing tomorrow?" The customer said, "I have to go to Chicago first thing in the morning for an important meeting." Sid put the customer on hold, gave his secretary some instructions, came back and talked to the customer one more time: "I'll see you on the plane tomorrow. I have the seat next to you."

"Do you have a meeting in Chicago, too, Sid?" he asked. Sid replied, "No. But this way I'll have you alone for two hours. And I can explain the whole program to you."

Yes, he made the sale and caught the next plane back to Philadelphia. That's converting a customer into a client.

Seven Suggestions to Creating Loyal Clients

This section highlights seven helpful suggestions to turning customers into loyal clients.

Suggestion #1: Give your best customers advance notice of ... everything

You mail much of your advertising third class because of the money saved. Not to these special customers. They receive everything first class because they are your first-class customers. You keep their names separate and apart from the rest of your mailing list.

When a sale is coming up, they are mailed first class and a few days earlier than the rest of the list to make sure that they're the first to know about the sale.

Having a fashion show? Not only are they the first to know, but they also receive priority seating.

A new line arrives at your business or items from their favorite brands. Your clients are the first to know.

> **True Tales**
>
> Create special promotions for clients only. Everyone expects you to have sales at holiday times (such as Washington's Birthday) and "trunk showings." But clients have SPECIAL events. You send your clients a letter in the mail saying, "You are invited for free to the concert at ...."

If you make changes in store layout, departments, or personnel, your clients are the first to know.

Your response to personalized promotions will be much better than the response to ordinary mailings because everyone wants to feel they are special. One way you can capture your clients' attention is to offer them an item or a service for free. "Free" is the most important word in the English language to capture the attention of people who shop with you.

Suggestion #2: Things that you would normally charge a small service fee to your customers are theirs ... free

For example: If you charge to mail packages, clients do not pay. If you charge to gift-wrap, clients do not pay. If you charge for a late payment, clients do not pay.

Suggestion #3: Give gift certificates from noncompetitive stores

This is a very special treat for your clients and very easy to do. You contact other businesses with locations near your own business.

You tell these businesses that you are willing to include a gift certificate from them to your special customers in your next mailing. It must be good value. You will not accept the "Take $50 off on your next $500 purchase." It must be given with NO caveats since you are introducing them to clients.

Most business will cooperate. If not, then they don't understand how to increase their sales. Check them off the list and move on.

Suggestion #4: Send free gifts at unannounced times of the year

In the morning mail, your clients receive a gift certificate for a popular item. Free. All they have to do is come to your business and pick it up by a certain date.

I sent a letter to my clients offering them our $10 canvas carry-bag, free, if they came to the store within the next week. We gave away more than 100 bags. Our shopping bags can become a significant form of advertising (and they can for you, too).

Since my business's name was "Gordon's Alley," I arranged to have a simple but good-looking canvas carry-bag screened with our name in very attractive large graphics. The bags were so cute that it became de rigueur for all high-school students to carry one.

When my clients came into my store for their free bag, almost without exception they bought something else. Remember, these people are clients. They won't take advantage of you. They appreciate the gift and "While I'm here, I thought of something else I could use …." When we added up the cost of the 100 bags against the additional, unexpected, would-not-have-been-made purchases, we were way ahead.

Gordon's Alley canvas bags became "traveling billboards" for my business throughout the community. Whenever my clients, school kids, and others went shopping or traveling, my business was advertised. Clients told us stories about visiting other states or countries carrying their Gordon's Alley bag and being stopped by strangers saying, "I've shopped there, too."

My canvas shopping bag became popular, much to my surprise, but after I realized that I had a "star," I promoted and promoted and promoted the bag:

- I created a separate department by offering many colors and a gym bag to go along with the basic carry style.

- ◆ I arranged to have monogramming of a first name available to personalize the bags. (No monogram charge for clients.)

- ◆ I advertised the bag on a prominent billboard, in the newspaper, and in our direct-mail pieces.

Suggestion #5: You're available when clients want you

You don't deliver on Saturday. But, if a client calls on Saturday morning and needs her son's pants altered for Sunday services, you ignore the rules and deliver.

Most requests CAN be honored by simply ignoring the rules.

If it makes good business sense, feel free to ignore the rules.

The most glaring error you can make in your courtship of clients is to promise something and not deliver it.

To make sure you can correct any foul-up, make yourself as available as possible. My insurance agent lists his home phone in the telephone directory. If I need him for an emergency (which always occurs after business hours), I can call him at home.

People Power

Douglas McCellan, a behavioral scientist, says, "An integral aspect of the nature of high achievers is that they respond to contingencies and adapt their style." That's you, if you want clients.

I returned to my store after hours if a customer needed a special something. The occurrences were rare but it was an automatic transfer of a customer into a client.

Suggestion #6: Give them the "extra" service that will set you apart

Several years ago, a colleague of mine told me about a great service. When he traveled to Switzerland and needed an overnight booking in New York City, he stayed at The Swiss Drake Hotel. Upon checking out, he would leave his bags with the bellman. The next time he saw his bags was when he and his bags each arrived in Geneva. That service made him a client.

Even though that particular service is no longer available for security reasons, the Swiss Drake Hotel still knows how to take care of clients.

Suggestion #7: Make sure you know who they are

When I check into the Kahala Mandarin Hotel in Honolulu and pick up the phone in my room, the operator says, "Yes, Mr. Raphel, can I help you." Okay, I know that my name appeared on a computer somewhere, but I feel important!

> **True Tales**
>
> You can wow people at the end of their shopping experience by having the cashier(s) say "thank you" and adding the person's name. After all, that name is on a credit card or a check, the methods most people use to pay for purchases. All it takes from you is to supply the training.

Dale Carnegie, who wrote about the importance of calling people by their name, said, "The average person is more interested in his own name than in all the other names on Earth put together."

I left Harry's Bar in Florence, Italy. As I walked out the door, the bartender called out, "Have a good day, Mr. Raphel, and please come back again." I was startled. It took me a few minutes to realize that my waiter had given my credit card to the bartender who rang up the check. But how many people have I told THAT story to …?

Added Value

Added value is the unexpected, unadvertised, unasked-for "extra." For example, at Thanksgiving time, my staff and I individually wrapped hundreds of little inexpensive gifts we bought at various trade shows. I had each cashier put them in the customer's shopping bag after a purchase was made.

> **Loyalty Lingo**
>
> **Added value** is the gift given to the customer as a "thank you" after the sale is completed. Unexpected, unadvertised, and unasked-for … but often remembered longer than the purchase of the original item.

"What's that?" asked the surprised customer.

"A 'thank you' for doing business with us" was the reply. Then, "I'm sure we say 'thank you' every time you shop with us. But it only seems natural at this time of the year to say 'thanks' one more time."

The customer, first confused, then astonished, and then pleased, would always stammer out a "Why, that's very nice" or a simple "thank you" and walk away, anxious to tell half a dozen of her friends what happened when she was shopping with us.

Impressive Impressions

Think about how businesses could really impress you and make you advance up the loyalty ladder from a customer to a client:

- ◆ What if ... carpet-company installers left a large bottle of carpet-stain remover with a thank-you note?

- ◆ What if ... after every automobile sale, the salesman left a "thank you" note in the car and a gift certificate with another note saying, "The first washing and waxing is on me!"

- ◆ What if ... the mail-order company, where I buy my hundred-dollar shoes, tossed in a polish with every order?

- ◆ Why doesn't ... my barber gives me a complimentary bottle of shampoo, sold only in barbershops, to sample, for future sales?

- ◆ Why doesn't ... my travel agent have flowers waiting in my cabin for my expensive week's cruise?

- ◆ Why doesn't ... the appliance-store owner, where I spent big bucks for a new refrigerator, deliver the refrigerator stocked with gourmet foods?

- ◆ Why doesn't ... the salesman who sold me my new copy machine include a dozen reams of paper with the thousand-dollar-plus machine?

- ◆ Why doesn't ... the law office send me attractive folders for the documents they just drew up? (Okay, Okay, forget the lawyers giving something free ....)

Would my reaction to these situations be pleased and satisfied and would I tell someone?

The list goes on and on. Whatever business you are in, there is something that relates to your business that you should give away for free, as added value, to your customers at the time of the sale. All they will do is make a decision to buy from you again in the future and to tell their friends as well.

On the Other Hand

I went to a restaurant and ordered dinner with some friends. Two of our entrees were not hot enough. We told the waitress, and she apologized, and then reheated the food to our satisfaction.

At the end of the meal she said, "I'm sorry for your inconvenience. We want you to have complimentary coffee and dessert." Yes, we bring our friends there again and again.

We also had lunch at American Express offices in New York City. They ordered lunch from a caterer for just the four of us. It arrived soon after with a big selection of homemade cookies. "She always does that," said our hostess, "Every order comes with something free."

Why don't restaurants include something free when they deliver take-out orders? A piece of fruit. A sample of the cake they bake daily.

I like the fact that the place I buy my seafood includes a half-dozen lemons.

I like the fact that the place I buy my annual firewood includes three boxes of kindling.

As a kid growing up on the East Side of New York City, Eddie Cantor (the famous comedian) delivered for a local bakery. One day, little Eddie asked his boss, "Why do you send 13 rolls to Mrs. Gross every week when she only orders and pays for a dozen?" The boss answered wisely, "Why do you think she orders every week?"

> **People Power**
>
> Morton Sloan, the President of Morton Williams Associates in New York City, says, "Getting the customer's attention is one thing. But keeping them coming back is the key to survival."

Customers think that …

◆ All supermarkets are alike: They all sell food.

◆ All banks are alike: They all sell financial products and services.

◆ All clothing stores are alike: They all sell clothing.

◆ All furniture stores are alike: They all sell furniture.

The list and thinking is as deep as the listings in the Yellow Pages. BUT, what if these businesses began to think out of the box and offered special services, then would you consider going back again and again not just as a customer but as a client?

"Customer Service Doesn't Work Anymore"

I just finished giving a customer-service seminar in Phoenix, Arizona, for art-gallery owners. One retailer came up to me and said, "You know, customer service doesn't work anymore."

"What?" I said, and asked her to explain.

"Well, it used to be the answer, but no more. You see, customer service brings the customer in the first time. But customer satisfaction brings them back." (Remember Feargal Quinn's "boomerang principle" described in Chapter 1?)

The retailer was correct. The point is that just providing ordinary customer service is not enough. It takes outstanding customer service to provide customer satisfaction.

Customer satisfaction is practicing Doing What You Promised You Would Do (DWYPYWD). DWYPYWD is delivering the deli tray on time, having the alterations finished when you say they will be done, not having to wait an hour at the doctor's office for a scheduled appointment. Poet Robert Service said it well: "A promise made is a debt unpaid."

Great service is keeping your promises. Customer satisfaction is making the customer so satisfied with your goods and services that they run around the community and bring more people to buy your goods and services. This satisfaction is a critical link to repeat and future business.

In order to stay in business, you need 20/20 vision to …

♦ Cut down the 20 percent of customers who leave you because of poor service.

♦ Add more people to the 20 percent of your customers who are clients by giving customers a steady dose of customer satisfaction.

> **Significant Stats**
>
> A Cambridge, Massachusetts, survey asked 1,500 people, "How well do service companies fulfill your needs as a customer?" Only one in ten said "excellent." They provide service. But they don't give satisfaction.

If you don't climb aboard the Satisfaction Express you might find that your competition has already left the station.

"Satisfaction research is one of the fastest-growing areas of research", said Simon Chadwick, CEO of Research International in New York. His company's business jumped 100 percent in one year and plans to double again the next year. Why? "It's a lot cheaper to retain customers than acquire new ones."

Developing a Loyalty Card Program

Recently I was working on a program for the staff at the Kahala Hilton in Hawaii. (It is now the Kahala Mandarin.) They gave their very best customers, people who booked at least 50 nights in the hotel, a Platinum Card that entitled them to free pickup and return at the airport via limousine, late checkouts, and a room ready whenever they arrived.

"But what about the ones who haven't yet reached this level?" I asked. "How about 25-room nights entitling me to another kind of loyalty card? Half the benefits but more than someone arriving for the first time."

The next morning they had a card and letter in my mailbox. The letter began, "Dear Mr. Raphel. Congratulations. You are the #1 holder of the Kahala Hilton's Gold Card."

They listed all the extra benefits I would now enjoy. Not all the advantages of the Platinum Card—but now I was personally committed to staying the extra nights so that I could have all the extra benefits of a Gold Card member.

What were they doing? Making me convert to a loyal client.

Developing a loyalty-card program is a long-time commitment to establish the card, maintain it, improve it, and add exciting new elements. Despite the work and commitment involved, I finally decided to initiate a loyalty card at my company because ...

> **People Power**
>
> Brian Woolf, the author of *Customer Specific Marketing: The New Power in Retailing* (Teal Books, 1996), says, "Treat all your customers alike ... but reward them differently."

- ◆ I belong to loyalty clubs.
- ◆ I receive discounts on food at my local supermarket.
- ◆ I receive room upgrades and special prices from hotels.
- ◆ I receive free airline tickets from my airline miles.

But I wasn't doing anything to reward the loyal customers of *my* business.

Where to Begin?

Start collecting literature from companies with frequent-buyer programs like airlines, hotels, gas companies, and major credit card companies. Read all their brochures, pamphlets, and letters, and then pick out the sentences that appear in most of them—they are the ones that obviously work.

Here's one of the great sentences that almost EVERY frequent-buyer program uses: "Your association with us and your annual volume of business places you in a unique group that requires and appreciates special recognition." How could anyone not continue reading THAT letter?

Now, start digging into your customer lists.

For example, I went through the list of customers on my computer and created a new list of those spending a minimum of $1,000 a year. This spending threshold made them eligible to receive a Gordon's Gold Card.

The final result was that nearly 500 customers were invited to become Gordon's Gold Card members. These 500 customers provided nearly $2 million in business every year.

Yes, I know 500 times $1,000 is $500,000. But remember, this was the minimum amount. Some of these customers spent $2,000 or $4,000 a year with us. One spent $12,500!

Deciding on the Rewards

Here are some ideas for "rewards":

◆ Offer a monthly free lunch at your restaurant.

◆ Send advance announcements by first-class mail instead of bulk rate.

◆ Provide a birthday present for the client and the client's spouse.

◆ Mail unadvertised special offers. (Note: I began a monthly mailing of these promotions only to Gold Card Customers with very special offers for them alone. Our cost was $500 a month or $1.00 for each one mailed. My lowest sales return from these monthly mailings was $4,000. The highest return was $23,500!)

◆ Find out what brands and items they liked best in your shops using a questionnaire. What brands and items did they want you to include in your selection? Where did they read, hear or see your ads?

As the result of querying my clients, I discovered that 75 percent of them listened to one radio station out of the several in the area. So I placed all our radio advertising on this one station.

The P.S.

In the letter that should accompany your client's loyalty card, along with their name, consider adding a P.S. and a gift certificate.

For example, my P.S. said, "We've enclosed a $15.00 gift certificate in your name to use in any of our shops." No minimum purchase was required. This was a pure gift.

Experience taught me that your good customers will rarely take advantage of you. I was not surprised to discover the average sale, when the $15 gift certificate was used, was $50. Translation: A profit on EVERY gift certificate.

I kept track of how much our Gold Card customers spent with us through the year from their sales slips. They each received a gift certificate at Thanksgiving for holiday shopping, to thank them for being a customer. The gift certificate was equal to 5 percent of their purchases for the year. The first year we gave away gift certificates totaling $5,000, which resulted in $50,000 in additional purchases!

Would we have done PART of this $50,000 in business anyway?

Yes.

Would we have done ALL that extra $50,000 in business without the Gold Card?

Absolutely, positively, unconditionally, NO.

The best result is the good feeling our clients had toward our business.

The Least You Need to Know

- ◆ Your better customers deserve unexpected rewards.
- ◆ "Added value" is a relatively inexpensive way to make your better customers feel important.
- ◆ Your business needs customer satisfaction, not just customer service.
- ◆ A loyalty card program can add significant profit to your business.

Chapter 8

Your Advocates

In This Chapter

- Special treatment for special customers
- Guaranteeing your business
- The advantage of being different
- The three R's for creating advocates

Advocates are the top rung of the loyalty ladder. They are people who not only consistently shop with your business but who also bring you others to shop with you.

What is the leading soft drink in the market today? Coca-Cola.

How about the leading soup company? Campbell's.

How about a soap company? Ivory.

Razors? Gillette.

Chewing Gum? Wrigleys.

That those brands are top in their respective categories today is not very surprising. But the surprising additional fact that you should know is that all these companies also were the market leaders in their categories for over 80 years.

How did these brands retain their popularity over such a long period of time? The answer is clear: These long-lasting brands created advocates. One satisfied customer told another who told another about the quality and reliability of the product. Customers became clients and clients became advocates. Advocates can spark continued growth in your business. And this chapter shows you how.

The Best Tender Loving Care (TLC)

Some businesses have figured out how to treat their advocates. Here are a few examples:

- A room and more: As an advocate, whenever I check into my favorite hotel, my room is waiting. Checkout for ordinary customers is noon. For me it's 6 P.M. And there's fresh fruit in my room with a "Thanks for coming" note from the manager.

- Savings and more: From my clothing store I receive special savings that arrive unannounced in the mail for my next shopping trip—and with NO minimum purchase needed to enjoy the savings. Know why? Because I'm an advocate.

The sections that follow provide some additional suggestions for turning your clients into advocates.

Take In-Depth Surveys

People will be glad to give you information if they know that you will use the information to the customer's advantage. For example, when you are approved to have an American Express Platinum Card, you fill out many pages of your background, history, likes, and dislikes. Questions range from the wine you drink to the novels you read.

The more American Express knows about you, the more selectively American Express can contact you for future purchases without annoying offers that don't interest you.

People will pay extra to be a Platinum Club member because of the special offers available with the care. As an American Express Platinum Card customer, you can participate in a back-stage reception with the star of a Broadway show. Or you can order orchestra seats for the opera. Or there are special tickets available for the U.S. Open tennis tournament. You pay for the tickets, but you are guaranteed seats at a popular event.

Call and Write

If a customer has not shopped with you for a while, call to find out why. Is everything okay? Have you done anything wrong? Is there anything special they need?

Write your advocates at least once a year. Tell them that they are "very special" (because they are). Send a list of the benefits they receive that are available to them because they are your best customers.

Ask these customers what else they would like from you. These customers are the best of the best. They rarely, if ever, will take advantage of you. They will like the fact that they are treated specially (wouldn't you?), and they might suggest a seemingly small request that you never thought important enough to consider.

True Tales
When you talk on the phone with a customer, SMILE! The person on the other end will know when you are smiling.
If you don't believe that a smile can be communicated over a phone line, try this simple test: Call a friend three times. Tell the friend that you will smile on only one call. Can your friend guess which one? Probably. In general, people guess correctly eight out of ten times.

Remember Their Names and Birthdays

In our store we sent our best customers a $15 gift certificate on their birthday. And another on the birthday of their spouse. They came, they saw, they bought. Because … we remembered.

Birthday rewards are a great marketing tool to keep advocates loyal. If you lack sufficient office staff, you can hire direct marketers who will work with your business to create and maintain a customized birthday program.

I previously mentioned cashiers thanking shoppers by name by looking at their check or credit card. Advocates should be recognized earlier in the selling process to create good feelings and more sales opportunities. To do this, in small businesses, it's a good idea to keep staff acquainted with an updated list of these very special customers. In medium to large businesses, a software program should be available to help sales people.

Special Handling

There are many ways to reinforce to the client how important she is to you. Here are some additional ideas, with proven examples:

♦ Exclusively yours. Did you ever think about giving out a private telephone number to advocates, so that they can place a reservation for a room, a meal, a ticket, an order (with no music or message hold)? It is an exclusive number, not available to a regular customer.

♦ It's not in my store, but what is it you wanted? Monty Dare sells sheets, blankets, and pillowcases in his store in Clacton-on-the-Sea in England. One day an 80-year-old customer called saying that she was a loyal customer. She wanted a bed. Monty doesn't sell beds. She said, "Well, go out and buy me a bed." Monty checked prices at local furniture stores, found the best price, and ordered the bed. But the furniture company's delivery truck had broken down. From his own company's warehouse, Monty arranged to have a trailer hooked up to a car, and had the bed delivered. In addition, he had the new bed installed and the old bed taken away to the local dump. She is now a confirmed advocate!

♦ My one and only. The "Personal Shopper" program inaugurated successfully by department stores makes great sense for advocates. Tired of shopping? Do you not know what to look for? Your own "personal shopper" first interviews you; finds out your likes, needs, wants; and then shops for you. Stores usually charge a fee for this service, but should consider giving it for free to their best customers.

♦ The joy of joining. Join the Intercontinental Hotel's Six Continents Club for a small fee and receive an automatic upgrade when you check in. Also included in your sign-up fee are special benefits, including the use of a conference room (usually $50 an hour) for an hour for free, and a night's stay for free, every time you renew your membership.

♦ Your way is my way. A Japanese manufacturer of bicycles offers totally customized products, produced and delivered to the buyer within a week of ordering. What a difference from Henry Ford's original dictum: "Give them any color they want as long as it's black." Henry Ford would not have made it in today's marketing world.

True Tales

Many companies are following the example of the Japanese bicycle maker and offer custom-made products for buyers. Examples include automobile manufacturers, clothing, and even art companies (where buyers can choose accent touches on existing colors in a limited-edition painting). Dell Computers is perhaps the best example of this type of company, making products exactly to the preferences of their customers.

When I think about businesses creating advocates through using special care and handling, I wonder …

- ◆ Why airlines don't have plugs for PCs next to all of their seats?

- ◆ Why insurance agents don't have after-hours telephone numbers available (when lots of accidents happen)?

- ◆ Why "banker's hours" are for the convenience of the banker and not the customer. Let's establish "Advocates' Hours"!

We can only hope that someday things will change!

The Power of Guarantees

One way to find and keep advocates is with the "Guarantee" you put on your products or services. Guarantees are one example of how, before a customer can be loyal to a business, a business must be loyal to the customer.

You-Be-the-Judge Guarantee

Norm Thompson in Oregon has a famous guarantee. Their mail-order company has trademarked their special guarantee, which they call their "You Be the Judge" Guarantee. What that means is that you decide if you are happy with their merchandise, and you are the sole judge of when that time should be. Not 30, 60, 90 days or even a year. If you're unhappy, at any time, just return the merchandise for a full refund or exchange. Your choice.

Guarantee in Your Store and on Your Card

Publix, a Florida Supermarket Company with markets in many states, has a guarantee that is in their stores and on their calling cards:

> We will never knowingly disappoint you. If for any reason your purchase does not give you complete satisfaction, the full purchase price will be cheerfully refunded immediately upon request.

> We have always believed that no meal is complete until the meal is eaten and enjoyed.

> (Signature of the CEO of Publix)

True Tales

My mother vacationed in Florida. I called and asked where she did her food shopping. "Publix" she said.

"Publix?" I asked. "But Mom, you have to go past three other supermarkets to shop there. Why do you go the extra distance?"

"Didn't you know, son," she answered, "Publix guarantees all the food they sell."

"But Mom," I said, "ALL the food stores guarantee all the food they sell."

"Really?" she said, "So how come they don't say so …."

A Whole Year of Reading Enjoyment—Guaranteed

Mother Jones magazine, annual winner of national awards, sells for a $10.00 annual subscription. Listen to their guarantee: "If at any time, for any reason, first issue, last issue, any issue, you choose to cancel, we won't keep your money. You'll get every penny back. "Wow. Powerful. You can receive the magazine for an entire year and then, if you decide you didn't like it, let them know and they'll send your total subscription back.

You'll find that very few people will ask for the refund after reading all the issues. About 99.5 percent of people are honest. Most business people focus too much attention on the small minority who will dishonestly take advantage of a guarantee.

True Tales

When we started a small book-publishing company, we looked to see what other business book dealers offered as a guarantee. We couldn't find any ("What?" asked one when we queried, "You're going to let them read the book and then return it! Ridiculous.")

We didn't listen to our competitors. Instead we offered a "12-month guarantee." Buy the book. Read it. Anytime, during the year, if they wanted to send it back for an exchange for another book or a refund, that was fine with us. We have sold thousands of books with this guarantee. You can count on one hand the number of books we have had returned.

Double Guarantee

"It's Fresh or It's Free." That's what Woolworth's Supermarket in New Zealand advertised. "If you're not happy with what you buy from our fresh-food department, we'll replace it AND refund your money."

Guarantee of Performance

One trend in the advertising business is a change—from percentage charging on services—to payment based on results. This guarantees the advertiser's best work.

Marketing Your Special Niche

Each of us as an individual has special strengths. It may be excellent memory, expertise in Elizabethan literature, the ability to run fast, in-depth knowledge of baseball statistics, or a combination of those strengths and others.

So has your business.

No matter what product or service you sell, you are doing something you think is ordinary, but it's not ordinary to your customers.

Inspire Advocates

In order to inspire advocates, who are your most profitable customers, you need to examine the ordinary things you do and begin doing them in an extraordinary way. At the same time, add unique products and services to create your special niche. It all begins with good ideas.

How can you come up with good ideas? Here are some ways:

♦ Read and read some more. This should include trade magazines, but also publications that do not solely concentrate on your business, such as the Sunday *New York Times* or *Forbes Magazine*. And make sure that you search the Internet for topics that interest you.

♦ Take a trip. Drive or take a train or airplane to the nearest large city that has lots of businesses like yours. Window shop. Look at the fashions. Begin to be passionate about what you see. Don't forget to visit art museums and "old towns." New experiences give you new insights into ideas that you can use in your business. If you can include some international travel, all the better. Your advocates will be impressed if you come back with ideas for different settings and unusual products.

Position yourself as doing something "different." Even a perceived difference can bring customers to you.

True Tales

Rollie LaMarche owns Picture This Gallery in Alberta, Canada. He is known far and wide in the gallery trade for service in his store and on his website.

He has an advocate who shops his gallery for a specific artist. One day this advocate called because he heard that one of his favorite artists just released new work based on Northern Canada.

Did Picture This have any of his new work in stock? Rollie said he did but that it would take a few days to pack and ship. "I'll come for it," said the advocate. He flew to the gallery in his own plane, landed in difficult weather conditions, picked up the artist's original (and most expensive) work, hopped back in the plane, and flew away.

The gallery was so loyal to him in the past, letting him know of the latest editions from his favorite artists, constantly keeping in touch, and satisfying his every request, that this advocate stayed loyal to Picture This by even picking up his own purchases.

Keeping Advocates

In the past ten years, the number of independent booksellers belonging to the American Booksellers Associations (ABA) shrunk more than half.

The main reason why is the competition from major book chains: Waldenbooks, Barnes & Noble, Borders, Wal-Mart.

Question: How have some independent bookstores survived?

Answer: They have a steady list of advocates.

Bookstores that survive offer extras like in-store events and specialization in certain areas. Michael Powell, owner of Powell's Books in Portland, Oregon, one of the country's largest book store at 70,000 square feet, says "You have to have a certain niche."

They stock and promote books by local authors. This niche creates loyalty among local consumers who take pride in indigenous authors. They want to assist members of their own community by buying these books. This makes the local community loyal not only to the authors, but the bookstore as well.

The Wall Street Journal quoted one independent bookstore owner who contrasted his store against the chains by saying, "They see books as products; we see books almost as children." And what customer would not be loyal to their children?

Reliable, Responsible, Rapport

How do you keep advocates as advocates? We recommend the three R's:

♦ You must be **reliable**: Because the number-one reason why people buy where they buy is "confidence," it makes sense that you promise what you will do, and then do what you say you will do. Accurately. Consistently.

♦ You must be **responsible**: You have a responsibility to the community in which you do business and live. Do you participate in civic activities? Do you encourage associates to do the same? How well do you handle all the requests from people (representing nonprofit organizations) who come through your open door for help?

Tom Haggai is Chairman and Chief Executive Officer of IGA, Inc., a global supermarket company based in the United States, comprised of 4,400 stores (and their wholesalers) in 44 countries. Tom knows and believes in the importance of community responsibility. He positioned IGA markets as different, separate from the competition, with the theme of "Hometown Proud."

Tom said, "We start with the premise that we are a community citizen and that we care about our community. Whether you shop with us or not, we're going to care about your town. We're going to serve you. We're going to take part in the community. We're going to support Little League, scouting, etc. We're not going to think that you owe us this business. We're going to earn your business and we thank you for letting us be here."

"Hometown Proud" permeates all the marketing of the IGA stores and their brands.

♦ You must have **rapport**: If people who shop with you are unhappy, for any reason, then you need to solve their problems. Your customers should feel you care about them. For example, my Volvo salesman calls me not only directly after the sale but also every few months to ask, "Is everything okay?"

Don't you want to be surrounded in life by people who are reliable, responsible, and with whom you have rapport? If the people in your business have these qualities, customers will flock to your doors.

The Least You Need to Know

- ◆ Reward your advocates through special services.

- ◆ How many ways can you guarantee your products and services?

- ◆ Find your niche and make it known.

- ◆ Remember to check up on yourself to see how you're doing.

Part  Making Loyalty Marketing Work Every Day

To win customer loyalty, you have to convince prospects and shoppers to become advocates of your business. Here's how:

First, make sure your employees have the right attitude. Then decide how to organize your business to put your customers first. You have to listen to what your customers are saying.

Once you've created a brand, an identity for your business, you will be able to attract and keep the customers you need to achieve long-term business success.

Chapter

First Step: Empowering Your Employees

In This Chapter

- ◆ Knowing what is most important to your employees
- ◆ Giving your employees decision-making authority
- ◆ Making sure that your employees know what they are selling
- ◆ Motivating your employees by providing incentives

In order for your business to compete, survive, and not be listed on the obituary pages of next year's financial newspapers, you not only have to find out what the customers want—and give it to them—you must also find out what your employees want ... and give it to them. Your employees are the key to your business success.

Here's why: When your customers first walk into your store, they see your employees. Your employees are the key to increasing customer loyalty. How they treat customers will make a lasting impression. Your employees are more than representatives of your business. In your customers' eyes, your employees are your business.

In this chapter, we'll talk about how your employees can make or break your business—and how to be sure that they become your business's strongest advocates. You can't build strong customer loyalty unless you first develop loyal employees.

Your Employees Know More Than You Do

Who is out front talking with your customers all day?

Chances are, it's not always you. As much as we would like to, the demands of running a business don't allow much time for the "head honcho" to sell to the customers.

So who is out here representing you?

Your employees, of course. And according to Feargal Quinn, CEO of Superquinn Supermarkets in Ireland, "My employees know more than I do." He knows that his employees listen to customers, because he has built a culture that responds to customers and rewards employees who pay attention to customers' concerns. And if you believe this and have confidence in your employees, then you must empower your staff.

How many times have you visited a store with a complaint, exchange, or question, only to be told, "I'll have to check with the manager on that"?

What is more frustrating to a customer than having someone NOT answer her question? Few retailers empower their employees to make decisions for the customer. But those who do are rewarded many times over with loyal customers who know that they have received an immediate response to their question or problem.

> **Loyalty Lingo**
>
> Employee **empowerment** is giving your employees the authority to make decisions on behalf of your business to help a customer with a question, concern, or problem, without having to consult higher management.

Of course, *empowering* your employees to act without consulting you requires a high level of trust in your employees. Such trust is achieved with a combination of training and experience.

Once it is achieved, one way to maintain that level of trust is to institutionalize employee empowerment. In many businesses, a dollar amount can be established by the management, and, up to that amount, the front-line employee has discretion to solve the customer's problem.

Once you truly believe that your employees can know more than you do, you will be willing to request their input on business decisions. Companies can do this easily through weekly meetings with their staff.

At these meetings, make sure you do the following:

- Talk about upcoming promotions and marketing programs that you are considering.

- Review the success (or failure) of recent promotions.

- Discuss new products that you are considering adding to your line.

- Ask employees which customers would be interested in the new merchandise.

- Show proofs of an upcoming direct-mail offer or newspaper ad before it is sent to the printer or newspaper.

In my retail clothing shop, I would often show my sales staff proofs of advertisements, brochures, and other promotional materials. Invariably, the employees would notice details that I had overlooked:

- "Why did you leave off the name of the store?"

- "You didn't say what day the sale starts."

- "I've counted 10 misspelled words ... so far."

My employees always pointed out something important I hadn't seen.

Why Your Most Important Customers Are Employees

If your employees don't understand your business, use your products, or enjoy what they do, how can they help your customers when they come to your business to buy? That's why it's important to think of your employees as your first line of customers.

Your job is to make your employees feel satisfied about their jobs. Then your employees will be sure to make your customers feel comfortable.

So ... have your employees use your products!

Here are some suggestions for a few specific businesses:

- For a restaurant, you want your employees to taste all the dishes that the chef makes. (Did you ever ask a waiter, "How is the swordfish?" only to hear, "I don't know, I've never tried it." That's not very helpful.)

- For a clothing store, you want your sales staff to wear the clothes you sell.

- For a housewares store, your employees should use the items at home so that they know what they are for and understand the quality of your products.

What follows are some suggestions to help make sure your employees are able to help customers who come into the business:

- Provide training

- Offer employee discounts

- Give employee identification

The sections that follow will give you more details.

Training

Before employees are allowed to begin work, they should receive training in the store's products and services. Each new employee should have a mentor, another employee who knows the business's inventory and is around to answer any questions or solve any problems that a new employee may have. Training employees is part of establishing the culture of a business.

There are many problems that occur very often in businesses. Customers may be upset because a product didn't work the way they thought it would. Customers might want to exchange clothes for a different size. These sorts of problems can be anticipated. All employees should be taught to respond to common problems in a common manner. This type of training helps to build a company's culture.

Employee Discounts

You should offer your employees a significant discount on the products you sell, so that they can become familiar and, indeed, like and use the products. When they enjoy the products and use them themselves, your employees will be authentic in their advice to your customers.

For example, your employee might say, "That light fixture will work well in your hallway, because I've seen it installed in several others with the same high ceilings."

Besides, do you really want your employees going to another store to buy the products that they are selling to other people? Just doesn't make sense, does it?

Employee Identification

Customers want to be sure that they know who your employees are and what their qualifications are. The exact way your employees display that information will depend on your industry. But it is helpful to identify employees in some fashion.

In a restaurant, for example, employees should have some sort of dress code. Depending on the formality of the restaurant, the dress code could range from t-shirts and jeans to suits for waiters. In an office environment that has customers, a standard shirt or even a nametag can work. The more the customer can identify employees by a dress code, the more comfortable customers will feel.

What Employees Really Want

In order to motivate your employees, you first have to know what they want to get out of working with you. We know that "money makes the world go around," according to the song in *Cabaret*, but how important is money to your employees in terms of job satisfaction?

A study conducted by Ken Blanchard of Ohio State University, author of *The One Minute Manager* (William Morrow & Company, 1983), sought the answer to that question. Blanchard surveyed 10,000 employees, asking what factors were most important in their jobs. They were asked to rank the factors from one to ten, with one being the most important factor and ten the least important.

He also asked managers and supervisors to answer how THEY thought their employees would answer.

Here's the survey—you fill each one out yourself before you look at the results. Rank from one (most important) to ten (least important). First rank them the way *you* feel about the factors in your own work life. Then try to rank them the way the survey showed that employers and employees chose.

Rank according to how you feel about the factors in your work life ...

	Your Ranking
Feeling "in" on things	_____
Appreciation of work	_____
Higher wages	_____
Working conditions	_____
Interesting work	_____
Job security	_____
Management loyalty to workers	_____
Promotion and growth potential	_____
Sympathetic help with personal problems	_____
Tactful discipline	_____

Rank according to how you feel employers would chose ...

	Employers Ranking
Feeling "in" on things	_____
Appreciation of work	_____
Higher wages	_____
Working conditions	_____
Interesting work	_____
Job security	_____
Management loyalty to workers	_____
Promotion and growth potential	_____
Sympathetic help with personal problems	_____
Tactful discipline	_____

Rank according to how you feel employees would chose ...

	Employee Ranking
Feeling "in" on things	_____
Appreciation of work	_____
Higher wages	_____
Working conditions	_____
Interesting work	_____
Job security	_____
Management loyalty to workers	_____
Promotion and growth potential	_____
Sympathetic help with personal problems	_____
Tactful discipline	_____

And here are the results of the Ohio State survey:

Ohio State Survey Results

	Employer Ranking	Employee Ranking
Feeling "in" on things	10	1
Appreciation of work	8	2
Higher wages	1	5
Good working conditions	4	9
Interesting work	5	6
Job security	2	4
Management loyalty to workers	6	8
Promotion & growth potential	3	7
Sympathetic help with personal problems	9	3
Tactful discipline	7	10

What a difference!

Employers said that "Higher wages" was the number-one-most important factor on the job. But the employees placed that fifth on the list.

Now, look what *employees* listed as first: "A feeling of being 'in' on things," which employers listed last. That was closely followed by "Appreciation of work," rated all the way down on the list as eighth by employers.

Your workers spend an average of 25 percent of any given week at their job. They want to know that what they do with one quarter of their lives is simply appreciated.

Charting Your Employees' Progress

What does this mean for your business and your employees? Simply this: Find ways to make your employees part of the decision-making process, so that they will actually be "in" on what's happening in the business. They will feel ownership in the business and be inclined to treat the business like it belongs to them. What a great group of employees you would have if everyone who worked with you thought of the business as their own!

> **People Power**
>
> Marshall Field, owner of Chicago's famous department store, was speaking to the wife of one of his employees. She introduced her six-year-old daughter to Mr. Field, who asked the young lady, "And what does your father do?" He expected her to name the department in the store where he worked.
>
> "Oh, this is my daddy's store," said the little girl.
>
> The mother, embarrassed, started to apologize, but Field replied, "No, don't apologize. I only wish everyone working here had that attitude. Then we would be the finest store in the world."

The success of your business can be specifically traced to a concept we call "The Psychology of the First-Person Plural." The question is this: Who comes first in your business, the employer or the employee? I think it should be the employee. Here's a simple test to see if it works in your business.

Listen to someone who works with you talk about his job. If you hear him use the first-person singular, sentences with the words "I" and "me," and you hear his reference to the company as "them," then you are listening to a problem. The words should be "us," and "we," and "our."

Rewarding Employees

If you want to ensure that your employees are treating your customers the way you want them to, you have to give employees incentives to do that.

As you have seen from the job factors that employees rank as the most important, motivation is more than just money. You can reward your employees in a variety of ways:

- Financial
- Promotions
- New responsibilities
- Recognition from the group

Let's take these one at a time.

Provide Financial Motivation

Review your current system for providing salary increases and bonuses. If your system, like many businesses, provides only for a percentage annual increase based on the increase in the cost of living, you might as well be the government, not a private enterprise.

What are you rewarding with that kind of system? Well, not leaving your employment, I suppose, but not much more than that. You're not sending any message to your employee that his or her behavior on the job is what you expect or desire. You must build in some financial incentives to reward behavior that you want your employees to have—innovative ideas, being extra helpful to customers, finding ways to cut costs—whatever it is that you want your employees to do.

To do this, you must …

- Establish standards for each job so that employees know what is expected of them.
- Get feedback on the employees' performance by observing employees at work, by soliciting customer comments about employees, by having employees rate themselves, etc.

◆ Attach a pay scale that responds to the levels of performance that your employees show.

◆ Each of your employees must have an annual (or more frequent) review session with management to discuss the employee's performance on the job. This allows for discussion between the employees and management about the workplace, the job, the customers, the expectations of both the employee and the employer, etc.

Don't underestimate the value of talking to your employees about their jobs. Most people love to discuss what they do, and especially want to hear when they have done it well.

People Power

Barry Schimel, a CPA with Aronson, Fetridge, Waigle, and Schimel in Washington, D.C., advises companies to eliminate the Christmas bonus. He says that a bonus tied to a particular time of year doesn't reward anything, and just becomes an expected part of the annual wages.

Making bonuses dependent on performance standards such as sales, increased productivity, or taking on new responsibilities sends the right message to the employee: "You are doing your job the way I want you to."

Award Promotions

Promotions are a strong motivator for employees. Be clear that there are opportunities for employees to move "up the ladder" in your company. Make sure that all employees have access to information about when new jobs become available, and encourage current employees to apply for promotions.

When a current employee is promoted, let all your employees know about it so they learn that good job performance is rewarded by promotions.

And *don't* promote people just because they have been around forever. Experience is a key factor in deciding who should take on a new job, but it is not the only one. If you promote a lackluster employee who has worked with you for 15 years, you'll only send the message to the rest of your staff that mediocrity is what gets rewarded in your organization.

Impart New Responsibilities

Giving your current employees new responsibilities not only helps your organization meet new challenges, it also empowers and encourages your employees.

Employees often become bored by doing the same job in the same way. When you offer an employee an opportunity to try something new, it forces her out of her rut. New responsibilities not only add to an employee's job enjoyment, they also make an employee more qualified to receive a new promotion.

By giving employees added training and added responsibilities you enable your organization to promote from within and help insure the long-term stability of your business.

Announce Group Recognition

Remember second on the list of employees' most important job factors? "Appreciation of work." Publicly recognizing an employee who makes a contribution to your business is a key motivator and will encourage other employees to do the same.

These rewards don't always have to be tangible; sometimes a simple "You've done a great job with this project" is sufficient and lets an employee know that his or her work is recognized and appreciated. Make sure that at the weekly staff meeting you mention any employees whose work is of the caliber you want everyone's to be.

Use all your resources to find out what your employees are doing. Many companies ask their customers to help them find employees who are good at providing customer service. They set up boxes for customers to give the name of an employee who was especially helpful or went beyond the usual to offer assistance. Employees named by customers are then eligible for "employee of the week" and receive prizes or a monetary bonus.

The Least You Need to Know

- Involve your employees in your business decisions; they constantly talk to customers and are a great source of information.

- Your employees are your first line of customers; treat employees well and your customers will be treated well by your employees.

◆ Your employees want to "be in on things" and want "appreciation of their work."

◆ Reward your employees with a combination of compensation, promotions, new responsibilities, and recognition. Satisfied employees lead to satisfied customers.

Chapter 10

Meeting Your Customers' Needs

In This Chapter

- ◆ Making sure that your business has a good personality
- ◆ Do you work bankers' hours?
- ◆ Using the four-mula for success
- ◆ The value of being likeable

After I finished a seminar in Anaheim, California, I went for breakfast in the hotel restaurant. I approached the cashier to pay the bill. He looked at me with a big smile and gave me the practiced line, "Good morning, sir! And how was your breakfast?"

I told him. "The coffee was so bitter I couldn't drink it. The melon was so hard I couldn't cut it. The pastry was so stale I couldn't eat it. Now what are you going to do about that?"

He looked at me, continued smiling, and said, "Well, I sure as heck won't ask anybody else!"

Although this host was asking the right question, he really was more concerned with just being pleasant than really taking care of customers' needs.

As a business owner, you can't just mouth words of insincere concern. Your customers are your business's lifeblood, and if your customers are not happy, your business will suffer.

How do you make sure you are really paying attention to what your customers want? It starts with your level of service, the quality of employees, and the look of your business. This chapter shows you how to put the package together and make your customers' satisfaction the lifeblood of your business.

It Has My Name on It

In order to make customers loyal to your business, you must establish an emotional connection with your customers. Customers describe your business the way they would describe a person.

Listen to their words: "Considerate. Caring. Helpful." Or: "Nasty. Mean. Hate to be around them."

If the personality of your business doesn't appeal to your customers, they will stop shopping with you. You should make sure your business acts toward other people the way you would act.

Sam Solomon was a manufacturer of fine children's coats. One day he walked into his stockroom and saw a group of coats ready to be shipped. He turned to the foreman and said, "The patterns of the side seams on these coats do not match. Rip them out and do them over."

The foreman protested, saying that this would be an extra cost, production schedule would be curtailed, and, besides, "Who will ever know?"

"I will know," said Sam Solomon. "Each coat has my name on the label."

When you are willing to put your name on your products and to promise your customers that you will stand behind your products, your sales will jump.

Remind Customers That You Care

My friend Herb Chavis sold automobiles for an automobile agency. When a customer came to buy a car, Herb would give him the price. The customer would go to a competitive dealer and then return to Herb and say, "Well, I'd like to buy from you, but another agency offered me a better deal." Herb asked to see the two printouts and then said, "This isn't the same. There's something on the page I gave you that they don't have." The customer looked over the two offers and said, "They look the same to me."

"Not quite," said Herb. "Look at the bottom of my page."

"There's just your name there," said the customer.

"Right!" said Herb. "When you buy a car from me, you also get me."

"I get you?" asked the customer.

"Right," said Herb. "When you buy your car from me, you also buy me. I'm here when you come back for any reason—a door light to fix or a rattle or something that doesn't work. Don't bring the car to the service department. Bring it back to me. I'll take care of everything. Is that worth the few extra dollars?"

The customer thought about what it meant to have someone who really cared, and decided to buy the car from Herb.

Having a personal relationship with customers will cut down on the number of dissatisfied customers. If you are making your customers happy, your business will skyrocket.

Significant Stats
Customer complaints about how they are treated have grown steadily over the past few years, according the Better Business Bureau. They received more than a million complaints in 1995. This tripled to three million in 2003!
More than 50,000 customers were asked if they were satisfied with their purchases in 2003. The "satisfaction index" dropped from 75 percent "satisfied" in 1994 to about 67 percent in 2003.

For customers to have faith in you, they must know what your business's reputation is. Without customer confidence, your business will fail.

One of my favorite ads, which ran more than 50 years ago, illustrates this point. The ad is so famous that it is reproduced in advertising anthologies and talked about in advertising courses all around the country. The ad is referred to as "The Angry Man Ad."

There is a picture of an executive sitting in his office chair, looking at the reader with a dissatisfied expression. Next to him is the copy that says …

- ◆ I don't know who you are.

- ◆ I don't know your company.

- ◆ I don't know your company's product.

- ◆ I don't know what your company stands for.

- ◆ I don't know your company's customers.

- ◆ I don't know your company's record.

- ◆ I don't know your company's reputation.

- ◆ Now—what was it you want to sell me?

Never believe that everyone knows who you are and what you do. If you believe that, you're suffering from a terrible disease called the Curse of Assumption. Even if people are familiar with you, they need to be reminded that you care about them.

Meeting Your Customers Needs, Not Your Own

Bankers' hours used to mean 9 A.M. to 4 P.M. on weekdays only. Bankers' hours were for the benefit of bankers, not customers.

However, once bankers started seeing the world through their customers' eyes, bankers' hours started to become customers' hours. It is not unusual to see banks open nights and on the weekend. ATMs are open 24 hours a day, and Internet banking lets people see their accounts at their convenience.

By making shopping convenient for your customers, you can make a big difference in your business. Here's a small idea I had that gave us a huge boost in customer awareness and respect:

The biggest day for our retail store was our New Year's Day sale. My family didn't really want to work New Year's Day, but we knew it was a good shopping day for our customers. We decided just to open the store for only three hours as an experiment.

The day of the sale, we came to the store an hour before we opened to check signs and merchandise, and to make sure everything was set.

True Tales

When we lived in Haddonfield, New Jersey, we helped organize a fair to raise money for our children's school. There were games, rides, and food ... and a lot of money was raised.

When the event ended Saturday afternoon, we were told to deposit the money in a local bank. However, there was something wrong with the key we were given to the bank's night depository. We had $7,000 in cash that we didn't want to keep at home for the weekend. But the bank was closed on Saturday.

So we went to the drive-in window of our personal bank, Commerce Bank. Even though the school didn't have an account there, the teller at the drive-in spent 15 minutes counting the money so that we could deposit it in our personal account just for the weekend. Even though he knew that the money was not staying in our account for more than a day, he was polite and helpful.

We arrived and saw several dozen people standing outside the store. We asked some of the people why they were there. They told us, "We wanted to be early and get the best buys ..."

We were amazed. We never had a dozen people outside waiting for the store to open in our 25-year history!

Shortly before noon, there were several hundred people lined up. We called the police for crowd control. Several policemen arrived and I asked for help when we opened the doors.

Fifteen minutes after we opened the doors, the police made us not let any more people inside. "Fire regulations," explained one officer.

For the remaining three hours, whenever 25 people left, another 25 were permitted to enter.

At the end of the day we added up the receipts and discovered, to our astonishment, that we did more business in those three hours than we had done in any WEEK of the year!

Through the years, the sale became a tradition. A place to see and be seen.

Our New Year's Day sale was a success for many reasons:

- ◆ We had the right merchandise at the right price.

- ◆ We picked out a day when many women wanted to escape their couch-potato spouses who were watching the big football games.

- ◆ Almost all other retail stores were closed.

The main reason we were successful is that we devised a sale that was good for our customers.

Four-mula for Success

We are always looking for ways we can add business. One simple way is a to increase the amount of customer contacts you make every day.

A banker in Nebraska tried this idea and made an $800,000 sale. Boeing tried it and sold a fleet of airplanes.

The sales are the result of a concept I call "Four-mula for Success," a four-step, easy-to-follow, guaranteed way of increasing your business.

I've told this idea in seminars around the world and as a consultant to individual businesses. Within a few weeks of telling the story, I always receive calls and letters saying, "I tried it. It works."

Your only commitment is that you set aside part of each day for contacting customers. You have your choice of four different approaches. You can do one from each category. Or four from one. Or any combination of four. The result is always the same: more business. Here they are:

- ◆ Four notes

- ◆ Four telephone calls

- ◆ Four personal contacts

- ◆ Four sales

I will describe each of these in the sections that follow.

Four Notes

Write four notes a day to your good customers. A letter saying, "I wanted you to know that your favorite brand just arrived." Or a short "thank you for being a customer" is fine. (THAT note will be passed around to friends until the letter frays at the edges.)

Think of it. When was the last time you received a personal note from anyplace where you spent money, telling you, "thank you"?

A personal letter to a customer today is rare in this world of e-mails and faxes. Few people receive personal letters. Today the main avenues of person communication are e-mails and instant messages from one computer account to another.

Staying in contact with your customer is good public relations, reminding your customer that you are still in business at the same stand, selling the same merchandise.

Four Telephone Calls

Instead of sending a personal note, you can make a personal telephone call. Ask anyone you know when the last time was that she received a positive phone call from anyone with whom she did business.

It happens quite rarely.

Now, imagine the reaction when you call, give your name, and your company's name, and thank the customer for their recent purchase with you.

A banker in a small town in Nebraska heard me talk about this idea. He immediately started calling four business accounts every day. One day he called to thank the owner of a local business who had borrowed a substantial amount of money. The owner was called out of a conference by his secretary, who assumed that any call from the bank was urgent. The businessman took the call.

The businessman called the banker back later that day. He said that the meeting he was in when the banker called was with a new business executive that just came to town and asked him what bank he should use. The businessman told him the story about the banker calling to say "thank you." The new business executive chose this bank with an initial deposit of $800,000.

Years ago, Argentina was in the market for new airplanes. Companies around the world were bidding for this lucrative business.

During the bidding process, Argentina won the World Cup in soccer—for Argentines, this was like winning the Super Bowl, the World Series, and the NBA championship all at once!

Boeing Chairman at the time was T.A. Wilson. He called General Jorge Videllya, then the president of Argentina, to offer his congratulations. Videylla was moved by the phone call and thanked him.

Shortly thereafter Boeing received the contract from Argentina for the planes.

Because of the phone call? Probably not. But, as they say in Brooklyn, "It didn't hoit."

Joe Girard was America's number-one automobile salesman (listed in the *Guinness Book of World Records* as such). He would attend sporting events in his city, and whenever the home team scored, he'd stand up and throw dozens of his calling cards in the air. Within the next few weeks, someone would come in with one of his cards to buy a car.

Four Personal Contacts

Most salespeople receive a box of 500 calling cards when they first arrive on the new job. They tuck them in their desk and the box remains half-filled a year later.

One sales manager I know uses a new box every month! Wherever he goes, he leaves his card. To the waiter or waitress at the restaurant. To the ticket-taker at the movie theater. When someone introduces him to a new person. "Everyone in business meets at least four new people every day," he told us. And each card only costs a few pennies. If only one or two who receives a card from out of the box of 500 buys something, you're way ahead.

Calling cards are really miniature billboards, reminding people to call you if they need what you have to sell.

Four Sales

All good salesmen remember the acronym AFTO: Ask For The Order.

A banker played golf every Saturday for years with one of his community's largest home builders. One day the president of the bank said to the builder, "Tom, we've been playing golf together every Saturday for the past four years. How come you don't have any money in my bank?"

And Tom answered, "How come you never asked me?"

People Power _____

Harry Truman was walking down a street in his hometown after a local election in which he was a candidate. He ran into an older woman whom he knew quite well and asked her if she had voted for him in the recent election.

"No," the woman replied.

Truman was stunned. He was sure that this woman knew and liked him. He asked why she didn't vote for him.

Her response, "You never asked me."

The moral is this: Never take a customer for granted.

Do one of each or any four of these techniques every day. The result is more than 1,200 contacts a year! If only one in ten people you contact respond, you made more than 100 EXTRA sales. These are sales you only have because you follow the formula for success.

The Importance of Being Likeable

When accepting her Academy Award, Sally Field turned to the audience and said, "You like me. You really like me!"

The power of charm is underestimated.

People don't merely pick out businesses on the basis of lower price. They want to go somewhere they can trust, a place where they feel comfortable.

A recent survey said, "People who enjoy shopping in a business will spend 20 percent more."

TV executives make a decision on who will anchor the news or what programs will be renewed based on what they call the "Q Factor." Translation: Does the viewer "like" the person he or she sees?

Political consultant and radio executive Roger Ailes says, "The biggest advantage in selling is the 'like' factor."

True Tales

Several years ago Lee Iacocca, then CEO of Chrysler Motors, gave a keynote speech to his dealers at their convention in Atlantic City. Here's what he said:

"Why does anyone buy a car from you? All cars are pretty much alike. They all have the same basic ingredients: an engine up front, seats in the middle, trunk in the back, and they travel on four wheels.

"Here's the difference. The customer buys cars from people they like. And so the question is what are you doing to make someone like you? Because if they like you, they'll have confidence in you. If they feel you're trying to help them make the right decision, they'll buy from you. They'll tell their friends and their friends will tell their friends, and pretty soon you'll have to open your showroom earlier and stay later to handle the crowds.

"Here's my message for you today: If you want to do more business next year, the answer is very simple: Make someone like you!"

The audience stood and cheered.

You have to instill yourself and your employees with the philosophy that you must be likable to the customers. That way you can avoid what happened to me recently while I was grocery shopping: I never saw the face of the cashier. She was so busy scanning all the items that her head was constantly bowed down, looking at the scanner. I had to pack my own bags. I was about to leave when I turned back to her and said, "Hey, at least you could say, 'thank you'!" She looked up and replied, "Hey, it's printed on the bottom of the receipt!"

No matter how hard you try to make your customers satisfied, you can never succeed unless your employees understand the importance of satisfied customers. Refer to Appendix C for a sample Direct Mail Letter Promotion.

The Least You Need to Know

- A good first impression can help build customer loyalty.
- Try thinking about your customer when you set business hours.
- Four customer contacts a day will greatly increase your business.
- Be likable to your customers and your sales will increase.

11

Listen and Learn

In This Chapter

- ◆ Why listening is important
- ◆ Four listening guidelines
- ◆ Speaking the same language as your customers
- ◆ Encouraging your customers to complain
- ◆ "Tell me what you want and the answer is 'yes'"

As with communication in any relationship, it is key that both parties understand what the other wants. Communication in business means to give your customers the information that they need to choose your business, your products, your services. Communication starts with listening. When you listen carefully to what your customer has to say, you can learn more about how to run your business than you could learn in any seminar.

This first step is to listen, and the second step is to respond. All too often we hear but don't really listen; we talk but don't really communicate. In this chapter, I'll give you tips on how to listen to what your customers want, learn from it, and then give them what they have asked for.

The Best Guest at the Party

A man was invited by a prominent hostess to her dinner party. Afterward, the hostess's guests told her how much they had enjoyed the man's company. The hostess was confused. He was no life of the party. He was, in fact, quiet and subdued. What quality did he have that appealed to her guests that she could not see?

At her next party, she introduced him to one of her guests and then, unobtrusively, remained in close proximity to hear what he said. It was very simple. After being introduced he would ask the person he just met, "Tell me about yourself." And then just … listen.

He listened to them talk about themselves. He encouraged them to tell him about their jobs, their family, their hopes, their dreams. Where would they like to go on their next vacation. Why? For how long?

> **People Power**
>
> Dale Carnegie, author of *How to Win Friends and Influence People* (Pocket, 1990) said, "You can make more friends in two months by being interested in other people than you can in two years by trying to get other people interested in you."

Later everyone told the hostess what a marvelous addition he was to the party. Why? Because people who listen seem to care more and be more open-minded. People who continually talk without listening come across as pompous, self-centered, and, often, narrow-minded. They interrupt and criticize. People who don't listen can receive a bad (although sometimes undeserved) reputation.

Listening is much more than hearing. If you "listen well" to someone, you not only hear the sounds of his words and the tone of his voice, but you also see his physical movement, his gestures, his body language.

At one time, Ben Feldman was America's number-one life insurance salesman. He lived in the small town of East Liverpool, Ohio, and, without traveling more than a few miles from his home, became the first insurance salesman to sell more than $25 million of insurance in one year. And then he doubled that figure. For more than two decades he was the leading salesman for New York Life Insurance Company.

When asked the secret of his success, he said there were three reasons:

1. Work hard.

2. Think big.

3. Listen very well.

Ben Feldman knew that he could not sell his product unless he knew his customer's needs. And he could not find out unless he listened.

Pay Attention to Listening

Not everyone knows how to listen. You may have to practice good listening skills before you can incorporate the art of listening well into your business acumen.

The following are three "listening" guidelines to help you win customer loyalty:

◆ Practice listening

◆ Be patient

◆ Make sure that you really listen to what your customer is saying

Each is described in the sections that follow.

Practice Listening

Listening is a skill that you can improve. Start today by forcing yourself to really listen to what everyone who talks with you is saying.

Look her in the eye. Hear her out. Do not let your mind wander, which can be a hard thing to control, since we hear four times faster than people can speak. But you'll find that if you think about how to listen, you'll start listening more carefully, remembering what people have said to you, and responding to their concerns.

Be Patient

Listen all the way through. Don't react too quickly. When you anticipate, you are changing directions on the road the customer wants to travel.

When we listen, at the same time we are planning out the words in our heads that we want to say in response. Don't. Try to listen to the customer's complete thought, and then take a moment to consider before you respond. (This is especially useful if you are listening to a customer complaint.) You'll find that when you let yourself do this, your responses will be better thought out and more on target.

Make Sure You Really Listen

There was a salesman who called on a drug store every week to fill inventory and to show new items. He always greeted the owner with a big smile and, "Good to see you. How's the family?"

The storeowner said, "Fine," and the salesman replied, "Terrific. Let me show you what we have for you this week."

Wondering if the salesman was really listening to his reply, the owner decided on a new answer. When the salesman appeared the following week and began, "Glad to see you. How's the family?" the owner replied, "Well, my mother-in-law jumped off a cliff, my wife had to go to a leper colony, and the children are lost in a forest."

Without missing a beat, the salesman answered, "Terrific. Let me show you what we have for you this week."

Don't be so concerned about making the sale that you neglect the basic rule in selling: "Find out what the customers want and give it to them." You can't find out if you don't listen.

That means listening to. Not listening against. When you listen against, you are not really listening. You are simply waiting for the customer to finish what he is saying so that you can start your prepared speech that has no relationship to what the customer just said.

You cannot communicate unless you take the time to listen.

The Great Communicator

"What we have here is a failure to communicate." Remember that phrase from the film "Cool-Hand Luke?" The consequences of the failure to communicate were pretty bad for Paul Newman, and they can be for you, too, in your business.

When a British national speaks of the "underground," she means a subway. To an American the word means a clandestine group. A "flat" to an American is a punctured tire. To an Englishman it is his apartment. A "boot" to an American is what she buys in a Texas shoe store. To an Englishman it is the trunk of the car.

Here we are, speaking the same language, but we can't understand each other.

Successful marketers know that you don't communicate with every customer the same way. Ad copy directed to teenagers is different from copy directed to senior citizens, which is different from copy directed to young families, etc., etc., etc.

Says Professor Wendell Johnson, "The degree to which there is communication depends precisely upon the degree to which the words represent the same thing for the receiver or the reader that they do for the sender or writer. The degree to which they do is an index of the clarity of the communication."

Translation: If I don't understand what you're saying, then I can't communicate with you.

It is easy to assume that everyone lives in the same conversational world. Not true. The next time you start to say phrases, abbreviations, initials, or acronyms to a prospective customer, think for a minute if these phrases inhabit your customer's world of understanding.

If not, you must take the time to explain what you mean. That's the start of communication.

True Tales

My community called a town meeting to discuss a controversial vote for an increase in taxes to pay for a $20 million addition to the local school.

The sides were pretty even. The pro-school forces selected a planner to sell the audience with reasons why they should support the referendum. Here are some of his actual words:

"Heterogeneity will be reduced by social innovations peripheral to major modification of certification requirements ... available climate for environmental and behavioral changes. The concepts are generalized and incorporated into the educational mainstream ... intrinsic protective of vested interests ... generally regressive factors and deteriorating conditions ... micro structure of achievement and learning ..."

There he was, in front of his audience to persuade them to vote in favor of the bond issue, and he was speaking in a foreign language.

No connection. No communication. The referendum failed. No surprise.

We've been talking about not being able to communicate when all parties actually speak a common language. But an even more basic mistake is often made when your customers communicate in a language different from yours.

This situation is not unusual in today's multilingual, multi-ethnic world. Many businesses, large and small alike, now operate in neighborhoods that have changed their ethnic base over time. The language spoken by the customers may no longer be the language of the business owner. If this happens in your business, make the changes you need to communicate with your customers. Try to learn the language. Make sure you have salespeople who speak the appropriate language(s). Carry merchandise that your customers are interested in buying. (How do I know what that is? Ask them—or have your bilingual staff ask them.) Run your advertisements in the language(s) of your customers, and in the newspapers, radio stations, and television stations they read, listen to, and watch.

Basha's Supermarkets in Arizona are known for their attention to the Hispanic and Native American markets they serve.

Their Bashas' Diné Markets are located on Native American reservations throughout Arizona. These stores specialize in the needs of Navajo, Apache, and Tohono O'odam customers with products such as Blue Bird flour for fry bread, as well as mutton and wool. Signs in the stores are in the native language. Bashas' also runs several markets that cater to the Hispanic community in Phoenix. Their Food City stores offer a full range of ethnic and Hispanic food varieties.

How Do You Communicate with YOUR Customer?

Here are four guidelines for effective communication that gains the confidence and trust of the customer:

1. Be specific.

   The more specific you can be about your business services or products, the sooner customers will understand your business. They won't have to ask questions. They'll easily make a decision whether or not to shop with you. Here are a couple of examples:

   > "Bring your film in and we'll have your finished prints in one hour."

   > "This is our guarantee: You'll never stay in our checkout line longer than three minutes, or take $2.00 off your total."

2. Understand the customer's problem ahead of time.

   Do research. Speak to people to find out what they, as buyers, want. It may well be NOT what you think they want.

3. Say what the customer wants to hear.

   A Midwestern bank was developing a mailing piece to invite their customers to a party celebrating the bank's million-dollar remodeling. The letter talked about the marble floor imported from Italy, ultrasonic elevators, state-of-the-art computers, hand-loomed carpeting.

   Then someone on the staff who was reading the proposed letter asked, "How is the customer helped by our spending their money on our bank?"

   His point was this: Take all the features and translate them into customer benefits. No more long teller lines; quick answers on loans; new ATM 24-hour banking; comfortable, quiet surroundings to maintain customer privacy.

   What is it your customer wants to hear? Less talk about *you*. More talk about *them*.

4. Be sincere.

   Communicating sincerely can't be faked. The customer will know in a few moments whether he or she believes what you say. Don't pander to what you think the customer wants to hear if you can't follow through. As in the rest of life, honesty is usually the best policy.

Your Customers as Quality-Control Inspectors

Encourage complaints. Urge your customers to tell you about problems in your business. If you are serious about winning their loyalty, then you want to know what they like—and don't like—about your business. This is something you can do only when you have confidence in your organization. You must be good to make this work. But it's a powerful tool for building customer loyalty.

The idea comes from Feargal Quinn of Ireland's Superquinn supermarkets. He tells how a consultant suggested that he bring "quality-control inspectors" into his supermarkets to make sure everything is done in a first-class manner. His answer was, "We have them. They're called 'customers.'"

At Superquinn, customers belong to the supermarket's points-based loyalty program. They save money by accumulating points based on purchases. Feargal decided to reward his customers by giving them "goof" points to add to their loyalty program for errors they saw. In this way, customers are encouraged to look for things that go wrong at the store.

Here are some examples: If they have a shopping cart with a wobbly wheel. If they find products that are out of date. If there are any empty checkout counters when three or more people are in line. Anything a customer finds that is not up to Superquinn's standards can be reported and the customer earns additional loyalty program points.

The key that makes this work, of course, is not only having the errors reported, but also to act on these reports. Feargal Quinn is convinced that customers are happiest after they have had a problem, if it is solved. He says that before a problem is present, customers are satisfied. When a problem arises, customers are dissatisfied. Then, when the problem is resolved and handled well, customers are even more satisfied than they were before.

"Tell me what you want, and the answer is 'yes!'"

This is the most powerful listening tool I ever put into action in my business. After my staff understood this philosophy, adopted it, and used it on a regular basis, we created loyal customers almost every time someone had a problem.

Here's how it works:

When a customer returns merchandise to your business or simply voices a complaint over your procedures, she is agitated and annoyed. She thinks that, based on her knowledge and experience with other businesses, you will not be sympathetic to her problem. She thinks that you will ask prosecutorial questions and accuse her of taking advantage of you with a frivolous complaint.

Here is the procedure I taught everyone to follow:

First, listen. The customer has probably rehearsed the entire conversation on the way to your business. He knows what he is going to say and, in his mind, knows what your answer will be. He will decide on a course of action ranging from raising his voice, to demanding a superior who will "REALLY listen," to storming out, and vowing never to return.

Do not interrupt him! Perhaps give an occasional and sympathetic "I see" or nod your head in agreement as he continues speaking.

Next, when he completes stating his problem (and undoubtedly repeating his unhappiness several times), wait a few seconds and then, in a quiet, slow, and sincere tone, look at him directly and say, "Tell me what you want and the answer is 'yes.'"

The customer will usually reply with a "Huh?" or "What's that mean?"

Your answer is, "That's it. Tell me what you want and the answer is yes. If you want a cash refund, that's fine. If you want new merchandise in exchange, that's fine. If you want us to compensate you for the cost of driving from your home to here and back, we'll be glad to do that. You are not allowed to leave our store until we feel you are 100 percent satisfied. I have listened carefully to your concerns and you are absolutely right. Now, all you have to do is tell me what you want and the answer is 'yes.'"

The customer's response is at first confusion, then disbelief, then, happy acceptance (and sometimes they're even apologetic about complaining in the first place).

This process makes converts out of unhappy customers, just about every time.

The Least You Need to Know

◆ When you listen to your customers, you'll learn volumes about your business.

◆ Make sure you really listen when a customer has a concern.

◆ Speak the same language as your customers do.

◆ Use customer complaints as a check of your quality.

12

Advertise, Advertise, Advertise

In This Chapter

- ◆ Profiting from postcards
- ◆ What's on TV?
- ◆ Profiting from e-mail advertising
- ◆ Using the internet to bolster your advertising

There is the old story about the man who had a hotdog stand near a highway. He had big signs on the highway telling people to stop and eat his hot dogs.

His son came home from college, and reviewed his father's finances. He told his father, "Your business is barely making a profit. Times are tough. You can't afford the billboards."

When the advertising signs were taken down, the hotdog stand immediately lost customers. In a few months the business was bankrupt. The son told the father, "See, what did I tell you? Your business failed because times are so tough."

Advertising is an important weapon in your business. Without advertising, your business will disappear like the hotdog stand. You need advertising to tell customers who you are, what you do, what products and services you offer, and what special deals you have for customers. The only way you can increase your customers' loyalty is to have them do business with you. Advertising is a vital ingredient in any customer-loyalty program.

In this chapter, we will describe some advertising methods that will help you interact with your customers. Our emphasis is on those methods that we have found to be particularly cost effective.

Postcard Mailings

I think of postcards as fun. I like to send out postcards that have interesting graphics or art. Think of designing a postcard the way you would design a billboard. You want a simple message that your reader can immediately understand. You need a call to action and a way to respond. In general, a postcard mailing can be a highly effective way to reach out to your customers. Here are some of the advantages of a postcard mailing:

- ◆ It is inexpensive. You can mail a postcard first class for about 60 percent of the price of a first-class letter. So, for every three letters you send out, you can send out about five postcards for the same cost.

- ◆ Postcards will grab the reader's attention. It is easy to throw a letter away without opening it if you think it is an advertisement. But most people will look at a postcard because it's so easy to read.

- ◆ It's a great way to clean up a mailing list. Every so often you should send a postcard mailing first class to your mailing list. Why? Because the post office will return all the incorrect addresses and give you addresses for customers who have moved. Then you can use the corrected addresses to bring your mailing list up to date.

Postcards can also be effective as part of a two-step or even three-step direct-mail campaign. You can use a postcard followed by a more detailed mailing to customers who ask for more information. That would be a two-step direct mail campaign. A three-step direct mail campaign would be a postcard, a letter and a follow-up phone call.

True Tales

In my business, I send a lot of oversized postcards. I send 5½ x 8½-inch postcards, which are much larger than the standard 4 x 6-inch postcards. The larger postcards are considered letters and require higher postage than standard letters. But the added real-estate on the cards gives me the opportunity to develop an arresting visual image. It also enables me to explain products and services in more detail than on the smaller cards.

In my research, I have found that oversized postcards have returns that are equivalent to a typical letter mailing, which has inserts, letters, response cards, etc. The oversized postcard is much less expensive to produce than a letter mailing with all the inserts. Oversized postcards, with their ease of handling, billboard-type impact and small production costs are becoming the direct-mail product of choice for my clients. They are surprisingly effective in political campaigns and for business-to-business mailings.

Advertisers use postcards to tell clients that a special mailing or special offer will soon follow. They also can be used as a follow-up to a more typical mailing piece reinforcing the main selling arguments of the larger piece.

On sales of products with a higher price tag, postcards can be effective for telling customers to expect a phone call about the product.

Postcards are a highly flexible form of advertising. Here are just some of the ways my clients have used postcards to bolster their customer advertising:

♦ As a greeting (with a specific offer) to new move-ins around a business location.

♦ As a birthday or anniversary greeting (with a special free offer) to customers with birthdays or anniversaries during that particular month. Businesses that I work with often screen their birthday lists and give their best offers (or giveaways) to their best customers.

♦ As a regular monthly offer to customers. When you have a mailing list, you should mail to the whole list at least twice a year. You should mail to your best customers with an offer at least once a month. Refer to Appendix C for samples of different types of postcards.

TV or Not TV?

The public perceives TV ads as the most influential, authoritative, exciting, and persuasive type of advertising. And TV reaches more of an advertiser's prospects each day than any other medium. And TV can help you target almost every major demographic segment.

Customers say TV is where they are most likely to learn about products or brands (which includes you). TV is also the primary source that adults turn to for news, local weather, traffic, and sports.

National advertisers use TV to reach the millions of viewers who watch sitcoms and national news events. But there is a TV tool (read "less expensive") to reach your neighborhood's smaller market as well. It's called cable advertising, now available in almost every home.

National brands also use cable advertising to target specific households. Said one brand manager, "We're canceling national campaigns in favor of local promotions. We look at each market as a separate entity."

You should also consider cable advertising. Most customers are located with 10 miles or less of your business. This means that you can reach your market area and create loyal customers at a very competitive cost versus other media (newspaper, radio, and direct mail).

TV combines sight, sound, motion, and emotion for powerful selling. But you must tailor your ads for this specific medium. Otherwise, you will lose the real advantages of this powerful medium.

Here are 14 rules for TV advertising:

1. The picture must tell the story.

   David Ogilvy, founder of the famed Ogilvy & Mather ad agency told his staff that the first rule for TV advertising is this: "The picture must tell the story." He asked them, if they turned off the sound of the commercial, would the viewer know what was being sold? If not, try again."

2. Mention your company's name and product up front. Then repeat it again and again and again, especially at the end.

3. Show the product.

   Car commercials simply showing trees, grass, and rivers don't sell cars, as Infiniti learned.

   Blue jeans commercials showing young attractive models in tight-fitting blue jeans do work. It attracts attention and creates interest in the teenage market.

More than any other medium, TV gives you instant identification. That's why all those politicians running for office show their face, their family, their pets, and their home.

4. Show how your product works.

   If your chairs are made of unbreakable steel, bang on them during the commercial. (Remember the Samsonite commercial of the gorilla throwing luggage around his cage?) Visual effects are powerful because TV is visual.

5. Use testimonials … *that make sense.*

   When football legend Joe Namath advertised women's panty hose, women watching were not convinced this was a reason to buy. Paying extra money for a well-known personality to sell your merchandise means, in many cases, that the viewer will remember the personality but not necessarily the product, unless it is closely identified to the personality.

   Tennis racquets from famous tennis players is good identification. Basketball shoes worn by well-known basketballs stars, okay. But having a heating-pad worn and advertised by a famous athlete for sore limbs? I remember it was Shaquille O'Neal but, uh, what was the name of the product again?

   The best testimonials are from real people in your own community. What a great way to create loyalty: Have good customers say your chosen words on your commercial. (You know the ones who will be creditable.)

6. Don't mention the competitor's name.

   When you advertise that your product is better than the competitor's, many viewers will only remember the competitor's name. So don't mention it.

7. Tight close-ups of the face are dramatic.

   That's why *60 Minutes* uses this effect. It's like talking face to face.

8. Grab the viewer's attention quickly.

   It is the same as the headline on a print ad. You only have the four or five seconds that the viewers will give you before they decide whether to keep watching.

9. Have a beginning, middle, and end.

   Think of each commercial as a mini-story. The viewer should be able to follow along, see the problem you present, and how you solve it (the benefit).

10. Be careful of what you say. Somebody's listening.

   Every word counts. Your audience is often listening even when they're not watching. They may leave the room during the commercial but can still hear the words.

11. Don't plan on revisions.

   They take time. And money. Your salesperson will review your selling message with you. Most will offer 'storyboards' to view, where you'll see sketches of the pictures and the words to be spoken. Ask yourself, "Is this being told in a persuasive manner with lots of benefits for the viewer?"

   If you wait to see the finished commercial and then decide whether to do certain segments over, you are asking to spend more money, because it takes more time than changing words for a radio spot or a newspaper ad.

12. Schedule TV ads during any season, but lightly in summer.

   Here's why: TV viewing decreases about 17 percent in the summer (remember all those reruns) but you pay the same for your ad! There are exceptions: If you are advertising summer products such as patio furniture, bathing suits, or suntan lotions, then it's fine to advertise in the summer.

13. Be wary of humor.

   Okay, the viewer may laugh. But will the viewer BUY? People buy for many reasons including (but not limited to) saving time, saving money, making money, protecting their family, and for comfort, health, and praise. But people don't buy because you made them laugh.

People Power

"People don't buy from clowns."—Claude Hopkins, the father of modern advertising

   Yes, humor does attract attention and can make people feel good, but you have to be very, very careful. Here's why: What makes one person laugh can make another person uncomfortable, uneasy, and unhappy.

14. Make it newsworthy.

   This advice works in every form of advertising. Is there a way you can tie your product/business into a local event? Special Olympics? Scholastic athletics? Community food drives? This association gives your business an added luster and creates a positive image.

The answer to TV or not TV is a resounding YES! Local cable advertising will make it possible for you.

E-mail: Quick, Inexpensive, and Effective Marketing

How do you communicate with your customers and potential customers? You could choose newspaper, radio, TV, or direct mail. Or you could use the fastest-growing marketing tool, the Internet.

The Internet gives your customers more ways to shop (and gives you more sales) but it also increases your opportunity to practice loyalty marketing through two marketing tools:

◆ **E-mails** are for fast computer communication to people whose e-mail addresses you have on file.

◆ **Websites** give you the opportunity to have your own home on the Internet, and to show your credentials and products to consumers who either know you or find your web address through a search engine.

The Internet gives you the unique opportunity to find, capture, and keep customers everywhere. You are no longer bound by a defined geographic market area. If you have a unique product or a unique offer, your loyal customers can be thousands of miles away.

E-mail enables you to send a personal message or sales offer to your customers faster than by direct mail from the U.S. Post Office (often referred to as *snail mail*).

E-mail has three major advantages for your loyalty marketing:

1. E-mail is less expensive than regular mail. No costs for postage. No envelopes. No paper.

2. E-mail is faster. Send an e-mail message and the recipient receives it right away! Direct mail takes a few days AFTER the time you've mailed your message.

Significant Stats
A survey by American Research Group asked adults and teenagers how they will make purchases in the year 2020. They gave these choices: in person, TV, telephone, or Internet. The Internet scored highest: 45 percent for adults and 46 percent for teens.

Significant Stats
According to a survey from Harris Interactive, "Seven out of ten consumers request legitimate e-mail marketing messages."

3. You can receive quick results by offering a special price for a limited time.

United Airlines knows that 7 percent of their customers make up 42 percent of their annual profit. They can identify them and give them special benefits. But how can they contact their other customers who use their services but not as often?

Answer: e-mail!

United uses e-mail for its loyalty marketing in the following ways:

- They offer special fares on their most traveled routes to their customers.

- They offer customers other special deals.

- By seeing what offers their customers respond to, United can then build once-in-a-while customers into loyal customers inexpensively and efficiently.

Used effectively, e-mail can help grow your customer's loyalty by increasing your communication with your customers.

People Power _____

"It is interesting that Larry Johnston (Chairman and CEO of Albertsons) says that going online (connecting to the Internet) is primarily a relationship-building device. This has been one of the central findings of our research at Michigan State University. Getting closer to the customer helps to strengthen their loyalty and get a greater share of their wallet overall. Good for Albertsons, which has quietly and systematically built the first almost-national network for grocery home delivery. If you live in a top-50 market anywhere in the U.S., it is coming to you." —Kenneth K. Boyer, Associate Professor, Broad College of Business, Michigan State University

How to Increase Your E-mail Marketing Effectiveness

Here are 16 e-mail marketing rules that will help increase the effectiveness of your e-mail advertising:

1. Sending e-mail to your own customers is much more effective than sending blanket e-mails to potential customers.

If your own customers receive your e-mail, they will open it and read your message, the same as they would if you mailed them a letter. If the message is *spam*, it is usually thrown away without being read.

2. Capturing e-mail addresses is necessary to build an e-mail marketing campaign.

   Make sure you receive permission from your customers to send e-mail to them. Customers who receive unsolicited e-mails will not be pleased. Ask your customers for their e-mail address on sign-up sheets in your place of business and in your regular mailings.

> **Loyalty Lingo**
>
> **Spam** is unsolicited e-mail, usually advertising sent to consumers and businesses without their consent. Spam is the electronic equivalent of junk mail. Today more than half of all e-mail is considered spam.

When your customer purchases from you online, include a "yes/no" item asking if they want to receive e-mail from you. Even though you have the e-mail address from the transaction, you still should get the customer's permission to send marketing e-mails. Most will say yes.

3. Don't forget to fill out the "subject" and "from" lines.

   Many e-mail writers don't fill out the subject heading to say what they're writing about. If the reader sees nothing in this space, they might easily assume that there is nothing to interest them. Think of the subject line as the all-important headline.

   The readers also want to know from whom the e-mail is sent. If you don't tell them, they may quickly delete what you sent them without reading further.

4. Include your name, phone, fax number, and web address.

   People want to know who is writing to them and how they can contact you.

5. Write a headline at the start of your e-mail that promises a benefit or provokes curiosity.

   Your object is not only to stop the readers but also make them keep reading. If your copy following your headline continues to provoke their interest—great! Just like a print ad on paper, someone who reads the first 50 words of your message will probably read the next 200 words!

Asking a question in the headline is a good attention-grabber, but you must answer it fast in the first paragraph or you'll lose your readers.

6. Know what you want to say.

People Power _____

"The consumer encounters 3,000 marketing messages per day. That's everything: Ads on TV, billboards, radio, newspapers, etc. Be specific! No long, rambling, explanatory copy." —Tim Sanders, Yahoo's Chief solutions officer

Tell the audience up front what you're writing about. Make it interesting. Make it believable. Offer a benefit. Provoke their curiosity. (Did we say that already? Good. It's worth repeating.)

7. Write short, effective, makes-a-point copy.

No long sentences (15 to 17 words is good). No long paragraphs (two to three is fine). The average person's attention span has decreased dramatically with the onslaught of messages received from all advertising media.

8. Check. And double check.

Have someone else check your e-mail message for clarity. You will be surprised how many times an objective reader will say to you, "What does this mean?" Or "You spelled this wrong." Your search engine spell-check will find words you've written incorrectly.

Once you've hit the "send" button, there's no taking those thousands of e-mails back. So be sure they are correct.

9. Write in a me-and-thee manner.

There is a direct-marketing credo that says, "Writing effective copy is like writing a letter to your Aunt Minnie." Your e-mail message should sound as though you're visiting your customers in their home and talking about something that interests them. Don't be afraid to use contractions because that's how people talk.

10. Make them want to come back.

Have the readers caught up with the message/story/offer you make so that they'll want to read your future e-mails.

11. Keep it short.

E-mail is not like direct mail, where the rule of thumb is, "Write as much as you want that will keep the reader reading." E-mails longer than one page (which means taking the time to scroll down and keep reading) are usually too much.

The exception to this rule is this: E-mail newsletters often require two or more pages that your customer will read as long as it's interesting. (See Chapter 15 for more about e-mail newsletters).

12. "Free" and "You."

These proven two words attract readers … and keep them reading, just as these two words do in other forms of advertising. This is a tried-and-true rule.

13. What day should you send e-mails?

If it's to a business, skip the weekends and Monday. The reason is that many businesses aren't open on weekends. When people return to work on Monday, your e-mail will be surrounded by dozens of other e-mails and will not receive the same attention as if it were mailed during the week.

> **Significant Stats**
>
> A study from EmailLabs says that Wednesday is the most popular day for opening e-mail messages, with 23.3 percent of e-mails getting opened, and Sunday is the weakest, with only 0.9 percent of e-mails getting opened.

Senior citizens tend to read e-mail every day. It's usually part of their routine.

14. What time of the day should you send e-mails?

About half of e-mails are sent between 8 A.M. and noon. Most are opened around 11 A.M.

15. When will you have a response?

Herschell Gordon Lewis, an acknowledged expert in writing excellent selling copy, says that about 25 percent will answer you right away. A total of one third will answer you on the second day, and another 25 percent on the third day. The remaining few will answer sporadically, if at all.

16. Give your customers the opportunity to "opt out."

At the end of your e-mail, include a little message saying that if they no longer want future e-mails from you, they can simply click the "reply" button and write in the subject line "Please cancel."

 **People Power**

"My goal is to collect 150 new e-mail names every month and to send out a new e-mail message to this list every two weeks." —Donald Kelley, owner of art galleries in Minnesota and Wisconsin

Also tell them that their e-mail address or personal information they give to you is never, ever shared with anyone else (and make sure you don't share it).

E-mail can be an effective, low-cost way of connecting to your customers. But unwanted spam is such a turn-off to people you should make sure you are only sending e-mail messages to people who want to receive them.

Marketing Through a Website

According to Biz-Rate.com, seven out of ten small businesses in the United States have a website. This is a 100 percent increase in only two years!

> **Significant Stats**
>
> Online retail sales in the United States grew 34 percent in 2003, reaching $72 billion, according to Forrester Research. This amounted to 5.4 percent of total retail sales in 2003, up from 3.6 percent the previous year. They estimated that Internet sales reached 6.6 percent of total retail sales in 2004.

Here's what makes a website exciting for small businesses: It levels the playing field. Now you have the opportunity to compete against the "big players" by creating a website that is appealing, easy to maneuver, with credible offers to a targeted audience. That audience is not limited to a specific location. Even if you have a small business you now have the potential to reach buyers around the world.

Another powerful goal of a website is to attract Internet browsers, who happen to land on your website (clicks), to entice them to visit your physical place of business (bricks).

You need a domain name to locate your business on the Internet. You can register the name of your website (domain) as long as someone else has not already claimed that name. There are a lot of places on the Internet you can go in order to see if the name you want has already been taken. Start by typing in "domain name" into a search engine.

The first page of your website is called the "home page." The home page is similar to the table of contents of a book or a magazine.

On the home page, highlight the name of your business. Include the most important information to briefly describe your business.

The home page is the beginning point for Internet users to navigate around your website. It should list all the major areas of your business so that a user can find the particular thing she is looking for. The user then can click on a specific area to find more detailed information.

People Power _____

"Here's the _First Rule of Web Advertising_: Stop the surfer in his or her tracks. You're at point-blank range when the surfer first lands on your site. _FIRE!_" —Herschell Gordon Lewis, President, Communicomp

How to Increase Your Website Marketing Effectiveness

Here are 13 rules to increase the effectiveness of your website:

1. Spend some time thinking about the name you want for your website.

   Here are two rules: Keep the name short, and make it reflect your name. (Our website is www.raphel.com.) Make it easy to type without making a mistake.

2. Tell customers about your website.

   Your website needs to be advertised and promoted. Place your website address on all your advertising: on your calling cards, your stationery, your invoices, and envelopes. Leave it on almost everything that leaves your business, including shopping bags, birthday greetings, and special announcements. (I've seen them on business delivery trucks!)

3. Capture the reader's attention at once!

   People read the web like they read highway billboards. They are moving with speed.

People Power _____

"When someone lands on your website, you have about 22 seconds to keep that person's attention." —Regina Brady, Internet pioneer

4. Organize your website so that customers can easily find what they are looking for.

   How long will prospective buyers wait for the information to come up on the screen? Less than you think. If they have to click to more than two places to find what they want, they will often give up and go to some other website.

5. Keep your website interesting. Not all browsers will buy right away.

   Usually customers will not buy the first time they check out your website. The average buyer will visit your website three times before placing an order.

6. Your website can be a "welcome mat" for your business or catalogue.

   Four out of ten people rank one of the Internet's most important uses as being "to look up information on products."

   Here's why: Most first-time buyers will visit your website before they come to your place of business. Your website becomes their "window-shopping experience." They'll "click" before they visit your "bricks."

   Catalog retailers, once threatened by the Internet, quickly discovered that the Internet increased their sales. The customer can buy any time of the day, any day of the year. It can be easier and faster to buy from a website than to place an order by phone.

7. Mailed catalogues do NOT cut back on sales from websites.

   A survey by the Millard Group found that 80 percent of consumers said that receiving catalogs in the mail influenced them to shop for the item online. They kept the catalog for reference to remember what they bought. In just one year (2003), the number of catalogs available online jumped 63 percent—from 3,733 to 6,097—according the National Directory of Catalogs.

8. Give a guarantee.

   Almost every business and catalog company has a guarantee, and the customer expects it! Guarantees give the customer confidence in what you're selling. Most research reveals that less than 2 percent of your customers will ask for their money back.

   Make it easy for the customer to contact you with any questions. Give them a toll-free number for not only handling sales but also for answering questions.

   Be flexible on the time they can send products back. Lands End and L.L.Bean don't set time limits on returned merchandise. Zappos is a shoe retailer whose website is continually cited as a good website model. (Look them up at www.zappos.com.) They give you a "365-day return policy." It's easy and it's free.

9. Give testimonials. Testimonials are praise for your business or product from customers.

   They give confidence to first-time buyers. Testimonials should be easy to acquire from your loyal customers.

10. Give a reason for buying from you this way.

    Some businesses offer free shipping. Others offer free return-shipping if you are not happy with what you bought.

11. Understand the importance of security.

    Customers are wary about giving their e-mail address, credit-card numbers, and other personal information. More than eight out of ten customers say it is important that a business tells them their information is secure and will not be shared with anyone else. A business that violates this trust can easily lose 80 percent of their customers.

12. Ask for relevant information from your customers.

    Ask customers their names, mailing and e-mail addresses, what they've ordered, and method of payment. Keep "method of payment" as the last item since that way they've already invested their time by placing the order. You want them to commit to the sale before you ask them how they should pay.

13. And, finally, …

    Send customers a "Thank you for the order" via e-mail, AFTER the sale is completed. Also remember to e-mail them again saying when the order was shipped.

Having and maintaining an interesting and entertaining website is becoming a must for any business. It is an important supplement to a physical store, where customers can communicate with and order from the business without leaving their houses. Try at least some of the advertising media described in this chapter. The more you reach out to your customers, the more they will decide to use your products and services.

The Least You Need to Know

- Postcard mailing is simple, visual, and cost effective.

- TV is the right medium for an exciting, visual connection to attract prospects and to remind customers who you are and what you sell. Cable TV advertising is a less expensive way to achieve the benefits of TV advertising.

- E-mail gives you the advantages of one-to-one advertising, and it is cheaper and faster than direct mail.

- The Internet give you the opportunity to have your own website in which you can offer your products and services to your market area and beyond. You can create great offers to inspire loyalty.

Chapter 13

Selling Rules!

In This Chapter

- ◆ How selling relates to loyalty marketing
- ◆ What you need to know about selling
- ◆ The making of a salesperson
- ◆ Closing the sale

In a successful company, everybody sells! The cashier, the accountant, the cleaning person, and the owner all sell. They are all proud of the company they work for, and they want to make sure everybody knows how great the company's services and products are.

While it is important that everyone in the organization wants sales to grow, it is crucial that your salespeople know the basic rules for selling.

As sales consultant "Red" Motley says, "Nothing happens until a sale is made." You can have the greatest products and services, tremendous advertising, an attractive business and superior personnel, yet your business will fail if your employees do not know the techniques of selling. This chapter will describe what you need to know for selling success.

Selling First—Then Loyalty Marketing

There is a strong connection between selling and loyalty marketing. Loyalty marketing is a long-term relationship between a business and a customer. In order to establish the relationship, there must be a customer. Selling is the technique that turns business prospects into customers. Then those first-time customers can be romanced, rewarded, and convinced to become loyal customers.

> **People Power** _____
>
> Harry Bullis of General Mills once told a convention of Northwestern Life Insurance representatives: "When I go out in the morning, I don't ask, 'How many sales will I make today?' I ask, 'How many people can I help today?'"

Selling is a means to an end. Making that first sale is an important first step in creating customer loyalty. If the first sale is satisfactory to the customer, there is the opportunity to earn the loyalty necessary for a long-term business relationship.

Show customers that you care about them; help them solve their problems; have them enjoy their shopping with you. Then the relationships lead to loyalty rather than simply making sales.

Learn Sales from Others

No one is born a lawyer. Or a doctor. Or a salesperson. A good salesperson can learn from selling techniques developed by other successful salespeople.

Before universities gave out degrees, a person learned a trade by serving as an apprentice to a lawyer or a blacksmith or a printer or some other occupation. There were no schools to give degrees in most professions. You learned by doing. By watching others excel in their crafts.

Next time you visit the Louvre, the Metropolitan Museum of Art, or your neighborhood museum, you may see, tucked away in one of the corners, a young artist, palette in hand, canvas stretched tight, trying to carefully recapture the mood and color of the famous painting before her.

The great writers, artists, musicians, merchants, salespeople became great not only by their latent talent but by copying that which preceded them. And having copied and learned, they then remade what has been done into their own individual tapestry.

In a similar fashion, you can learn how to sell by watching successful salespeople. Watch how they listen closely to customers before the sale. The best salespeople are the best listeners. They know that only by truly understanding their customers' needs will they be able to make a sale.

Watch how successful salespeople give customers alternatives. They rarely ask a "yes" or "no" question. They give their customers choices. When a customer chooses between two or more alternatives, the customer is basically selling herself. Only when a customer has narrowed down exactly what she wants does the salesperson ask for the order.

A good salesperson solves needs. The salesperson's motivation is to satisfy a need or solve a problem. The financial rewards only come after a customer is truly satisfied.

One of the questions we are frequently asked is, "How do I sell the products and services in my business?" People want to know the secrets of selling which apply to the business they are in. They ask us:

How do you sell …

- Furniture?
- Trucks?
- Food in a supermarket?
- Credit cards?
- Hairspray?
- Eyeglasses?
- Repair work?
- Bank services?
- Insurance?
- Mobile homes?
- Art?

The answer to all questions: THE SAME WAY.

As a businessman and speaker, I was asked to give seminars for a variety of companies around the world on selling the products or services of the particular company, with little or no relationship to my basic selling experience in retail clothing.

But once committed to giving selling advice to other businesses and other industries, I made a study of selling techniques and found the basic techniques in selling were the same.

There are only four basic techniques of selling:

1. Know the product or service you are selling. The more you know the benefits (and possible problems) of the products you are selling, the more able you are to steer a customer to products or services she needs.

2. Take care of the customer. The sale only starts when the money changes hands. By following up with customers and servicing customers, you are paving the way for future sales.

3. Understand the customer's problem(s) and solve them. If a customer comes to you with a complaint, consider it an opportunity. Once you solve a customer's problem, he will start recommending your services to all his acquaintances.

4. Give the customer a reason to buy. Once you have listened to a customer's needs, you can close the sale by listing the advantages of buying now.

Whether you own a furniture store or a bank, a dry cleaner or an insurance company, the four techniques listed above will work. The more you practice these basic techniques, the more your business will prosper.

Facts and Fiction About Good Salespeople

Salespeople are vital in distinguishing your business from your competitors in the eyes of your customers. But a lot of people have the wrong idea about how salespeople achieve selling success.

Here are some commonly held misconceptions about salespeople, and the real facts.

> **People Power**
>
> Ed McMahon, Johnny Carson's TV sidekick, remembers when he was selling kitchen gadgets on the Boardwalk in Atlantic City with two other pals—all in their early 20s—Jack Klugman and Charles Bronson. He said, "None of us was born with that sixth sense for handling audiences. We all learned it the hard way."

Fiction:

> *Sales people are born, not made.*

Fact:

- ◆ Successful salespeople come all sizes, shapes, colors, descriptions, and both sexes.

- ◆ They acquire their talent through observation and by learning what works and what doesn't through experience.

Fiction:

You just need a winning smile and a good personality to be a good salesperson.

Fact:

- ◆ Success is most often gained through preparation.

- ◆ The more you know about your product, the more you sell.

- ◆ The more you know about your competition, and, most of all, about your customers, the more you sell.

- ◆ The more you know why anyone should buy what you have to sell, the more you sell.

Fiction:

Successful salespeople are Type-A personalities. They work at great speed, all hours, ignoring family and friends, and develop illnesses more quickly.

Fact:

- ◆ Some do.

- ◆ Some don't.

- ◆ Recent studies say that good salespeople are actually healthier than the general population.

- ◆ They are more excited about accomplishment and are not focused on retirement.

Fiction:

Successful salespeople are solely motivated by money.

Fact:

- ◆ Salespeople look at money only as a way of keeping score.

- ◆ Money is not the goal.

- ◆ They want personal achievement and accomplishment.

We had a friend who started a shoe and fashion business in New York City's Greenwich Village in his late 60s after years of learning and selling dance and fashion merchandise. At age 90, he still owned and managed his successful business.

Fiction:

Salespeople must be young.

Fact:

♦ The average age of new salespeople is mid-30s.

♦ Many start selling later in life.

♦ Age is not a necessary ingredient.

What Makes a Good Salesperson?

Several years ago, the insurance industry faced a dilemma. For decades the industry noticed that more than half of its newly employed salespeople left after the first year. And 80 percent left within three years.

The cost of recruiting, selecting, and training new salespeople, added to the money spent on salaries and expensive account amounted to more than $50,000 for a sales recruit that left after one year.

The insurance industry found out that these sales recruits left because they did not know the basics of selling. No one had taught them what makes a good salesperson. By teaching insurance salespeople how to approach customers and how to convince customers to buy, the insurance industry was able to dramatically lower the number of defections of salespeople.

What did these insurance salespeople learn? What does makes a salesperson tick? We've interviewed and observed some of the best salespeople in the country and found there are certain characteristics that top salespeople share. Here they are:

♦ They work hard.

♦ They are driven by a desire to succeed.

♦ They are always learning and improving.

♦ They are intensely competitive.

♦ They are unhappy with how things are and want to make them better.

♦ They learn from their failures.

♦ They believe in themselves.

The First Selling Ingredient: Empathy

David Mayer and Herbert M. Greenberg, psychological consultants at the Marketing Survey & Research Corporation of New York, conducted seven years of research on the question of what makes a good salesperson. Their conclusions, written nearly four decades ago for the Harvard Business Review, are still quoted and used as guidelines by many organizations.

They said that a good salesperson had to have two key characteristics: *empathy* and ego.

Why Empathy Is More Than Sympathy

Empathy means understanding the needs of customers. Watching them while talking to them. Adjusting to how they act and react. Not having a memorized sales talk that is the same for everyone.

> **Loyalty Lingo**
>
> **Empathy** *("I feel your pain")* comes from the German word "einfühlen" used by Freud and, later, by Heinz Kohut. To be empathetic is "to feel or find one's way into another's state of mind."

Empathy was not always a part of selling.

In 1887, John Henry Patterson of National Cash Register (now NCR) created the first modern sales team, giving them their own territories. This meant that they could form relationships with the customers.

Patterson gave increases based on how much they sold. He soon discovered that certain salesmen outsold others. He asked his best salesman why he was so successful. His answer was, "I have perfected a memorized sales speech."

Patterson was impressed, and printed this presentation under the title, "How I Sell National Cash Register." His salespeople were told to memorize the contents if they wanted to keep their job.

Selling has evolved over time. Yes, it is important to have a prepared sales presentation that lists all the selling points and overcomes major objections. But this is only a guide to the empathic salesperson. He or she must change, modify, and adjust the words to what benefits the customer. Because this is what shows the salesperson's concern and loyalty to the person buying the product.

Trust Is a By-Product of Empathy

When you are empathetic to customers' problems, they trust you and are more willing to buy from you.

Why is this important?

A recent survey said that only 10 percent of Americans associate the word "trust" with the word "business." What an indictment of the selling profession!

In the past 10 years I've stayed in about 150 hotel rooms across the United States and internationally. I've always fill out the customer comment card in the room with a compliment or criticism, and include my name and address because I want to know if I will hear back. Do they have empathy with my response?

Of the 75 comment cards I've left at the front desks or mailed back, I received answers from 5!

One that did reply was Marriott. I later found out that Bill Marriott personally read 10 percent of the 8,000 letters and 2 percent of the customer comment cards received each month.

Was this a reason why Marriott's occupancy rate was 10 percent higher than normal? Yes. Because Marriott responded to complaints when customers were unhappy. Marriott showed itself to be empathetic with the feelings of its guests, thus generating a high degree of trust.

Empathy Can Be Expressed in Advertising

Allstate Insurance Company prepared a direct-mail piece for their agents showing a "typical" white American suburban family: husband, wife, two children, and a dog.

Said the African American salesman who looked at the piece, "Doesn't look like *my* customers."

Said the Hispanic salesmen, "Doesn't look like *my* customers."

Allstate quickly printed two additional brochures. Same copy. Same selling points. But now the sales staff had a choice of the photo on the cover: a white couple, a Hispanic couple, or a black couple.

The result was a very effective mailer because Allstate understood the importance of empathy in their advertising.

Empathy Can Solve Problems

When GE first offered its toll-free number to answer customers' problems about GE products, the naysayers were quick to ridicule what they said was a cost-increasing way to do business.

However, this turned out to be a huge marketing success for GE. The GE Call Center developed 750,000 of the most-asked questions (and answers) in their library. GE did a cost analysis of this service versus their sales, and discovered that the value was four to six times the cost.

Empathy paid off!

Empathy is NOT sympathy. It means selling with concern.

It means understanding the needs of the customers. It means solving the problems of the customers with your products or services.

The Second Selling Ingredient: Ego

Ego is the necessary second ingredient of a successful salesperson. When ego is combined with empathy—in proper balance—you have a winning combination.

♦ *Strong empathy but little ego.*

   This will make you well liked but not sales-oriented.

♦ *Strong ego but little empathy.*

   This can make you disliked. The sales you make are done through force or intimidation. No long relationship can develop. It certainly does not lead to loyalty.

♦ This is the successful salesperson's ego:

   He has a basic need to succeed. The customer is merely a way to achieve this goal. He has self-confidence.

   He is a strong believer in "imaging." He sees himself throwing the pass for the touchdown, breaking the track record, and always making the sale.

   Here is the philosophy of a salesperson with a strong ego: "If I'm not making sales, it's not the weather, the economy, or the time of the year. It's *me*. And if I AM making sales, it's not the weather, the economy, or the time of the year. It's *me.* After all, somebody's buying something from somebody. Now, how am I going to have them *buy from me?*"

◆ *A salesperson with ego sets goals.*

Murray's father, Harry Raphel, set goals. He wanted to be a member of the "Million Dollar Club" and had a calendar on his desk showing how much insurance he had to sell every day, every week, every month, to make that goal for the year.

And yet, less than 1 percent of salespeople have written goals.

Harry Raphel sold insurance during the depression. He had a "debit"—a geographic section of the community assigned to him where he sold policies and returned every week to receive a payment—usually 25¢ or 50¢. When he came home in the evening he would tell stories of people he had met and insurance he had sold. He was proud to be a good and successful salesman.

One day he went to a woman's home to collect the weekly premium. She told him it was difficult for her to be home when he came. He said she should simply leave the premium book and the quarter in her mailbox and that he'd sign it and pick up the money. She thanked him.

He did this for several weeks. One day he came to this home, opened the mailbox, and saw his premium book with the quarter, and he also saw another premium book with money enclosed from a competitive company. His ego was challenged.

He rang the bell. The woman came to the door. He said to her, "Are you mad at me?

She replied, "Of course not. Why do you ask?" "Well," he said, I've been coming here every week to collect your premium, and today I found another insurance company's book in your mailbox. How come?

And she said, "Oh, do you SELL insurance? I thought you were just a collector."

My father convinced the woman to buy insurance from him. He convinced her he was not just a collector. My father said to me, "From that day on, whenever I spoke with a prospect, I'd say, "I'm a salesman. And I sell insurance. Every year I will meet with you about your insurance needs to change or add policies."

The Selling Profession

Selling is one of the few professions that does not depend on advanced education. Psychologist Walter Dill Scott said, "Success or failure in selling is caused more by mental attitude than by mental capacities."

This does not mean good salespeople don't need an education. They do—but they must have knowledge of the products they sell. It is not unusual to see people who sell sophisticated medical equipment in the operating rooms of major hospitals watching the skilled surgeons use this high-priced equipment. The salesperson who made the sale is there to advise, suggest, and watch over the procedure.

A successful salesperson understands why people buy. This information can be invaluable to businesses in trying to ramp up the loyalty and sales of their customers.

People Power _____

Elmer Wheeler was America's number-one salesman in the 1940s. Wheeler went to see King Gillette, owner of Gillette blades, and said, "I have six words on this folded piece of paper. If you decide to use them, you pay my fee. If you don't, I leave."

Gillette took the paper, unfolded it, read the words, and wrote out a check. Here are the six words: "How are you fixed for blades?"

Some executives of America's drugstores asked him how to increase sales at drugstore food counters. He gave them the phrase that immediately put more money in the register. When a customer asked for a malted milkshake, the clerk asked, "One egg or two?"

The Petroleum Institute asked him to come up with a phrase to have people buy more gas. Wheeler gave them three words that increased sales across the country. When someone pulled up to a station for gas, the attendants were instructed to simply ask this question: "Fill 'er up?"

It's Never Easy

Being a successful salesperson often means having to overcome obstacles. Salespeople often have long and irregular hours. They often need to travel to appointments and be away from home for days. They face rejection, knowing that many of their prospects feel they are an unwelcome interruption in their daily work. Salespeople often have to make cold calls, imposing themselves on busy people who are not really interested in the salesperson's products.

Most people find it difficult, if not impossible, to know that when they wake the next morning there is no promise of a wage or benefits from a company. Independent salespeople must create these opportunities themselves.

However, there are benefits to selling that can help overcome the tough life salesmen face. There is the thrill of making a big sale which rivals the thrill of scoring the winning touchdown in a football game.

There is also the more quiet joy of helping a customer find the right products to make his business a success. There is comfort in knowing your products can enrich people's lives, and a challenge in overcoming the obstacles every salesperson faces.

Creating Loyal Customers

Loyalty marketing is just as important to salespeople as it is to anyone else in business. Once a trusting relationship is established, salespeople spend less time chasing sales and more time solving problems for their customers.

From a salesperson's point of view, an established customer is much more of an opportunity for sales than a cold call. The reason is that the established customer knows and trusts the salesperson. That customer will be interested in a new product the salesperson is now handling. The established customer will also be more willing to accept a salesperson's advice on the amount of items to buy, what sizes to carry, what colors to order, etc.

Established customers also can become advocates for salespeople, introducing them to new accounts and providing references for people skeptical of the salesperson's products. The more salespeople cultivate their loyalty customers, they will have an easier time increasing their sales and finding new customers.

Close vs. Close

There's a very entertaining and revealing scene in David Mamet's Pulitzer-Prize-winning play, *Glengarry Glen Ross*, where the sales motivator played by Alec Baldwin gives a chalk talk to a group of real-estate salesmen on the techniques of making a sale. Some of the real-estate salesmen have grown complacent, and Baldwin's characterization of the enthusiasm needed to complete a sale is compelling.

Baldwin prints the letters "A B C" on a blackboard and tells the sales force that the letters stand for "Always Be Closing."

His point is this: No amount of training will make you successful if you don't know how to close a sale.

Okay—I'd be first in line to agree that the object of selling is to get the order.

But I believe that the close of the sale to a prospect should begin a sales relationship with that prospect, or that the close of a sale with a customer should continue the relationship.

People Power

"The sale merely consummates the courtship at which point the marriage begins. How good the marriage is depends on how well the seller manages the relationship. Will there be continued or expended business, or troubles and divorce?"
—Theodore Levitt, *Harvard Business Review*

Be Careful How You Close the Sale

To allow the close to define the sale defeats the primary value in selling, which is the "lifetime value" of the customer. You can't have that if you *close* the door and walk away after making the sale.

Don't *close* the sale. *Open* relationships.

Here's why: A sold customer is expensive to replace. Think of the time and effort it took to bring someone to the point of buying what you have to sell.

Shouldn't the goal be one of investing in the long-time value of the newly acquired customer? The opportunity for loyalty marketing begins after you made the sale, but only if you *begin* the relationship.

The end of a first sale is really the beginning of the NEXT sale. The more involved your business is with your customers, the more they will remain loyal customers and also recruit new customers.

Be Close, Not Closed

What if the letter "C" in the "Always Be Closing" credo was changed to "concerned" or "caring" or "compassionate"? Being close defined in that sense enhances your goal of creating customer loyalty.

Make the customers feel as if they came to visit you in your home and you said, "Draw your chair up close."

A good example of this closeness AFTER the sale was what happened at a convention of the Little People Association (LPA). They contacted several hotels in several cities. The Marriott in Salt Lake City offered them good pricing and many amenities. The LPA agreed to the terms and booked the Marriott for their convention.

Was that the end of the sale? The close?

Hardly.

A story in *The Salt Lake Tribune* told what happened when the little people arrived.

- A low check-in desk was set up in the hotel lobby.

- Step stools or milk crates were placed in guest rooms, the gift shop, and at the main registration desk to help conference attendees reach sinks, wall-mounted thermostats, and hangers in closets.

- Wash cloths and towels were placed on the backs of toilets

- TV remote-control devices were moved from the tops of armoires to the night stands.

"We got down on our knees and walked through our rooms. It proved a totally different perspective. A lot of the time you take things for granted," said Dusty Casey, Marriott's director of hotel operations.

They didn't stop after they made the close. They continued by understanding the needs of this customer. They stayed close to them.

The Least You Need to Know

- Selling that leads to loyalty has to include caring about the customer.

- Good salespeople are not born with the ability. It is acquired by learning from good salespeople.

- To succeed, good salespeople have to develop both empathy and ego.

- Closing the sale should not be the end, but rather the beginning of a customer relationship.

Chapter 14

Branding: The Ties That Bind

In This Chapter

- ◆ Creating your image in the minds of your customers
- ◆ Developing the components that make your brand
- ◆ Using your brand in your total marketing package
- ◆ Developing customer loyalty to your brand
- ◆ Preserving your brand

We've all heard of customers being loyal to a brand. That, in fact, is the Holy Grail of retailing—creating that magic "brand" that resonates with buyers so much that they choose that product above all others in the same category.

The pinnacle is when the brand name becomes the de facto name of the product category. Kleenex. Xerox. Coke. iPod. Levis. Band-Aid. Vaseline. Q-Tips. FedEx.

You can begin to create the same kind of loyalty from your customers when you successfully brand your business.

Think of branding the way it was done in the Old West: The rancher had his "brand" seared into the hides of all of his cattle. That way every cow was clearly part of that ranch, and was set apart from all other cattle. Your business's brand should set you apart from the competition and make you stand out in the minds of customers.

The Importance of Branding Your Business

Let's start with my definition of branding. Branding is the way you identify your business for the public. Branding creates an image of who you are and what you do. Your brand exists not on paper as a logo, but in the minds and actions of customers, who choose your brand over others. We see branding as a relationship between a customer and the product, service, or business.

Why should you brand your business? Here's why:

◆ Branding separates you from the competition.

◆ Branding creates trust, simplifies choice, and saves time and effort.

◆ Branding builds a bond between the product and the consumer.

◆ Branding is a unique business identity including (but not limited to) personality, quality, and likeability.

However, you don't have to be a major corporation to develop a brand. Small companies can create an image just as powerful as large corporations. Your business's brand should be explicit and should easily define who you are and what you do.

Vermont Spirits, a small distiller of vodka that makes its product from milk solids, uses bottles with a drawing of a cow on them. This gives the customer immediate recognition of what makes this vodka different.

People Power

According to Tom Peters, "Branding is more—not less—important than ever if you want to stand out in the crowded marketplace."

You build your relationship with your customers through your brand. Branding is a necessity for finding, capturing, and keeping loyal customers.

Your brand name should create a distinctive image in the customer's mind. It should make people think immediately what business you're in, what benefits your business provides, and why you're better than the competition. When someone moves into your community and asks her neighbor, "Where's a store I can shop for (name of a product you sell)?" the name of your business should be the automatic answer. Then you'll know you have developed a clear brand in your customers' minds.

Ways to Create a Brand

Branding is part of your total marketing package. This means that the colors you use in your logo, your bags, your slogan, and the special look of your advertising, marketing, and promotions—all of these are parts of your overall marketing strategy.

First and foremost, YOU must decide what your business is all about. Answer these questions:

◆ What is my core business?

◆ Who are my target customers?

◆ What is my business image? (Is it homey, formal, modern, old-fashioned, creative, organized, etc.?)

> **True Tales**
>
> UPS changed their marketing approach a few years ago by committing to the color "brown." Their drivers wear brown uniforms, their trucks are brown, and they even refer to themselves as "Brown" in their advertisements.

All too often, business owners neglect answering these simple questions and don't develop a strong sense of the essence of the business. Without this knowledge, you can't project a clear image to your customers of your special brand.

Once you know who you are, how do you create your brand, your particular image that stands out in the customers' minds?

Creating a Slogan

Ideally your slogan should include your name, or make people think of your business. For example "The Big Apple" immediately brings up the image of New York City.

> **True Tales**
>
> The owner of Burpee seeds once appeared in a TV interview. He was asked to tell about his most successful promotion. He said it was his slogan. "We have the best slogan in the world," he said. Here it is: "Burpee's Seeds Grow!"
>
> "The first word tells you who we are. The second word tells you what we sell. The third word tells you what it does. Burpee's Seeds Grow!"

Here are some examples of famous slogans that include the name of the business or product:

1. "You're in good hands with Allstate"

2. "With a name like Smuckers, it has to be good"

3. "Next to myself, I like BVD best"

4. "Doesn't your dog deserve ALPO?"

5. And my company's slogan that branded our retail complex as a destination shopping area: "If it's Saturday, it must be Gordon's Alley!"

All of these slogans help the customer understand the product better, are easy to remember, and most importantly, mention the product name. Since slogans are meant to be repeated many times, customers will hear your business' or product's name over and over when you include it in your slogan.

Creating a Logo

Logos, like slogans, help customers identify your business immediately. And also like slogans, many of the best ones include the name of the product or business. In fact, for many businesses, the logo can be simply a typographical version of the business name—no cute drawing or picture needed. Some examples are logos for such companies as:

- IBM

- Coca-Cola

- Gap

But for others, a picture conjures up the brand even better than words could. Some examples include logos for:

- Apple computers

- Target's target

- The CBS eye

- The Nike swoosh

- Shell Oil's shell

- McDonald's golden arches

Either way, have a competent graphic designer create your logo. It doesn't need to be complicated, but you will need it in print-ready and digital versions for use on signs and in advertising. Give the designer direction about your business and what you envision your logo to be. Then get several ideas before you settle on one that really says, "This is my business's brand!" to you.

Once you have developed your slogan and logo, *use them*. Use them in your advertising. Use them on your signs. Use them on your letterhead stationery. Use them on your business cards. Use them on your paper bags. Print them on your receipts. Use them in every communication that goes to potential customers, because they will reinforce your brand in the minds of your customers.

Slogans and logos that identify you and that you use consistently are valuable creative advertising tools. Use them in concert with all basics of print and broadcast media and in-business marketing.

Becoming an Expert

You should learn all you can about whatever you are selling. Attend seminars. Join associations and civic clubs. Become active in your community. Encourage others in your company to be experts as well.

Eventually you and your associates can be on a panel or speak at a seminar or club meeting. Giving expert information brands your business as the best in your field.

Another way to appear as an expert is by writing a feature story for your local newspaper or appearing on local radio or TV talking about your area of business. Local papers are often looking for column writers on various topics, as well. For example, if you own a garden-supply business, you could approach your local newspaper about writing a weekly column on gardening tips. Once such a column is established, readers will begin to write in with their questions, and you'll never be at a loss for topics.

Being an expert is a great way to enhance your brand and promote loyalty. Who wouldn't want to be the client of the CPA who talks about money management on the radio, the realtor who writes the newspaper column about how to buy and sell your home, the physician who is interviewed by the local TV station about health issues? They have the "brand name" of being the best in their fields.

Your Brand Is Your Name

There was once a store called, "The Little Shop on the Corner." Let's hope they (1) never get bigger and (2) never move. Their name limits them to stay small and stay put.

We often recommend that clients use their own name for the store's name when starting a new business. After all, the name has meaning—it's the owner, right out there with his or her name on the sign!

Your name is easy to brand, because it is individual and sets you apart from other business names. That makes it easy for customers to remember.

Walk down the main street of your town or through your local mall. You'll find that national chain stores as well as one-location mom-and-pop stores are often named for the owner. It's a tried and true branding technique that has worked for many years.

Using Your Brand on the Internet

When Harry and David, the Fruit-of-the-Month-Club guys, introduced their website, they said, "Our website is an extension of our brand."

They understood that website marketing does not stand alone. Your website is part of your total marketing package, and is yet another way to reinforce your brand. Extending their brand to the web gave Harry and David increased sales and increased customer loyalty by giving their customers another way to buy their products. Their website showcases their gourmet food products with the same beautiful color photographs of their enticing specialty food items and the same folksy descriptions of the products.

If you have gone to the trouble and expense of developing a website for your business, make sure that it reflects your brand. As with the logo, I recommend professional web developers to help you here. Naturally, the mechanics of how the website works must be correct. But equally as important is how the website "feels." It should be immediately recognizable as your business and yours alone, using the brand that you have developed.

A great example of a small business that has developed a website that "looks like them" is from a manufacturer of baby clothing, Zutano, based in northern Vermont.

As soon as you click on their home page, you understand the brand. The graphics are in keeping with their colorful, modern baby clothes. The website has examples of each of their lines of clothing, but it is not overwhelming in size. Their love of babies is evident—there's even a section in the site where they post baby pictures of little customers wearing their clothes!

Small business or large, if you have chosen to market on the web, be sure that you use the web to extend your brand. Internet marketing is quickly becoming a major source of sales for many businesses. Don't waste a strong opportunity to build your brand with a mediocre Internet site.

What Your Brand Does for Your Business

What's the value of branding your business? Why go to the trouble and expense of making sure you create and present a consistent image for customers?

Because you'll get plenty of return on the investment you make branding your business. Your business brand does several important things for your business:

♦ Establishes how you are different from your competitors

♦ Builds your image in your customers' minds

♦ Builds more loyalty from your customers

♦ Creates your business' identity

Establishing Your Point of Difference

Stanley Marcus, the creative genius of the Neiman-Marcus department store, was once asked what the difference was between his store and Saks Fifth Avenue. "Aren't they both department stores carrying fine merchandise? How can you say you are different?"

His answer: "There are many ways of playing any part on the stage. Watch five different actors and you have five different renditions. I often feel that running a store is like running a newspaper. Newspapers all have access to the same news. But one comes out like *The New York Times* and one comes out like the *Daily News*. They all have the same basic material, but one editor likes sex on the front page and the other wants international stories."

Stanley Marcus chose as his point of difference to make customer satisfaction paramount for Neiman-Marcus. While the store is known for its extensive collection of designer fashions, it stands out from its competitors with its over-the-top customer service. Stories abound about customers who brought back merchandise that the store never sold, saying, "It was given to me as a gift and I want to return it," and the return was made, no questions asked.

According to Marcus, customer service was his brand.

Building Your Image

Wal-Mart wants you to think of their brand as synonymous with low prices. Their slogan says it all: "Always low prices. Always." But they also try to brand themselves as the down-home, small-town friendly store, and manage to do it, despite the fact that they have become the world's largest retailer with enormous, 200,000-plus-square-foot stores.

How have they developed a brand that is opposite to the reality of their business?

Their use of image advertising to enhance their brand has helped to create their folksy, friendly image. Television ads trumpet Wal-Mart's charitable giving, emphasize their hiring of senior citizens as front-door "greeters," and highlight long-term employees who have been promoted through the ranks.

Wal-Mart's brand is one of their most valuable commodities, protected and nurtured with all their marketing might.

The company is a great example of the importance of the brand and its power over customers.

Building Loyalty

When someone has a positive experience with your brand, he or she is more likely to buy that product or service again, rather than a competing brand. Brands are trusted friends who have proved their worth through the years.

Customers have built-in habits when shopping. They are loyal to businesses with whose brand they are

> **True Tales**
>
> Leo Burnett, founder of the Leo Burnett Publicis Groupe advertising agency, was hypoglycemic. One day during a meeting he collapsed, and asked someone to quickly get him a candy bar. Before the person could leave the room to bring him the candy he said, "Make sure it's a Nestlé." Now *that's* an example of the true meaning of brand loyalty.

familiar. It makes shopping with the company or buying the products a comfortable experience.

When I go shopping for a car, the first place I look is always the Volvo dealership. I have learned from Volvo's advertising all the safety and performance features that make their cars so reliable. I have experienced a good relationship with the Volvo service department. I have heard good things about Volvos from other people who drive Volvos. All these experiences, feelings, and advice from other people, coupled with Volvo's advertising, have created a strong brand identification for me. When I want a car, I will always try Volvo first.

> **People Power**
>
> "The consumer needs to build a relationship with the product, and the product needs to have an identity. When you weaken a brand, you weaken brand loyalty." —Professor Susan Fornier, Harvard Business School

Creating Your Identity

For my own retail clothing shops, I developed a brand of exclusivity and uniqueness in the merchandise. My store became known for having clothing that no one else carried. I actively promoted and advertised clothing that we bought on European buying trips: winter jackets from Finland, baby knits from Italy, children's sportswear from France.

But the percentage of inventory from these signature items in my shops was less than 10 percent! The remaining inventory was merchandise also seen and available at the local department stores. But customers knew us as "the store with all that great merchandise from other countries." Our brand "aura" of quality and exclusivity extended, in our customers' minds, to everything in the store.

Brand-Aid

As much as you strive to create a brand that means something to the public, there is always the possibility that something can go wrong. When calamity strikes, you must act quickly to preserve your image.

Celebrities, for instance, go to great lengths to develop an identity that resonates with the public. Ex-governor of Vermont Howard Dean was perceived for a long time as a serious anti-war candidate who would give President Bush a run for his money. However, after losing the Iowa primary, Dean tried to encourage his supporters by saying that he would bring the fight for the Democratic nomination to a number of other states. His exhortation was given wide media play, and many commentators and voters decided that his message to the troops sounded like a wild man screaming. Try as he might, Dean could never regain the mantle as a serious candidate, at least not in 2004.

Basketball superstar Kobe Bryant received a blow to his image when a hotel worker accused him of rape. Criminal charges were later dropped, but not before Bryant lost a great deal of public esteem.

Martha Stewart's business enterprise took a significant hit when Ms. Stewart was first indicted, and then convicted, of lying to federal agents.

Just as celebrities must fight hard to maintain an image with the public, your company must make sure that your best asset, your brand image, does not suddenly disappear.

Some of the factors that can hurt a company's brand image include ...

- ◆ A business losing its brand appeal through its own misdeeds or mismanagement.

- ◆ A business trying something new that confuses and upsets its client base.

- ◆ The actions of outside people that hurt a company's brand image.

Each will be described in the sections that follow.

Business Misdeeds or Mismanagement

A company that mistreats its stockholders or cheats the public can quickly fall from grace.

There have recently been a number of instances of brands losing their allure. When a company's chief officers try to enrich themselves at the expense of customers or shareholders, a once-thriving business can quickly disappear. Enron, which had the public and the business magazines anointing it as the paragon of the new ideal corporation, quickly lost any public support as financial irregularities appeared.

Even companies that survive can have a difficult time of managing customer perception when a chief executive falters. Tyco, a conglomerate of many successful companies, saw its share price plummet when its chief executive was accused of enriching himself at the expense of the company.

There is no easy way to overcome the misdeeds of mismanagement of top executives. Often the only recourse for a business is to have its board of directors act quickly to conduct an investigation and fire anyone who was involved in the wrongdoing.

Trying Something New

A business should be commended for trying to advance new products or offer new services. However, sometimes a business may be too hasty in ridding itself of a brand or image that the public is confident about.

A case in point is Coca-Cola. At one point, Coca-Cola decided to replace its signature drink with a brand called "New Coke." After much testing, Coca-Cola was convinced that this new brand would be quickly embraced by the public. The new drink had a sweeter taste than its replacement.

The public quickly reacted. But the response was not what Coca-Cola wanted to hear. The public wanted its old Coca-Cola back. To Coca-Cola's credit, it quickly reintroduced the original soda under the brand name "Coca-Cola Classic" and gave the public a choice between this brand and the New Coke.

The public voted with its pocketbook. Eventually, Coca-Cola discarded New Coke, and Coca-Cola Classic became Coca-Cola again.

The lesson here is not that innovation is bad. Rather, companies should be careful before discarding something that the public likes. Once buying habits are set, they are very tough to change.

The Actions of Outsiders

You cannot always protect yourself from people trying to do your business harm. But you should strive to let the public know that you will go to great lengths to protect the integrity of your brands.

A classic case of a brilliant response to tragedy was Johnson and Johnson's response when some Tylenol capsules were tampered with and a few customers were poisoned. Rather than trying to tell the public that Tylenol was a safe product, the company quickly made a major financial decision to recall all the outstanding Tylenol bottles. The company quickly geared up to produce tamper-proof packaging. The quick response reassured a nervous public. There was an initial financial loss but a long-term gain of keeping the public's trust.

Outsiders can also harm your brand by trying to imitate your success. Many companies are threatened by companies that try to steal a brand's luster.

For example, Rolex is a brand that stands for the highest quality of watch making. Rolex sells high-priced watches that are a status symbol for many people.

Other companies try to steal the brand image that Rolex has developed by producing inferior imitation products. They make the products look like Rolex and put on the Rolex name but they are not Rolex watches. This counterfeiting can hurt a company like Rolex if the company lets the practice become widespread.

Many other established brands have been the victims of brand rip-off. Products like Louis Vitton handbags and Calvin Klein jeans are often counterfeited by fraudulent merchants who want to create the allure of the well-known brand with an inferior product. But the value of the brand is so key to these businesses that they spend hundreds of thousands of dollars to find and prosecute the people who are responsible.

The Least You Need to Know

◆ Your brand tells your customers who you are and what you do.

◆ Use your brand identification in every phase of your advertising and marketing to your customers.

◆ Branding is part of your total marketing package, including slogan, logo, website, and all of your advertising.

◆ Branding done right leads to loyal customers.

◆ You have to react swiftly to protect your brand if it is threatened by inside or external forces.

Part  Putting Together a Loyalty Program for Your Customers

Now comes the fun part.

If you've accepted the fact that returning customers are the key to your business, then you'll be open to ideas for making your customers come back to your business again and again.

One of the most cost-effective ways you can reward your customers is by putting together a loyalty program. A loyalty program is a win-win proposition for business owners and customers.

This part of the book will show you how and why loyalty programs work and how you can start a loyalty program in your business.

Information Is Power!

In This Chapter

- ◆ The importance of gathering customer information
- ◆ Building your database
- ◆ Why you need a computer
- ◆ Tracking customer visits and spending
- ◆ Why your customers want to give you information

In order to succeed, you have to run a good business. That's a necessity. If you own a retail store:

- ◆ Your premises must be clean
- ◆ Your employees must be friendly
- ◆ You must carry the type of merchandise your customers want

If you have a professional practice:

- ◆ You must not keep your clients waiting
- ◆ You should have a courteous staff who help your clients with all their questions
- ◆ Your offices should be first rate

But all of this is not enough to ensure success in your business.

To do that, you must develop a long-term relationship with your customers. You need to learn the following about your customers:

- Name

- Age

- Address

- Gender

- Birthday

- The amount of business they do with you

- The items they want to buy

- Their responsiveness to sale items

The more you know about your customers, the easier it will be for you to grow your business.

Information is the name of the game.

The ability of your business to find out more about your customers has never been easier. Computing power is cheap, and it is getting cheaper by the day. Now is the time for your business to invest in information-gathering. The more you know about your customers, the faster your business will grow.

Why You Need a Database

Al Lees, Jr., and his son Albert Lees ran a supermarket in Westport, Massachusetts, for many years. It was a one-store operation that had been founded many years ago by Albert's grandfather.

Al and Albert worked in the store every day. They greeted their customers, tried hard to stock merchandise that their customers wanted, and generally ran a very good operation.

After long consideration, they decided to start a loyalty card program in their store. They gave out loyalty cards to their customers and revamped the pricing of the goods in their store. If someone presented a loyalty card, he or she received a better price on many items than someone who did not have a card.

After a few months on the loyalty program, it was time to start looking at the data. They ran a report from the *database* that showed their top 25 customers in terms of their total amount of purchases.

The Lees were in for a shock! They could only recognize seven names on the list. Al and Albert Lees had been working every day in their single-store supermarket and yet they had no idea which customers spent the most money at their store.

As Albert says, "We made it a point from that day on to memorize our top 25 customers. We greeted them by name, bagged their groceries, and were immediately responsive to any of their requests. We recognized that our best customers were our most profitable customers, and we went out of our way to service them."

They realized that the lifeblood of their business was their customer base. Gathering data from their loyalty program made it easier to provide the level of customer service they wanted for their best customers.

> **Loyalty Lingo**
>
> A **database** is information about your customers and their shopping habits that you collect and store. You can use the information in your database for many purposes, including marketing.

Collecting Information Isn't Rocket Science

There are many ways to collect information about your customers. These include questions at the register ("Could you tell me what zip code you live in?"), to sweepstakes or raffles, to sign-up sheets for loyalty cards.

Before you decide how to collect information, you should first decide what information you need about your customers. Here are several categories of information that could be helpful to you (similar to the ones we mentioned at the beginning of the chapter):

- Name and address of your customers
- Birthdays and other demographic information about your customers
- Items that particular customers purchase

The sections that follow contain details on each of these categories.

Names and Addresses of Your Customers

Your customer's name and address is necessary for any written communication. If you plan to e-mail your customers, also ask for an e-mail address. However, people hate *spam*. So you should ask for permission to send e-mail messages and you should inform your customers that you will not sell or give away their e-mail addresses to any third parties.

> **Loyalty Lingo**
>
> **Spam** is unwanted e-mail sent to consumers and businesses without their consent. Today, more than half of all e-mail is considered spam.

There are several ways you can collect your customers' names and addresses (and other relevant information such as birthdays).

- You can ask customers if they want to be part of a private mailing list and receive special offers.

- You can have a sweepstakes or raffle and have customers fill out a form that asks for their name and address.

- You can start a birthday club or a kids' club and have customers sign up to receive special benefits.

- You can go to a list broker and buy names and addresses of people who live near your business.

Once you have your customers' names and addresses, you should enter them onto a mailing list. A mailing list will help you to be able to sort your customers by where they live, and also to print labels so that you can send your customers letters and postcards.

Birthday and Other Demographic Information

A typical direct mailing that advertises a new credit card or offers a magazine subscription generates less than half of 1 percent response. Out of every 200 people who receive the mailing, only one person is likely to sign up for the magazine or credit card.

In contrast, a message from a business offering customers a free gift on their birthday will usually generate a 30 percent or greater response. Casel's Supermarket in Margate, New Jersey, often has as many as 70 percent of their shoppers redeem a birthday offer.

Why does a birthday mailing cause response rates to be 60 to 140 times higher than a typical direct mailing? A birthday mailing goes to people who are already your customers. In contrast, a credit-card mailing will go to a wide variety of prospective customers, usually picked on the basis of their income, location, and credit rating.

Also, people like recognition on their birthdays. If they don't use a gift certificate or special offer that you give them, they may feel as if they are missing out on a present.

Other demographic and lifestyle information about your customers can help you sell your merchandise more effectively. For instance, if you run a sporting goods store and have a list of your customers who play tennis, a mailing to those people for a racquet sale will be far more cost effective than if you send a notice of the sale to all your customers.

The more you can tailor your customer information in ways that match the types of goods and services you are trying to sell, the better your results are going to be.

True Tales

One of the best salesmen I know used to send his life-insurance clients a postcard a month before their birthdays. The card said, "I know it's not your birthday yet, but I wanted you to be aware that life-insurance rates will go up when you turn a year older. Now would be a great opportunity to increase your policy before the new rates take effect."

The card was very successful in generating a lot of business for a very small cost.

Items That Particular Customers Purchase

The more specialized your business, the more you should try to keep track of customers' purchases. For instance, the owner of a hardware store might find it difficult keeping track of all the items that all his customers buy. However, if you are a travel agent selling package cruises, it would be great to know where your customers have gone previously, so that you can recommend some new opportunities for future trips.

Similarly, art-gallery owners will want to keep track of which artists their customers purchase, so they can remind those customers who like a particular artist that a new print or painting is for sale.

As another example, when I was in the clothing business, I would take a camera on buying trips to Helsinki, Finland. I would take pictures of the latest models of winter jackets and have postcards made out of the pictures. While still in Helsinki, I sent the postcards to our customers back in America, telling them that I had just picked out their new winter jacket.

The response was overwhelming. People called every week and wanted to know when their jacket was coming in. The reason this promotion was so successful was that I targeted a group of people who had bought that particular type of product in the past.

How a Computer Can Help

Suppose you want to find out a list of all your customers who spent more than $100 over the last two months. Or a list of customers who had responded to a mailing campaign. Or a list of people who had shopped with you more than two times in the last 12 weeks.

It's easy, if you keep track of your customers and their purchases on a computer. Using a computer to look at customer data can help you with merchandise and marketing. It can let you know which items sell everyday and which sell just during specials. If you look at sales by time of day, it can also help you to figure out how many people you need in your business during lunchtime or during the afternoon rush hour.

This use of customer data is part of a big change that has swept over the customer-loyalty landscape in the last 15 years. The price of collecting data has greatly diminished. Computers are faster, computer programs are easier to use, and the price of hardware and software has dropped considerably.

Where it once took giant mainframes to keep track of customer data for large companies, those same companies are now keeping track of vast amounts of data on desktop machines.

Here are some basic rules to follow when you begin to build a database on a computer:

> **True Tales**
>
> Remember the old phrase, "Garbage in, garbage out"? It still applies today. Make sure that you put the correct information in the correct places. We know of a company who recently did a mailing but somehow put their customers' city where the address should be. Result: Their mailing had to be redone at a big expense.

- Try to buy off-the-shelf software. It is far more likely that you will find a product that's right for you than it will be to find a programmer who can create a custom system cost effectively.

◆ Buy the hardware support agreement. Usually I shy away from buying maintenance agreements, but if you have a lemon of a computer (which happens more
often than you might think) or if you have software problems, a maintenance
agreement can be a lifesaver.

◆ Try to limit the amount of people inputting data into your computers. You may
think that data input is something anybody can do, but if you just let one or two
people do your input, you are bound to have fewer mistakes and a more consistent database. I am constantly surprised by how badly well-meaning and intelligent people can mess up a computer file!

Recency, Frequency, and Monetary (RFM)

Once you have the basic customer information (such as name and address) safely
inside your computer, you can then concentrate on the three basics of customer
targeting—*recency*, *frequency*, and *monetary*.

Your most valuable customers are the ones
who ...

◆ Came in recently

◆ Come in frequently

◆ Spend more money than other customers

This is why you want to track this information
in your customer database.

Loyalty Lingo

Recency is when a customer last spent money in your
business. **Frequency** is how often
a customer comes to your place
of business. **Monetary** is how
much a particular customer has
spent in your business.

True Tales

A friend of mine runs a supermarket, and a customer came in asking if she could suggest some flavors of ice cream that the store currently did not carry. Our friend looked
up the customer on his database and found out that she was one of his top-10 customers. He came back to her and said that he would add any flavors she wanted to his
selection. He realized that not having those flavors was just going to send one of his
best customers to a competitor.

Tracking Recency, Frequency, and Monetary

In order to be able to use RFM data, your business has to gather the relevant information into a computer. Here is all you need to do:

◆ Record the dates that your customers come into your business.

◆ Record each separate time a customer comes in as a separate visit. Do not group all customer visits in one record.

◆ Record the total amount of money a customer spends when she comes to the business.

You can get more sophisticated than this. You can track the specific items a customer buys. You can try to ascertain a customer's profitability by recording whether a customer only buys sale items or buys full-price items. You can see if a customer responds to a particular mailing or newspaper ad.

All these additions to your database will make it more complete, but you should probably start with just the basics. Keep track of every time your customers come in and how much they spend when they visit your business.

Using RFM Data

The next step is to use the data you have gathered. An easy way to use this data is to divide your customers into groupings. R1 would be customers who came in most recently; R2 would be customers who came in a while ago. F1 would be customers who come in frequently; F2 would be customers who come in less often. M1 would be your big spenders; M2 would be people who spend less while shopping with you. You can divide your customers up into more categories, but these groupings are fine to get you started.

Once you have grouped your customers into these categories, you will have eight different types of customers:

R1F1M1

R1F1M2

R1F2M1

R1F2M2

R2F1M1

R2F1M2

R2F2M1

R2F2M2

Each of these customer types has distinct characteristics. For instance, an R1F1M1 customer would be one who shopped recently, shops frequently, and has spent a lot of money. This is a valuable customer. An R2F2M2 customer would be someone who hasn't come in for a while, doesn't shop frequently, and doesn't spend a lot of money. This kind of customer has less value to your business.

One of the primary ways you can use an RFM classification system is to lower the cost of your advertising. Sending a mailing to an R1F1M1 grouping will bring better results than sending the same mailing to an R2F2M2 group.

You can also use the classification scheme to better understand your customers. For instance, customers who are in R1F2M1 and R2F2M1 are customers who do not come in very often, but spend a lot when they do come in. These may be customers who live far away but tend to stock up when they shop with you. These customers could be very valuable although they do not shop very often.

In contrast, customers who are in R1F1M2 come in very frequently but do not spend a lot when they are at your business. They like your business, but are mainly browsers or purchasers of low-cost or sale items. Even though these customers come in frequently, they may not be that valuable to your business because of their lack of volume.

Another interesting exercise is to see where your best customers come from by looking at the RFM statistics in terms of geography. By finding out where your best customers come from, you can increase your marketing in those geographical areas.

New Ways of Gathering and Sharing Information

One of the most cost-effective means of gathering information is developing a list of your customers' e-mail addresses. Once you develop an e-mail list, it is cost effective to communicate with your customers through e-mails. I have found in my business that a monthly newsletter keeps customers informed of what's happening in my business and can let them know when we have new merchandise or are having a sales event.

Here are some tips to having a successful e-mail newsletter:

- Only do mailings to customers who have requested them. Nobody likes unwanted e-mails.

- You don't always have to advertise sales or specials. Customers may be turned off by excessive advertising.

- Tell your customers to send the e-mail newsletter to their friends. Have an easy way for newcomers to sign up for your list.

An e-mail newsletter works best when you have a website for your business. On a simple website, you can have a home page that describes your business an "About Us" section that has information about the business's principals. You can have a section where people can sign up for the e-mail newsletter and you can have an archive section for previous editions of the newsletter.

If you become more ambitious, you can add other sections to your website that describe your products and give people a chance to order those products.

But you don't have to get started with a complicated website. Having a place on the Internet that describes your business is a good idea, and it is probably better to start small, test out some ideas, and then grow your website.

The Principles of Participation Marketing

Alan Rosenspan is a marketing professional who has won numerous industry awards. He believes in participation marketing, where customers not only give you permission to market to them, but actually become involved in the marketing process. Here are Alan's Five Principles of Participation Marketing:

1. Really know your customers. Make sure that your database is accurate, and ask customers to correct mistakes in your records.

2. Generate feedback at every opportunity. Start with a questionnaire and think about creating a customer-satisfaction survey.

3. Involve customers and prospects as much as possible. Emulate Dell Computers, which lets customers decide how much memory their computers have, as well as which accessories they want.

4. Market on your customers' schedule—not yours. Diaper companies do this well by giving new mothers coupons that they can use when they need it.

5. Make customers feel vested in your success. The more that customers become involved with you, the more likely they are to recommend your business to other customers.

Participation marketing is the wave of the future. Too many customers have been burned by "spam" e-mail to have much faith in unsolicited advertising. By making your customers a vital part of the marketing equation, you increase the level of customer trust and make customers look forward to reading, not discarding, your message.

Your Customers Want You to Collect Data

Many businesses are concerned that their customers are worried about their privacy rights. And we devote a whole chapter to making sure you protect your customer's privacy (see Chapter 22). But most of your customers are more than willing to exchange information for rewards.

Significant Stats

More than two thirds of Americans now have loyalty cards for supermarkets. Millions of Americans now have credit cards that earn them frequent-flyer miles, and millions have also signed up for programs at casinos to record all their bets in exchange for rewards.

In the supermarket industry, successful loyalty programs record more than 80 percent of dollar transactions from people using their loyalty cards.

These transactions take place because there is an implicit negotiation going between the businesses and their customers. If the dialogue were spoken, it would go something like this:

Business: "Okay, Ms. Customer, I will give you better prices on products you like if you give me a little information about yourself."

Customer: "Sounds good. But why do you need information about what I buy?"

Business: "Well, I want to know who my best customers are that so I can reward them. It will also help me in my marketing. I can send offers to just those people who want to use them."

Customer: "That sounds all right. But you're not going to give anyone else information about me, are you?"

Business: "Not at all. I'll only use it to send you offers and rewards. I promise not to share your information with any third party."

Customer: "Sounds good. It's a deal."

While these words are never spoken, they are the backbone of loyalty-marketing programs. Most customers are willing to participate in a loyalty program if they are able to gain sufficient benefits, such as lower prices on products and services that they want to buy.

So make sure your loyalty program meets the needs of your customers as well as your business. The more information you have about your customers, the easier it is going to be for your business to shape your marketing and your rewards.

The Least You Need to Know

◆ Your business should gather information about your customers.

◆ The basic information you should gather is customers' names and addresses and their purchase history with you.

◆ Using a computer, you can sort your customers into groupings based on purchase history for marketing purposes.

◆ Customers will give you information in return for rewards.

Chapter 16

Winning Big by Using Customer Information

In This Chapter

♦ Using customer information for much more than giving price breaks

♦ Grouping customers according to how profitable they are

♦ Finding out where your current customers come from

♦ Some customers are not worth keeping

♦ Using what you know about your current customers to market for new customers

Do you ever watch poker on TV? Certain players always seem to rise to the top. They seem to have the uncanny ability to read their opponents' habits and to look right through the backs of the cards and make the winning bet, time after time. These winning poker players do not rely on luck. They use their experience, knowledge of odds, and information from how other players bet their chips to know what cards other players have.

Businesspeople who use loyalty information successfully are like those top poker players. They make the right moves because they have more information than their rivals. They win the big payoff by gathering information.

You are competing against other businesses and wagering your resources on marketing and merchandising. In this chapter, you will learn how to use your database of customer information to win your big payoff: more sales and more profits.

Ways to Use Your Customer Information

Now you have started to collect information about your customers. You know where they live, how often they shop with you, and how much they spend.

But what can you do with this information? And what other kinds of information should you collect?

Start with knowing who your very best customers are—by name and by face. Make sure those customers get the best service your business can possibly give. These customers are undoubtedly on the "advocate" rung of your loyalty ladder (see Chapter 8), so they are your most valuable customers in many ways. You cater to the wishes of your best customers. You build your store around their needs. You market more to your best customers and you try to encourage your next-best customers to shop more often and spend more with you.

> **People Power** _____
>
> Don Gallegos tells a great story about catering to one of his best customers. At the time, Don was president of King Soopers, a division of the large supermarket company Kroger. King Soopers' big competitor was Albertson's Supermarket.
>
> One of Don's best customers told him that although he did most of his grocery shopping at King Soopers, he preferred the taste of Albertson's private label applesauce. Don knew what he had to do. He went right over to Albertson's and bought a case of their applesauce.
>
> Then Don brought the customer into his office. He said, "We'll always have this applesauce in my office for you so you don't have to make an extra trip to Albertson's."
>
> "Oh, by the way," Don added, "The applesauce is cheaper here than at Albertson's."

Once you and your staff understand who your best customers are and the power of keeping them happy, it's time to go back to your customer database. Examine the data this time not by individuals but by groups of customers.

Most loyalty program software breaks down the customers by deciles—the top 10 percent in terms of sales, the next 10 percent, and so on.

The sections that follow highlight some of the ways you can use customer information to delight your customers and increase your profitability.

Merchandising Mix

Just because you sell a lot of a product doesn't mean the product is profitable for your business.

In an optical store I know, there is a line of optical frames imported from Italy. There are also several lines of lower-priced frames from the United States.

If you looked at the sales figures, you would see that the U.S. frames outsold the Italian frames by 3 to 1. However, if you dug a little deeper, you would also find out these facts:

- ◆ The U.S. frames only sold really well during big sales.
- ◆ The Italian frames had a much higher mark-up than the U.S. frames.
- ◆ The optical store's best customers tended to buy the Italian frames.

After examining these sales figures closely, the optical store discontinued a couple of its U.S. optical frame lines and put their emphasis on Italian frames. Profits soared.

The lesson is that gross profits don't really mean that much. You have to concentrate on the bottom line and cater to your more profitable customers.

Marketing Profitably

How do casinos decide whom to invite to their private parties and tournaments? How do catalog companies decide who gets how many catalogs? Why do you receive different credit-card offers than your neighbors?

The answers to these questions relate to information that customers have provided in one way or another to businesses. The more information a business has about its customers, the more it can tailor its advertising to achieve profitable results.

When I visited a casino in Atlantic City, I noticed that a large percentage of people playing the slot machines stuck personalized cards into the machines before they started playing. These cards do the following:

♦ They let consumers rack up bonuses based on their volume of play.

♦ They provide information to casinos so that they can determine who their largest players are.

♦ They give casinos other information such as how long people play at various machines, and what time of day the machines are being played.

All of this information is analyzed by casino management who can then make judgments about the relative advantages of different sorts of slot machines as well as which customers are most valuable.

Information Bonuses

There are some measures beyond how much customers are spending that are available when you start to look at customer data. These include …

♦ What time of day and what days of the week you do your most business (this will help you match staffing to busy times).

♦ Which customers will respond to which kinds of promotion (some customers are very responsive to direct mail; others throw mail offers away).

♦ Items customers buy at the same time (lawn fertilizer and wheelbarrows (maybe you want to merchandise these two together).

When you start looking at the purchase histories of your customers, you'll begin to get a much clearer idea of how your customers utilize your services and how you should change your business to meet the needs of your best customers.

True Tales

A good way to utilize customer information is to form clubs. Form a baby club for people who buy diapers. Form a coffee club for those who purchase more than their share of coffee beans. One of the most successful types of clubs has been formed by wine sellers. They invite their best customers in for tastings, offer discounts on supplies, and recommend wines in a monthly newsletter. Wine sales soar when you can identify people with similar interests in wine to gather together and exchange information.

How to Determine Customer Profitability

All customers are not created equal.

When you go fishing, you not only have to go where the fish are, you have to go after the big fish. If you catch minnows, you'll only have to put them back.

What sort of measurements should you make to determine customer profitability?

First, begin with the recency, frequency, and monetary measures I described in Chapter 15. Customers who come in often and shop a lot tend to be your best customers.

However, there are other measures of profitability you must be mindful of:

♦ Try to single out customers who pay for goods with higher margins. These are customers you should romance.

♦ Single out customers who are responsive to advertising. These are great customers because if you find them, you can advertise to this group more frequently.

♦ Single out customers who are sale shoppers. You may think that these customers are not as valuable (because of the lower net margin on sales items) but these customers can be invaluable to you when you are reducing inventory or getting rid of closeout items.

In order to determine the net margin of merchandise, you must be able to determine the cost of the goods sold and the price at which the goods were sold. Retail price only fits into the net-margin equation when there are no reductions or discounts given on the item.

People Power _____

Casinos call them the "sharks." They are the people capable of losing (and winning) a million dollars a day. Casinos will go to great lengths to wine, dine, and lure these "sharks" away from their casino competitors.

When they are at the casino, there will be tables specially roped off with larger limits for these big players. The casinos are willing to pay thousands of dollars in giveaways, trying to meet these players' needs.

Who are the "sharks" in your business? What are you doing to capture them?

Where Are Your Customers Coming From?

Here's a good exercise for you. Buy a giant map of the 10 miles around your business. Ask the next 100 customers you have to give you their exact address. Place a pushpin on your giant map for each of these addresses. After you have placed 100 pins on your map, you will have a good idea where your customers are coming from.

Why is this a good idea?

Because the most important information you can find out about your entire customer base is where your customers live. By finding out your customers' addresses, you can determine where and in what media it will be profitable for you to advertise. You can find out the carrier routes (subdivisions of zip codes) where your customers live and see if your customers live in carrier routes with high, medium, or low average incomes. Once you know the *demographics* of your current customers, you can reach out to other potential customers with similar demographics.

Loyalty Lingo _____

Demographics are the study of information about people including race, births, marriages, mortality, and so on.

How far people will travel to your business is based on two characteristics:

- The uniqueness of the items you sell
- Where your competition is located

If you are a middle-of-the-road hardware store or dry cleaner, chances are strong that most of your customers live close by your store. There are of course exceptions in sparsely populated parts of the country where there is not much competition.

However, if you sell fine art, or, better yet, a specific kind of art not available from competitors, collectors may travel hundreds of miles to see what you have in stock.

In general, for most businesses, the bulk of their customers will live at most a five to ten-minute drive to their place of business. That is why advertising beyond a five-mile radius from the place of business is going to quickly lead to diminishing returns.

Finding out the exact location of your customers within the five-mile radius will permit you to refine your marketing even more.

The more you know exactly where your customers are coming from, the less you have to pay in advertising costs.

Discouraging Unprofitable Customers

The climax of every episode of Donald Trump's hit TV show "The Apprentice" is when "The Donald" gathers the candidates in his boardroom, looks one of them straight in the eye, and says, "You're fired!"

Ouch. Firing hurts. But you have to take the same attitude to some of your customers. If they're costing your business money, or if they don't fit into your market niche, you may have to get rid of them.

Sol Price founded Price Club, the first store that only let customers shop if they belonged to a certain group or paid a fee to be allowed to shop. Price Club was the predecessor of stores such as Sam's Club and Costco, which offer special discounts to members.

Sol Price believed in the concept of the *intelligent loss of business*. Price only wanted to deal with customers who believed in his philosophy that his stores were the "purchasing agent of the customers." Here were the foundations of Price's business model:

◆ The retailer would try to buy merchandise at the lowest price from the manufacturer, charge the bare minimum markup to the consumer, and stand behind the quality and workmanship of the product.

Loyalty Lingo

The **intelligent loss of business** is achieved by only meeting the needs of customers who agree with the goals of your business. For example, if you sell high end jewelry you may decide not to carry imitation diamonds for people who cannot afford your products. On the other hand, by opening a store that only sells items for less than one dollar, you are turning away people who want higher priced brand-name merchandise.

- Price Club would engage in very minimal advertising.

- Price Club would not let consumers use any form of credit.

- Price Club would charge customers a yearly membership fee to defer its expenses.

Although Price Club as an ongoing enterprise has vanished, some of Price's concepts have continued very successfully in other formats. Warehouse clubs and even the pricing policies of discounters like Wal-Mart and K-Mart have their origins in Price Club stores. One idea of Price's that has not stood the test of time was his refusal to let customers use credit, specifically credit cards. This dose of paternalism has not withstood the public reliance on credit.

Like Price, you have to determine where you want to exercise the intelligent loss of business. You can choose to limit variety to increase your specialization and inventory on items you sell best. You can make it harder for people without loyalty cards to buy merchandise from you at discount prices.

> ### Significant Stats
>
> Many companies who have adopted loyalty programs have made the determination that a portion of their customers is not contributing to the bottom line.
>
> Here is an amazing statistic: Many supermarket companies have increased their net profitability 30 percent without increasing gross sales at all!
>
> How do they do it? Supermarkets traditionally offer specials that are available to all of their customers. Supermarkets with loyalty-card programs only offer the specials to customers with loyalty cards; the rest of the customers pay much higher prices. Thus by instituting a loyalty program, they can offer specials but still receive high markups from customers who do not bother to sign up for a card.

Encouraging Profitable Customers

Even more important than discouraging unprofitable customers are promotions and marketing initiatives to encourage profitable customers.

Businesses who are successful at gathering customer information are ahead of the curve in providing benefits to their best customers. They can …

- Have catered private parties available to certain customers based on their spending habits.

♦ Offer bonuses (free turkeys at Thanksgiving, 20 percent off any shopping trip, a free pair of sunglasses) to customers who meet specified spending criteria.

♦ Offer rewards such as tickets to sporting events and/or artistic performances and/or museums and zoos.

By offering special benefits, retailers can make reward programs the core of their business. For instance, Best Buy began their Reward Zone loyalty program in 2002. Within two years the company had signed up more than 3.5 million customers throughout the chain.

Best Buy's program costs members $9.99 a year. Some of the benefits to members include the following:

♦ They get exclusive free CDs.

♦ They are allowed to critique new music releases.

♦ They are invited to sneak previews of hit movies and attend other members-only events, such as getting free tickets to music festivals.

Future possibilities include tiered membership (where rewards vary according to your tier) and a possible business-to-business program.

Offering New Services

Some companies are beginning to use information from customers in innovative ways, by broadening the categories of items they can sell to loyal customers. For example, Tesco's (a large supermarket company in England) and Costco in the United States now offer customers financial and insurance services as well as food and general merchandise. Those companies have learned that their best customers will be interested in buying other services from them, even if they are not directly related to the reason why the customer's began shopping at the store.

In fact, Tesco uses the Internet to offer a wide variety of new services to its current customers. It has also started a profitable Tesco-branded bank. This *horizontal leveraging* of customer assets is one of the most exciting uses of customer information.

> **Loyalty Lingo**
> **Horizontal leveraging** is using customer information gathered in one business to offer other business services to customers.

Creating Business Partnerships

Another use of customer information is business partnerships. Suppose that you own an art gallery and I own an upscale restaurant. We do not compete with one another. Yet, many of our customers enjoy the finer things in life. There may be ways that we can join together and share mailing lists and maybe do some cooperative advertising because we are going after the same type of customers.

It also makes sense for businesses to share information if they are in the same location. For instance, businesses in a shopping center can run cooperative mailing and advertising programs because customers often visit multiple stores on a single trip.

When I ran Gordon's, the clothing store, I invited nearby merchants to share advertising costs. We would put together a full-page newspaper ad or a direct-mail piece and just charged each merchant who wanted to participate a small percentage of the cost. It worked well for everyone. I was able to defray some of the cost of our mailing, and the other merchants were able to reach a large audience at a small percentage of what it would cost them to advertise alone.

Will My New Customers Look Like My Old Ones?

Your new customers don't have to physically look like your old customers. But you want them to have one characteristic in common. You want your new customers to be interested in the products and services that you sell. In order to do that, it pays to start with your current customers and the information you have about them.

Here's a good use of customer information:

- ◆ Examine your database for your best customers (use the recency, frequency, and monetary system described in Chapter 15 for starters).

- ◆ Determine the geographical areas where your best customers come from.

- ◆ Add to the mix any demographical information you have about your customers (age, gender, income).

Then try to find other customers with similar characteristics to your current customers. In fact, there is a good chance that your future customers will look a lot like your current customers. Maybe not in physical appearance, but your future customers will have many of the characteristics that your current customers have.

The first step is geography. If many of your customers come from the same town, that is a good place to go shopping for new customers. Whatever the reason why all those customers are coming to you (ease of traffic, income matching the goods you sell, your reputation in that neighborhood), they are all advantages that other people located in that town can take advantage of.

If there are certain characteristics that apply to your business (for example, if you sell women's clothing), you will obviously want to narrow your list to the kinds of people who are most likely to buy your product (women).

Consider working with a *list broker*. The more information you can give a list broker (where your customers are located, what their age and gender are, etc.) the more easily the broker can come back to you with a list of new customers that resembles your current customer mix.

> **Loyalty Lingo**
>
> A **list broker** is someone who can produce lists of consumers based on criteria such as location, age, gender, income, and home value.

You might also think about limiting your radio and TV cable advertising to those areas and those audiences that match your current customer profile.

If you're a bigger business, you might want to consider doing some more intensive profiling of your customers. There are demographic companies that can take your current customer list and append demographic information such as family income, age, house value, lifestyle interests, and so on. This information can be quite valuable when you begin looking for other customers who look like your current customers.

The Least You Need to Know

- You should spare no effort to satisfy the wishes of your best customers.

- You should provide better rewards and market more intensely to your best customers.

- Knowing where your customers come from can be valuable in reducing your marketing costs.

- Like Donald Trump, you have to "fire" unprofitable customers.

- Your future customers are going to have similar characteristics to your present customers.

Chapter 17

How It Works at Your Business

In This Chapter

- ◆ Using incentives to bring your customers back
- ◆ Increasing business at the register
- ◆ Giving your customers unexpected surprises
- ◆ Don't forget to include the kids!

Many business owners look at their customers with the wrong frame of mind. They expect loyalty from their customers. They think, "I've provided a good location, I've spent my time picking out the best goods, I've hired the best help, and therefore I expect my customers to be loyal to my business."

Wrong, wrong, wrong. These business owners don't realize that customer loyalty works the other way. Sure it is important to provide a great facility with fine merchandise and helpful employees. But that is only the beginning of the process. You also have to figure out mechanisms so that YOU can be loyal to your customers, not the other way around.

This chapter discusses some of the innovative ways you can make your customers want to come back to your store. Customers will not come back time after time because of some imagined debt to you. But if you can make shopping a fun experience or if you can provide some rewards and lures to make your customers come back, you will achieve customer loyalty. But you have to earn it, not expect it.

Bounce-Back Programs

The theory behind *bounce-back programs* could not be simpler: The customer is in your store. How can you entice him or her to come back time after time?

Here are some of the types of bounce-back programs you should consider for your business, and information about each:

> **Loyalty Lingo**
> Bounce-back programs are incentives created by a business to make a customer come back to shop again and again.

- Continuity and stamp programs
- Jackpot programs
- Games
- Direct-mail programs

Continuity Programs

Continuity programs, as their name implies, are programs designed to have visitors come back to a business because they want to continue to buy one in a series of related items.

At one time, supermarkets used continuity programs extensively as a way to have customers come back into their store. The supermarkets would sell a set of encyclopedias at a reduced price. Each week a new volume of the encyclopedia would be offered. Consumers would come into the supermarket week after week to purchase the new additions.

Continuity programs are the basis of highly successful programs such as the Book-of-the-Month Club and various music and video clubs. You receive several books or movies or CDs for free or for very little money. In return, you agree to buy a certain number of books or movies or CDs in the future (at reduced club-member prices). The whole enterprise is designed to give customers good values and to keep offering them incentives to continue to buy.

Now here's a quick test to show how old you are. Do you remember collecting S&H green stamps at supermarkets and gas stations and putting them into stamp books, which could be turned in for gifts at storefront redemption centers?

If this strikes a chord, you may also remember Chubby Checker and hula-hoops. Started around the turn of the twentieth century, green-stamp programs reached their heyday in the 1950s and 1960s, when 80 percent of American households saved stamps in books.

Green stamps were a way to keep customers coming back for more. Now green stamps have been updated to S&H Greenpoints, which are automatically added to your account when you make a purchase at participating retail or online stores.

Greenpoints appeal to the collector in all of us. There is something compelling about collecting baseball cards, or matchbooks, or salt and pepper shakers, or stamps, or shells, that makes us want to keep adding to our collection.

You can do the same thing very simply in your business. If you run a bagel shop, give customers a card where you punch a hole every time they buy a dozen bagels. Make 10 purchases and your next dozen bagels are free. Customers who have the card tend to keep it and want to buy more from your store. If you have a convenience store, you can offer a card that entitles them to a free gallon of milk every time a shopper has bought a total of 10 gallons. If you have a dentist's office, you can offer a free cleaning to every new patient.

If you entice shoppers to come back to your business again and again, you have a program that spells success for your business.

Jackpot Programs

The jackpot program is fun, exciting, and designed primarily to increase business from your current customers. Here's how it works:

◆ Any or all of your customers can enter your jackpot program. There is no purchase required.

◆ Each week the customers have to come in and register for the program. Again, no purchase is required.

◆ A drawing is made the first week of the program. If the customer whose name is drawn has come in that week, he or she is eligible to win the jackpot. The jackpot can start at $100 the first week, and the grand prize increases $100 each week.

The excitement starts building when there is no winner. You can put a sign in your window announcing the jackpot prize … $300, $400, $500. When the prize reaches $1,000, the excitement mounts and the employees get caught up in the game. And of course, the more customers who walk in your business every week, the more sales volume you will inevitably do.

Make sure that your program complies with state laws on sweepstakes. Most of the time, if the sweepstakes is open to everyone and there is no purchase requirement, there will be no problem. But different states have different requirements, so check this out thoroughly before you begin.

Games

Everybody loves games. Games are a fun way to make your customers want to do business with you.

One of the favorite games I've seen was blackjack, designed by Stan Golomb, who sold the promotion to hundreds of dry cleaners.

Here's how the promotion worked:

♦ The dry cleaner's hand had already been dealt. The dealer had a 10 and a 7.

♦ The customer had the jack of spades and another card that had to be rubbed off at the store.

♦ The customer got a percentage discount from her cleaning order depending on the card underneath: 10 percent for a hand of 18, 20 percent for a hand of 19, 30 percent for a hand of 20, and a whopping 40 percent off for a blackjack.

Each customer was guaranteed to have a winning hand. This was one of Stan's best-selling promotions, and he reported that dry cleaners doubled or tripled their business when they tried blackjack.

Customers loved the program. It was a little bit like owning a lottery ticket without the initial expense.

True Tales

When I did promotions at my clothing store, I made sure that there were three tear-off coupons in each mailing.

One of the coupons was only usable the day of the sale for special merchandise. A second was a mystery coupon, which entitled the shopper to a minimum of 5 percent and a maximum of 50 percent extra discount on selected sale items. The third coupon was for the customer to enter a drawing in which the winner received a free trip to a vacation spot.

Customers loved all the promotions, which gave them extra reasons to come into the store on the day of the sale.

Direct-Mail Programs

Another type of bounce-back program is a direct-mail program. Whether you are a hardware-store owner or a lawyer, a chiropractor or a greeting-card shop owner, direct mail is an efficient way to reach out to potential customers. You can develop a mailing list, increase your business, and find loyal customers just by doing direct mail.

Here is a simple way of developing a mailing list of customers who buy from you:

1. Determine the carrier routes (divisions of zip codes) that are the best prospects for your business. (You can start with the carrier routes closest to your store).

2. Mail to one third of the addresses in the carrier routes with an offer that can be redeemed in your store.

3. When the person you mailed the card to comes in, make sure you collect the card that was mailed to them (see #5).

4. At the end of three months, you will have mailed to every household in your market area.

5. Make a list of those households who have responded. And ask for their names when they come in!

6. Continue to mail once a month to people who responded to your blanket mailing.

7. Once you a year, you repeat the process of mailing to all the households in your area.

After a few years, you will have a great list of people who respond to your mailings.

Other ways of using direct mail on a regular basis are birthday programs, new move-in programs, and programs geared to people who meet certain criteria, for instance, people who earn over $75,000 a year for an upscale art gallery. (People with higher incomes presumably are more interested in the products carried by an upscale art gallery.)

True Tales

Birthday clubs are very popular in the restaurant industry. Chains like TGIF and Denny's ran very successful birthday promotions for years.

We work with a chain of restaurants in the south whose customers have signed up to receive offers on their birthdays. Each month the chain sends out hundreds of birthday offers and has response rates of over 30 percent.

The chain tries to make a profit on the birthday card redemptions but they really like the program because it rewards their customers. The customers appreciate the recognition on their birthdays and are delighted at the recognition when they come in.

At the Register

One of the most critical stages in a customer's interaction with your business is the time he is at the checkout counter. It is a small window of time when you can successfully guide the customer to future transactions. It is also a time that you can handle any complaints or returns the customer might have. If you handle any difficulties with a smile and a pleasant attitude, the customer will want to do business with you again.

Let's first look at some of the things you can do to encourage customers to spend more money with you while they are checking out:

◆ Offer customers a chance to sign up for a store-branded credit card. The customers usually receive a discount of 10 to 20 percent for signing up for the card at checkout.

◆ Give customers a gift certificate for an amount (based on their purchase) for their next visit to your store. This is an in-store rewards program. You want to encourage customers spending more than $100 to visit you again and again.

◆ Work with manufacturers, distributors, suppliers, or noncompeting retailers to offer discounts on future purchasers of selected products. For instance, if someone buys Coke at your store, you can give her a discount on a purchase of a six-pack the next time she comes in.

Marketing firms in the supermarket industry have made the issuance of coupons at checkout into one of the biggest marketing opportunities for supermarket owners.

Some of the programs encourage shoppers to buy more of the products they currently like. A buyer of Heinz ketchup might get a coupon to stock up on ketchup (or other Heinz products) the next time he shops.

Other programs encourage customers to switch to competing brands. A buyer of Crest toothpaste might receive a coupon for Colgate or vice versa.

Manufacturers pay the cost of these programs. The supermarket owners provide the manufacturers with access to consumers at a critical time in their buying experience.

In addition to offering customers incentives, the register is a place to gather some vital information about your customers.

Just ask each customer what zip code she lives in, match it with her gross purchases, and you have the start of a very informative database. By finding out which zip codes your better customers come from, you are well on the way to starting a marketing campaign to areas where your customers reside.

You can also use the checkout as a means to building a mailing list. You can invite customers to join a birthday club, a loyalty program, or to just ask them if they want to receive special offers from the store. In all of these cases, you can have the customers fill out a short form, and you have started a mailing list.

Of course, the register transaction is also a place where your employees have to be careful with handling customers.

The register is where customers bring back merchandise for an exchange or a credit. This is an opportunity to make the customer happy by not hassling her about the return or exchange. A certain portion of your customers will not like what they purchased. The more you treat those customers with warmth and respect, the more they will enjoy shopping at your business.

True Tales

Before the widespread availability of credit cards, our clothing store had a generous layaway policy. Customers who couldn't afford to pay for all their clothing at one time, could put a small deposit on items they wanted but couldn't immediately pay for. We would hold the merchandise for the customer until they had the cash to buy it.

Credit cards have largely replaced the need for layaways, but many businesses now give customers cash advances at the register. Some businesses have automated the process for their larger customers, who are entitled to cash advances of up to $200 on their credit cards without any time-consuming authorization.

Delighting Your Customers

Richard George and John Stanton are professors of food marketing at St. Joseph's University in Philadelphia, Pennsylvania. They are also experts in customer service—entertaining business audiences around the world with their knowledge of how to grow a business by catering to customers.

George and Stanton's book, *Delight Me … The Ten Commandments of Customer Service* (Raphel Marketing, 1997) shows why businesses must go beyond customer satisfaction to customer delight. Without meeting that high delight barrier, George and Stanton say that customers will be satisfied but won't come back.

Here are some examples George and Stanton give of how employees and businesses can delight customers:

♦ The salesperson telling the customer how he can save money.

♦ A red rose given to every female customer at a restaurant.

♦ Giving customers several ways to talk with you and order with you from their home (including a toll-free number for out-of-state customers).

♦ A travel agent who knows by city the client's hotel and car-rental preferences and books them accordingly.

♦ A car dealer who provides customers with new cars as loaners when their cars are being serviced.

Customer information can be a crucial component of delighting customers. Knowing customers' birthdays can enable you to send them a greeting and gift on that special occasion.

Knowing what type of merchandise a customer wants can enable you to call her up when her favorite artist has a new print for sale or some of her favorite shoes have arrived in stock.

True Tales

Customer information can play a large role in delighting your customers. Here is an example:

You can pick out the top 5 or 10 percent of your customers based on total purchases, and surprise them with tickets to a ballgame or concert.

You can, as a friend in the supermarket industry did, have a promotion offering turkeys for $2 a pound (less than 50 percent of retail) when customers bought over $200 in groceries over four weeks. Then you can give the turkeys away at no cost to the customers!

If your state laws permit it, you can have a wine-tasting with fine wines in elegant surroundings, only for people who have joined a wine club.

The Importance of Children

One of the most important questions all business owners should ask themselves is, "What am I doing to attract children to my business?"

This may sound like a marginal part of your business. After all, children rarely have a lot of money and do not often make the final decision on purchases.

But children are quite important to your business because …

♦ Children will be the future customers of your business. The sooner you acquaint them with your business, the better off you are.

♦ Children can use the "nag" factor to influence their parents' choice of which business to go to. When children are happy, so are their parents.

♦ In many types of consumer purchases, parents will actually defer to the wishes of their children. Children have large influence over toy purchases and some food items.

So, if you attract the child, you attract the parent.

True Tales

Think about starting a Kid's Club at your business. Here's how it works. The child is actually enrolled in the program. The child receives a bonus (a cookie or a toy) whenever she comes into the business. The child also receives a special gift on her birthday.

These programs are successfully used by a number of businesses. Supermarkets are very successful with these sorts of programs. They also do very well when they have a special Kid's Week with all sorts of rides and games in their stores and parking lots.

A fast-food restaurant can successfully use a Kid's Club (Burger King has a long-standing program for kids) as can a children's clothing store or a children's shoe store.

Kids, like their adult counterparts, love to join a club that is going to give them recognition and rewards.

Stew Leonard owns a small chain of very large supermarkets in Connecticut and New York. The supermarkets are totally geared toward kids. There are singing milk cartons and cows that moo when you pull their tails. There is a petting zoo in the parking lot and tours of the store for schoolchildren.

Stew also goes around to neighborhood schools, tells the kids about his supermarkets, and gives away gift certificates for free ice-cream cones. When mom and dad are dragged to the store to cash in on the free ice cream, they often shop for the household groceries.

Stew's whole philosophy is that if you have a store that is kid-friendly, the whole shopping experience becomes that much easier for adults.

The Least You Need to Know

◆ Customers like games and special promotions. The more involved they become, the more loyal they become.

◆ Checkout can be the most crucial time of the customer's experience in your store. It's a chance to make offers for the next visit and gather information that you can use in marketing.

◆ Customer satisfaction is not enough to keep customers. You must delight your customers.

◆ Children are your most important future consumers, and they can help bring your business profits today.

Chapter **18**

What Specific Industries Are Doing

In This Chapter

- ◆ Industry-specific loyalty programs
- ◆ How "commodity"-type businesses use loyalty programs
- ◆ Taking the guesswork out of providing customer rewards
- ◆ Improving profits with returning customers

Loyalty programs take different forms in different industries. Where there is frequent customer interaction but low prices of goods, such as in the supermarket industry, there is an incentive to give consumers an advantage for coming in frequently to the same store.

Other industries have different challenges. Casinos in Atlantic City and Las Vegas want to make sure that their best customers don't want to stray to the competition. Airlines want to romance their customers with visions of free vacations when they fly frequently.

Credit-card companies try various partnerships to attract consumers by appealing to that consumer's lifestyle or group affiliation.

Small-business owners can develop programs to make customers want to come back to win prizes or earn rewards.

Each of these different types of businesses has developed specialized programs to lure customers back for more business. Although some of this information has appeared earlier in this book, it takes on added meaning when it is associated with a particular industry. By examining the different ways these industries appeal to their customers, you can come up with a plan to develop customer loyalty in your business.

Airlines: Where the Loyalty Craze Started

America is a big country. And the world is an even bigger place. Business travelers and even vacationers have to fly often and sometimes many miles to reach their destinations.

Because Americans fly so often, and because airline flights are a relatively expensive item, people have always loved the idea of getting free or reduced prices on their air travel.

Because airline miles have become so popular, it is hard to remember that frequent-flier miles are a relatively new program for the airlines. Frequent-flier programs were introduced in 1981 by American Airlines. Shortly thereafter, United, Delta, and TWA came out with their own programs. The basic idea is that every time you fly you earn points that can be redeemed for future flights.

True Tales
Today, according to frequentflier.com, there are more than 70 frequent-flier programs worldwide and over 100 million people enrolled in these programs. Some of the big U.S. carriers have over 20 million people enrolled in their own programs.
Ten million rewards are issued by the airlines each year, and, as a general rule, about 5 percent of airline seats are set aside for frequent fliers.
The most popular routes? No surprise there. People cash in their frequent-flier miles to go to popular resort locations like Hawaii and popular overseas destinations like London.

Frequent-flier miles have proven so popular in this country that credit cards are now offering frequent-flier miles in return for credit-card activity.

A recent article states that the number of frequent-flier miles outstanding has risen at a rate of 20 percent a year, two and a half times as fast as the supply of dollars.

Although airlines continue to promote the accumulation of these rewards, the experience of the airline industry offers these warning signals:

♦ Too much success can actually lead to customer dissatisfaction. When too many people try to redeem their rewards at the same time, they may be frustrated over frequent flier limited options and limited seating.

♦ Frequent-flier miles, despite their popularity, have not proven to be a cure-all for the airline industry. Other factors, such as terrorist attacks and threats, and increases in the cost of fuel, are far more important to the bottom line.

♦ When all the airlines adopt similar programs for frequent-flier miles, the use of those miles as a marketing tool becomes minimized.

The danger in the frequent-flier program is this: the best customers may not feel that the program adequately compensates them for their loyalty to one airline. The airlines are each making a deal with the consumer: "You fly with our airline whenever possible and we'll give you great rewards."

If an airline's best customers come to feel that they are not being treated properly, if the availability of the rewards are quite limited, or if the customers feel that there are too many hurdles to jump over to claim the rewards, then the bargain is broken. Customers will discount the worth of the rewards and spread their air travel around. The whole opportunity of frequent-flier miles will have been wasted.

True Tales

The ultimate frequent-flier plan was announced by USAir to persuade funeral directors to use their airline when sending bodies across the country.

This promotion established a TLC (Tender Loving Care) card and announced it with the headline, "Introducing: A Higher Level of Care." After 30 shipments, the funeral director received one free trip within the United States or Canada.

When the story was written in the trade magazine, Advertising Age, here were some of the comments from advertising executives and other readers:

♦ "We wanted to be first out of the box."

♦ "Northwest tried the idea, but it died."

♦ "It almost makes dying worthwhile."

♦ "It's really a 'Frequent Dier' program."

Supermarkets: The Rise and Reign of Loyalty Cards

Supermarkets generate a large proportion of food sales in this country. They are marketing machines, giving manufacturers space to display their goods in layouts designed to help consumers find the foods and general merchandise they need.

Supermarkets have been around since 1859, but their dominance of the retail food business really started in 1918, when Clarence Saunders opened the first self-service grocery retailing system in Memphis, Tennessee. His store was called Piggly Wiggly, and the name persists in stores around the country today.

Supermarkets have proven to be an ideal format for manufacturers to display their goods and for retailers to practice one-stop shopping. Because shoppers visit supermarkets far more often than other retail outlets (an average of three times per week), supermarkets can gather a much larger percentage of a consumer's wallet than other retailers who see their customers once or twice a month.

True Tales

The giant retailer Wal-Mart has realized the business benefit of having customers come to their stores more often.

Wal-Mart's typical store used to be a 60,000-square-foot discount store. But now its typical store is a 120,000- to 200,000-square-foot supercenter, which includes a large supermarket.

Supercenters have proven to be a very profitable format for Wal-Mart. Now, Wal-Mart is the largest retail enterprise in the world, as well as the number-one supermarket chain in the United States.

Loyalty marketing in the supermarket industry typically takes the form of a plastic card, which identifies the customer with a number that is scanned when the customer checks out.

Here are some of the ways that supermarkets have used the information gathered at checkout to interact with and reward their best customers:

- Free turkeys for customers buying up to a certain dollar figure in the weeks before Thanksgiving.

- Free tickets to baseball games for selected customers.

◆ Partnership programs with benefits at noncompeting retailers, such as American Express and McDonalds.

◆ Sweepstakes promotions that give cardholders a chance to win vacations in Hawaii and other resort locations.

The advent of loyalty cards has given supermarket operators a chance to give special benefits and discounts to their best customers. It has made advertising more productive. Some supermarkets have eliminated newspaper advertising in favor of directly corresponding with their best customers via newsletters.

Loyalty cards also give supermarkets an opportunity to practice *customer management* techniques.

Loyalty Lingo _____

Customer management is a method of making decisions based on the buying habits of customers. Traditionally, supermarkets have engaged in category management, for example, treating ice cream as a category that would be managed according to product sales. Customer management enables supermarkets to base their buying decisions on the likes and dislikes of their most profitable customers.

A **cherry picker** is someone who shops only to take advantage of sales and specials. This type of shopper shops at many different stores and usually has very little loyalty to any one store.

One reason why loyalty programs are so popular in the supermarket industry is the amount of people who are *cherry pickers*.

In fact, most supermarket customers shop at several supermarkets on a regular basis.

A recent study in the supermarket industry showed that only 20 percent of supermarket shoppers confined their shopping to one supermarket per week. Fifty-three percent shopped two supermarkets and 27 percent shopped three supermarkets or more!

However, 72 percent of people's food shopping was done at the customer's primary store. These studies show that shoppers tend to go to their primary store for large purchases, but shop other stores for special items or because the other store is running an attractive sale or special.

When shoppers are asked why they shop at their primary store, convenient location and store deals rank above a frequent-shopper program in importance. This is despite the fact that more than two thirds of Americans carry one or more supermarket frequent-shopper cards.

For most supermarkets, their loyalty card functions as paperless coupons. Customers present the card at checkout and receive that week's discounted price for the products on special. It's just like snipping out coupons from the weekly circular, but easier. But there is much more that supermarkets can do with the information they collect in their loyalty programs. Unfortunately for the supermarkets, it is rare for a store to use the data in a way that will really make a difference in their business.

Until supermarkets start following the lead of other businesses that make better use of frequent-shopper data, they will never receive the full benefit of issuing frequent-shopper cards.

True Tales

Marv Imus of Paw Paw Shopping Center in Paw Paw, Michigan is one of the strongest believers in listening to his customers. He uses his loyalty marketing program to receive valuable information about how his customers shop his store.

Imus made some analyses of specific categories. He found that in one group of products the lowest selling item in the category was the most profitable. Traditional category management techniques would have prompted him to eliminate the item (because it did not sell in great quantities) or raise its price (to squeeze more margin out of a low turnover product).

However, Imus' loyalty data showed that the product was purchased by some of his best customers. He did not want to disappoint those special customers, so he kept the product and did not raise the price.

Casinos: Growing an Industry with Loyalty

Casinos sell dreams. The ability to win a lot of money in a short amount of time is the lure of gambling, together with the ability to have experiences that are a little bit exotic in a locale that caters to your every desire.

But casinos are backing up those dreams with a very solid pattern of rewards to keep their best customers coming back again and again.

Did you ever notice that casinos have rows and rows of slot machine players who are careful to insert their player cards in slot machines before they begin to gamble? And did you notice the casino games players who are careful to give the pit bosses their name and address before they start rolling the dice or playing blackjack?

All these players are making sure the casino counts their activity at the gaming tables and the slot machines. The more these players gamble, the more rewards they will receive.

Casinos use the information they obtain from players in several important ways:

Loyalty Lingo

A **comp** is a reward issued by a casino to a customer. A comp can be for a meal, hotel room, cash, gifts, and so on. Comps are usually based on the amount a customer bets. The more the bet, the greater the value of the comp.

- They can determine who their best players are and reward those players with gifts and *comps*.

- They can keep track of which customers respond to the offers and other marketing efforts of the casinos.

- They can determine precise statistics of how much particular customers bet. The more customers bet, the more profitable they will be in the long run for the casinos.

Casinos now are becoming much more sophisticated about making sure they collect as much information as possible about their customers.

Harrah's Casino has a program that links the slot play of its 15 casinos. The program is called "Total Rewards" and it records the action of more than 70,000 players at once at all the Harrah casinos.

With this program in place, Harrah's customers can win cash back every time they play, as well as earning points toward comps such as food, hotel reservations, and shows. Depending on their play, slot plays also receive special offers as well as premium rewards, which go as high as a cruise and a new car.

The incentives Harrah's gives its customers and the ability to link customers' play at different casinos is further-reaching than many of its competitors. However, loyalty marketing is alive and well throughout the industry.

Casinos have recognized that customers like the knowledge that even if they lose at the casinos, they will earn rewards through their play. They will be solicited to come back with free lodging, and they will be invited to tournaments where they can win a lot of money for a little stake.

One of the most successful casino marketers over the years has been John Romero. He has relied on direct-mail letters over the years that meet or exceed the competition's best offers.

But Romero does it in a way that is personal and playful. He writes customers in a way they would expect to hear from a friend, not the impersonal letter people often receive from a large corporation.

Whether Romero is offering the biggest shrimp cocktails in town or a free night's stay, the tone of his correspondence is friendly and personal. That is why he has survived in a tough marketing environment for 40 years.

Casinos are such big and efficient marketing machines that many of them have brought their direct-mail operations inside the casino enterprise. Many companies have their own staff people to write and design promotions. A few have even become printing companies, finding it less expensive to buy actual printing presses themselves than to farm out the work.

Credit Cards: Affinity Marketing

If you are a middle-income or upper-income family with a decent credit history, watch out! Your mailbox is probably flooded with all sorts of solicitations from credit-card companies. They all sound inviting and the offers are outstanding ("No interest on purchases for one year!", "Free Balance Transfers!", "No Annual Fee!"). But you probably have three credit cards in your wallet already and you see no need of keeping track of a fourth one.

Banks who issue credit cards are trying to gain more traction with people who already have and enjoy a similar product. To differentiate their products, banks try numerous strategies:

- ♦ Offering cards with no annual fees.
- ♦ Offering cards with very low interest rates on purchases (or balance transfers) for an initial period of time.
- ♦ Offering cards with an affiliation to a group or cause.

The problem is that no-fee cards are the industry standard. Offering cards with low interest rates for initial periods of time can lead to unprofitable results. If consumers started only using cards with no interest rate or a very low interest rate, banks could actually lose money on transactions.

However, the one bright spot in the industry's recent marketing campaigns has been *affinity cards.*

The problem for credit-card issuers is this: Many of the banks that offer credit cards to consumers are now offering very low or nonexistent interest rates for specified time periods. And almost every company seems to offer no-fee cards. How can a bank that wants to issue a new credit card make its offer stand out from the crowd? How do you gain attention when everyone else has a similar message?

> **Loyalty Lingo**
>
> An **affinity card** is a card that has a tie to a specific charity or organization. For instance, a card that pays a certain amount to a charity for each amount charged to the card.

The solution: Find a new message! And that's where affinity marketing comes in.

If you went to John Doe College, you will almost inevitably find an offer to sign up for the John Doe College credit card in the mail. Not only do you get to flash a credit card with the name and picture of your college printed right on the card, but money is also donated to the college every time you charge something to the card.

If you think that your college is doing fine, then why not sign up for a credit card with an affiliation with your favorite charity or sports team or hobby? Banks are now teaming up with every organization with a significant number of members, graduates, or a big-enough mailing list.

The benefit to the organization is revenues from the bank offering the credit card. The advantage to the bank issuing the card can be significant.

Because of the success of affinity credit cards, recently a whole new type of credit card has emerged. These are co-branded credit cards, which have the backing of a bank but also carry benefits from a major corporation.

> **Significant Stats**
>
> Synergistics Research Corporation has found that fully 20 percent of consumers have credit cards with some sort of affinity or co-branding. These consumers said that the affiliation was a major factor in their usage of that particular card.

Examples include the AT&T Universal Card, the GM Card, and the Shell Card. One of the benefits of the GM Card, for example, is that you can use 5 percent of your purchases toward paying for a new car.

The ability to use credit-card purchases as a way to buy other wanted items makes sense to consumers. Consumers also react well to helping charities out when they buy something they want. As long as consumers respond well to offers linking credit cards with other companies and charities that they like, the number of these programs will continue to grow.

Small Businesses: Prizes Keep Them Coming

When you have a shoe store, dry-cleaning business, or hardware store, or even if you are a tax preparer or other professional, you are facing several difficulties in making your customers more loyal:

 ◆ Your business is viewed by many consumers as a commodity business and will shop with you only on the basis of price.

 ◆ Most of your customers purchase fairly inexpensive items or services.

 ◆ Customers do not attach a notion of fun or excitement to the prospect of going to a hardware store or dry cleaner or dentist office.

It is precisely because many small businesses can be a ho-hum affair for many customers that your business needs a dose of entertainment to boost sales.

In the long run, most businesses are operating under the same loyalty principles. Whether you run a restaurant or a dry cleaner, an airline or a jewelry store, you are looking for ways to attract and keep really good customers.

By focusing on your better customers, you will lower your marketing costs. You will match rewards to spending. You will have a solid base for continuation of your business when times are tough.

People Power

Stan Golomb was a friend of mine who died recently after a long life in advertising and marketing. His specialty was the dry-cleaning business, and he was always looking for a promotion that helped him "Find, capture, and keep customers," which is the title of a book Stan wrote about his experiences in helping dry cleaners market their business.

Here are some of the ways Stan helped dry cleaners promote their business:

- New move-in cards sent to everybody who just moved into town.
- Birthday cards and promotions sent to customers on their birthdays.
- Saturation mailings to homes near dry cleaners offering $5 off their next cleaning bill.
- Promotions offering cash back or free silver coins to customers who came back to the dry cleaners often.
- Games such as blackjack giving customers a chance to get a big discount or free cleaning.
- Premiums such as calendars, magnets, soap, and golden hangers to encourage customers to come in more often.

The Least You Need to Know

- Airlines reinvented their industry when they focused their customers' efforts on becoming frequent fliers.

- Supermarkets prosper by using loyalty cards to identify the purchase patterns of their best customers.

- Casinos may be the most advanced industry in terms of tracking the transactions of their customers.

- Credit-card companies have discovered that becoming partners with charities and well-known corporations help sell them their products to consumers.

- Small business owners need loyalty programs to instill a sense of excitement and fun in their customers.

Specific Types of Loyalty Programs

In This Chapter

- The profitability of two-tiered loyalty programs
- The flexibility of points-based loyalty programs
- Charging customers to participate
- Using employees to start loyalty programs

Once you are convinced that a loyalty program makes sense for your business, you have to decide how you are going to reward your best customers.

In this chapter, you will see how the loyalty concepts explored in other chapters can be used in specific programs designed to keep your current customers and attract new customers.

There are no restrictions on the type of loyalty program you can start in your business. The only limits are your imagination and the enthusiasm of your customers for the program you devise.

Here are some of the interesting things that businesses have done when starting a loyalty program:

◆ Involve other businesses. If you are a jewelry store or an art gallery, there is nothing that says you can't offer lunch at a local restaurant for your best customers. All you need to do is strike up a deal with a restaurant you like. They'll be glad to participate.

◆ Give family members a special bonus. One restaurant I know gives a free meal to every member of the family on their birthday.

◆ Tie a loyalty card in with a debit or credit-card program. This option is used by many large companies in Europe and is starting to work here.

This chapter discusses some of the more common types of loyalty programs businesses use. Your business can choose one of these types, be a combination of a couple of different types of programs, or you can do something totally novel. Before you make your choice, let's see what other businesses are doing.

Two-Tiered Card Programs

Imagine that you are a small business with lots of competition in a very mature industry with total sales of over $400 billion per year. Also imagine that with just one change in procedure you could increase your net bottom line 25 to 30 percent with no increase in sales and no increase in marketing costs. Would you adopt that policy?

You bet. And that's exactly what a hundreds of supermarket businesses did in the 1980s. The supermarkets introduced a loyalty card that made all their specials and temporary price reductions available only to club members. The supermarkets then charged everyone who was not on the card program full price for merchandise.

Here's what happened in a nutshell:

◆ Total store sales remained around the same.

◆ About 20 percent of transactions were not recorded on cards. These people did not receive markdowns on the goods they bought.

◆ Marketing costs went down because the stores could market exclusively to club members.

Loyalty cards became the rage in the supermarket industry. Many stores started card programs and about two thirds of all adults became card-carrying supermarket loyalty-card members.

True Tales

Some people forgot their cards when they came to buy groceries. To resolve that problem, stores began issuing tiny bar-coded cards that fit on a key ring.

Other supermarkets had a simpler but elegant solution. The shopper's telephone number became their card number. Now you did not even have to bother to carry a card around with you. If you remembered your phone number, you were all set.

Two-tiered programs are very simple to initiate and fairly simple to operate. However, most supermarkets do not take advantage of the data possibilities inherent in these programs.

Most supermarkets start the two-tiered programs with the best intentions. They collect the information about customer purchases at the cash register, and after a few months they begin delving into the data and then start marketing programs for their best customers.

However, several factors cause most supermarkets to disregard most or all of the data they are gathering:

◆ No employees are assigned to dealing with the collected data on a full-time basis. The loyalty-card program is usually assigned to the company's marketing department, which, in the case of single-store operators, is usually the owner of the company.

◆ It is too much of a burden to try to develop customized marketing programs for best customers in addition to the store's normal marketing efforts.

◆ Just having a two-tiered program brings in extra profits. There doesn't seem to be a reason to extend the program beyond the basics.

Some supermarket chains use the *data-mining* possibilities in two-tiered programs to profoundly change their business. Some small stores like Lee's Supermarket in Westport, Massachusetts, and Green Hill Farms in Syracuse, New York, actually use their loyalty programs as the basis of their marketing, merchandising, and store operations.

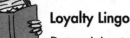

Loyalty Lingo

Data mining is a method used to examine the information gathered from customers. Data-mining can show how customers change their buying habits based on incentives. It can also show how often new customers come back after their initial shopping trip, as well as which customers are buying which items in the store.

Other large companies such as the Tesco chain in England use information gathered in their loyalty program to offer banking and other financial services to their customers.

The basic benefit of two-tiered programs for businesses is that they don't have to be a lot of work. Either someone has the card and gets the discount, or doesn't have the card and is charged full price.

Because of the bottom-line benefits, this has proven to be a popular program. But at its most basic, a two-tiered program doesn't really reward loyalty. It only divides customers into two classes, those who have cards and those who don't.

To really create a loyalty program, a business has to be willing to examine the data created by a two-tier program.

Points Programs

Points programs are a simple concept and a popular type of loyalty program. Every time you purchase an item at a business, you receive points. Typically, you receive one point for every dollar you spend. Your better customers will like these types of programs, because the more they spend, the more they are rewarded.

Businesses have a lot of options to offer their customers who earn points in a loyalty program:

- ◆ They can offer customers cash back: A customer can receive, for example, one dollar back for every 100 points earned.

- ◆ They can let customers use their points to purchase items in a catalog that may be unrelated to the business where the customers earned the points.

- ◆ They can give customers some other benefit (such as air miles) for making charges on a credit card or spending money in a store.

The points earned are commonly related to the amount you spend (e.g., one dollar spent = one point). However, points can be earned in other ways, too.

Airline frequent-flier programs let people earn points based upon the distance they fly. One mile flown = one point.

Some businesses let customers earn points from other businesses. For instance, a supermarket might give customers two dollars for every dollar they spend in the supermarket. They might also give customers one point for every dollar they spend in a noncompeting bookstore or sporting-goods store.

True Tales

Feargal Quinn's Superquinn supermarkets in Ireland have an interesting way of rewarding customers. They issue customers "Goof Points" for pointing out mistakes the store makes (wrong pricing of items, broken shopping carts, and so on).

Superquinn has figured out that rewarding customers for finding mistakes empowers a whole new army of volunteer quality-control officers. This program has the double benefit of rectifying mistakes and making sure that people don't feel bad about pointing out flaws in the operation.

Points are a very flexible mechanism for rewarding customers. If you find that your store is not very busy on a Tuesday, by all means, increase the number of points that your customers can earn by shopping on Tuesday.

If you have some especially profitable items in your store that you want people to buy, give them more points for buying those products. Points are the way to micromanage your store and your customers by giving people extra inducements to do the things you want them to do.

Points can be used as an add-on to a two-tiered pricing program. For instance, you can give rewards for just using your loyalty card. You can also offer points for using your card during a special promotional period (for example, collect 500 points in the three weeks before Easter and win a free ham).

As loyalty author Brian Woolf, who was at one time CFO of the large supermarket chain Food Lion, has pointed out, companies that establish a points program should be aware of the financial obligations established by the program. Below are some statistics from one of Woolf's studies.

Assuming that 80 percent of your customer's transactions are done with loyalty cards (a worthwhile goal) and that customers redeem 80 percent of the points they earn, here is how much company sales must increase to break even with a points program:

◆ 6.8 percent if incremental sales yield 10¢ per dollar

◆ 4.5 percent if incremental sales yield 15¢ per dollar

◆ 3.3 percent if incremental sales yield 20¢ per dollar

◆ 2.6 percent if incremental sales yield 25¢ per dollar

The bigger your margins, the less you have to increase sales to break even with a points program.

Because businesses are free to adopt any rules they want for points programs, they can make rules that tilt points programs in favor of their better customers:

◆ They can require customers to use their points within 12 months (or 24 months) or lose any benefits associated with the points.

◆ Businesses can establish thresholds that customers must meet to earn points. For instance, points can only be earned if a customer spends $400 during a specified period of time.

◆ Points can be restricted to only certain items that a vendor sells, either higher-priced merchandise or merchandise that the merchant has a high gross margin on.

Loyalty Lingo

Customer segmentation is a way of treating some customers differently from the rest of your customers. Usually customer segmentation is done on the basis of purchases, although segmentation can be done on other factors such as age, geography, or type of item purchased.

Points programs can be used as a way of dividing the customer list for marketing programs. For instance, a special offer could be mailed only to customers who earned 400 points during a specified period. The business owner can make any rule he or she wants. Points accumulated are a great way to segment a database into customers who deserve special rewards and those who don't. This process is an example of *customer segmentation*.

You can also offer customers ways of redeeming points that cost you less money or even do not cost you anything at all.

For instance, some companies offer a travel bonus: Earn 1,000 points and you can use those points to receive a $100 vacation gift certificate.

One credit card offers magazine subscriptions for unused frequent-flier miles earned when using the credit card. Many people have not earned enough points to win a free trip, but they are anxious to use their frequent-flier points. Offering a magazine subscription may not cost the credit-card company much money (depending on the deal they strike with the magazine) but the customer will feel good about having a use for extra frequent-flier points.

> **True Tales**
>
> A business can have several different levels of benefits and not require customers to pay anything at all. Customers self-select their level of benefits by the amount they bet at the casino.
>
> The upper level of casino patrons receive the benefits of private clubs, special seats at performances, luxury hotel rooms, salons, limousines, and so on. For casinos, these special guests more than make up for their rewards by their level of play inside the casinos. These high-rolling customers more than make up for the costs of entertaining them by the amount they collectively lose when gambling.

Buying Into Loyalty Programs

Many businesses have decided that it is not worthwhile to keep all their customers in their loyalty programs. Because many loyalty programs have no costs associated with signing up for them, many customers sign up and then forget all about the program.

It's different when you pay for a loyalty program. Customers who pay realize that they have a stake in the program and are careful to take advantage of the program. They feel cheated if they pay money and don't participate. A financial involvement makes people become better customers.

Take the Barnes and Noble book chain for example. They sell a membership for $25 and their concept is very simple. As a member, you receive a 10 percent discount for any books you buy in Barnes and Nobles stores. You also receive a 5 percent discount for any Internet purchases at the Barnes and Noble website.

Significant Stats

Here's how the Barnes and Noble concept works in practice, assuming that you make all your purchases at Barnes and Noble stores rather than the website.

- If you buy $100 worth of books per year, you save $10.
- If you buy $250 worth of books per year, you save $25.
- If you buy $500 worth of books per year, you save $50.

The math makes the membership proposition obvious. If you buy over $250 worth of books, it pays to become a member. If you only shop Barnes and Noble occasionally, it's not such a good deal.

One of the concepts that has worked out very well for large discounters is the "club" concept. Companies such as Sam's Club and Costco charge their members a premium every year for the opportunity to shop in their businesses.

These members then get to take advantage of the enormous buying power of the large discounters. These discounters say that charging a fee helps them create the infrastructure and retail settings to sell goods to consumers at very close to cost.

Another way customers can buy into loyalty programs is by joining a club which has special membership benefits.

For instance, Larry's Markets in Washington State offers an Epicurean Association with several benefits for customers. For a $40 sign-up fee, Epicurean Association members receive benefits that include the following:

- 15 percent discount on wine purchases
- Selected cases of wines at 10 percent above cost
- Invitations to wine- and food-tastings
- 20 percent discount at an upscale hotel chain
- 10 percent off selected food products

Members also receive other benefits and rewards, including a subscription to The Epicurean, a special newsletter written for Epicurean Association members.

The concept of paying for loyalty benefits makes a lot of sense to retailers. When they have club members instead of customers, they are dealing with a more focused group of buyers, people who have a stake in the business.

Book of the Month Club and Columbia House music and video clubs have built their whole business around the concept of paying members. The way these clubs work is that members initially commit to buying a certain number of books or CDs or videos over a certain time period.

In return, Columbia House and Book of the Month Club commits to giving members a certain number of free products, and tells its customers that they can receive discounts on all their purchases.

These clubs used to have provisions that required members to contact the club if they did not want the monthly product sent to them.

Because many people did not want to have to notify the club when they did not want to make a purchase, most of these clubs changed the notification requirement. Today, most clubs only require members to contact them if they do want to buy a product.

True Tales

Many airlines have introduced a paying membership fee to help distinguish their better customers. All customers can be involved in a loyalty program by collected frequent-flier points for reduced or free air flight and other travel discounts.

However, a certain segment of the flying public wants more benefits. They like to enjoy private clubs at airports and to be able to upgrade their seating accommodations when extra seats are available.

So, airlines like United created special clubs that catered to their most frequent fliers. For a fixed amount of money, customers can be treated like special guests at airports and on flights.

Some enterprises (like airlines) have evolved into having two sorts of loyalty programs for their customers. For the masses there is a frequent-flier club, which entitles them to receive bigger and better benefits the more miles they fly. For fliers who really want the next level of service and comfort, there is a United Club (and most of the major airlines have their own version of this sort of club) where passengers can relax in comfort before flights and also have other perks like special seating privileges.

Employees and Loyalty Programs

Employees are the most critical component in making a loyalty-program work. They are your customer interface, and like all other customer contacts, this one must be handled properly to ensure customer satisfaction.

Front-end employees interact with customers at the cash register or counter. They must make certain that the program data is collected and input correctly. Are they asking customers to put their names and addresses on a mailing list? Or are they helping customers to complete a detailed sign-up form, and presenting a temporary loyalty card until the actual card arrives in the mail? Either way, employees must be carefully trained about the program and coached to handle customers politely during the process.

Customers will have questions about the loyalty program. Employees must be knowledgeable about the program so that they can answer customers' questions correctly.

Employees who sign up customers for your loyalty program need to understand the mechanics of the program. They should know what the benefits of the program are for the customers and be able to explain those benefits fully.

Because employees are such a crucial part of the mechanics and support of the loyalty-card program, such programs must be designed with employees in mind.

Employees can be very useful in the start-up phase of a loyalty program. Many businesses start their loyalty programs with a two-week testing period. During that testing period they only let employees use loyalty cards. This serves a double purpose: It gets employees used to handling the loyalty program and it tests the system for glitches.

By getting employees involved early in the testing and implementation process, businesses can make sure that their loyalty programs can have a successful formal launch.

People Power

Tom Haggai, the CEO of IGA supermarkets, believes that IGA employees are all "customers" of his store. He says: "It is important to remember that your 'customers' are also the people who report to you. They are your primary customers. The people who buy the groceries are the customer of your customer. Owners and managers must treat the person carrying out the bags of groceries to the car as graciously as they treat the person who paid for the bags of groceries."

The Least You Need to Know

- There are several different methods to distinguish between holders of loyalty cards and other customers.

- Two-tiered programs are simple to administer, and they lead to advertising and big profits from people who don't join.

- Points programs give businesses a great amount of flexibility but can be costly.

- Some businesses feel that charging customers to enter a loyalty program increases profits and participation.

- Employees should be involved in the beginning stages of any loyalty project.

Part 5

Putting It All Together

Once you understand the importance of customer loyalty, how to move customers up the loyalty ladder, and how to put together a loyalty program, you can start devising a winning loyalty program for your business.

First, recognize the potential problems. You must make sure that you satisfy any privacy concerns your customers may have. Next, you should study how other companies have achieved great success by catering to their best customers.

Finally, you can design and implement a loyalty-marketing program that is best for your business.

Chapter 20

Problems with Loyalty Programs

In This Chapter

- ◆ Loyalty-marketing pitfalls
- ◆ Protecting your customers' privacy
- ◆ Not using customer data
- ◆ Keeping your program interesting
- ◆ Including your employees in the program

Let's remember the purpose of a loyalty-marketing program: an information-gathering tool, a reward mechanism for customer behavior, and a means of marketing your business. That's a lot of functions for one program!

It's no surprise, then, that plenty can go wrong as you pursue your goal of winning customer loyalty.

Some of your customers will be unwilling to give you the information you need to track their purchases. They may be concerned about their privacy, about how you will use the information you gather.

The rules of the programs may be confusing to customers and possibly even to your employees. The programs may be expensive to implement. Some customers may forget to bring in their loyalty cards but still demand the benefits of the loyalty program. Other customers may even question the fundamental fairness of loyalty programs.

But if you try to anticipate difficulties, if you treat customer questions and even complaints with a smile, you can overcome these barriers with success. This chapter describes what you should know about possible pitfalls as you begin the serious task of encouraging customer loyalty.

The Right to Privacy

The Supreme Court of the United States has found that a right to privacy exists in the United States Constitution. And you'd better make sure that you protect the privacy of your customers or your business will run into considerable trouble.

Everyone Knows Everything

Just think about how many different types of organizations collect information about individuals:

♦ Internet websites. When you visit a website, it is likely that information will be collected about your interests and shopping patterns. Many sites attempt to collect as much information as possible, and scams have been set up to try to collect and use personal identification and financial information about web users.

♦ Marketers. The more information a marketer has about you, the more relevant the advertising material the marketer can send you. Financial information is useful to marketers but it can be dangerous for you if it falls into the wrong hands.

♦ Businesses. Many businesses are now enticing customers to open store-brand credit cards to earn discounts on initial and subsequent purchases. To be approved for a store card, customers must give financial information to the store and be approved by a credit agency. The store card may be useful to the consumer, but she should be aware that her financial life is now available to a business where she shops.

People Power _____

"I think every consumer has to realize that every policy is different, offering varying levels of protection and varying provisions," Andrew Shen, a policy analyst at the Electronic Privacy Information Center, told *CRMDaily*, noting that privacy policies generally are unreliable. "There is no single thing guaranteed by all privacy policies."

Keeping Customer Information Private

Many businesses have adopted a three-point program to ensure that the privacy rights of their customers will be protected:

1. Businesses make sure that their programs are opt-in programs. Information about customers will not be collected unless the customer agrees to it.

2. Information that identifies specific customers will not be sold to third parties under any circumstances. Information that identifies specific customers will not be shared with any third parties without the customer's specific authorization.

3. The customer can rescind the right he or she gives to a business to collect sales information at any point in time.

These sorts of protections are set up by businesses because of the growing feeling among many consumers that personal information about their spending practices will be shared with other businesses and possibly governmental organizations.

Don Peppers and Martha Rogers, in their book *Enterprise One to One* (Currency, 1999), suggest that businesses adopt, publicize, and use a "Privacy Bill of Rights," which should spell out ...

♦ The kind of information generally needed from customers.

♦ Any benefits customers will enjoy from the enterprise's use of this individual information.

♦ The specific things the enterprise will never do with the information.

♦ An individual's options for directing the enterprise not to use or disclose certain kinds of information.

♦ Any events that might precipitate a notification to the customer by the enterprise.

They caution that if customers are reluctant to give a company information because of distrust, the company will have to "buy" the information in the form of greater and greater incentives and discounts.

Websites such as www.no-card.org warn consumers against signing up for supermarket loyalty programs. They say that various governmental organizations, including health and law enforcement, will have legal rights to secure information from supermarket organizations. They also claim that there are no guarantees that other third parties may not be able to access specific customer information over time.

The Good, the Bad, and the Ugly

The growing ability of companies to track information is indeed a double-edged sword. On the positive side, the more information a company can track, the more it can tailor offers and messages to the specific needs of each shopper. Also, the company is able to personalize the shopping experience, as if the business were small enough to know all its customers by name. A customer-loyalty program can enable a business to send the customer birthday greetings, or greet the customer by name when he or she checks in at a hotel or airport.

On the other hand, the greater the information gathered, the greater the potential for harm. For instance, if an insurance company knows that a particular customer is taking medication that indicates that customer is at a greater risk for a heart attack or stroke, would that information justify the insurance company charging that customer higher rates or even withdrawing coverage if it deems the risk too high?

Most of us would not want this to happen. The companies collecting the information say it will not happen.

A new privacy danger is looming on the horizon. Called RFID (Radio Frequency Identification), these are product-identification tags that go far beyond the capabilities of today's bar codes. RFID tags can be embedded into a product, thereby staying with the product itself for a long time. The RFID tag can be read at a distance from the item, and without the specific orientation to the scanner that is required to read a bar code. This may enable retailers to track customer behavior at levels that endanger the privacy rights of the consumer.

A customer could be tracked walking through a store by monitoring the customer's RFID loyalty card. A retailer would be able to know if a specific customer stopped near an advertising display, if the customer picked up the item, put it back on the shelf, chose a similar item instead, and so on. The "Big Brother" comparison is obvious. Privacy policies will have to address this and other new technologies as they are developed, to avoid a general consumer backlash to loyalty programs.

Wal-Mart is the biggest proponent of the RFID tags. They plan to include them on all their products within the next few years. The biggest retailers have the most detailed information about consumer behavior—that's something that frightens some trade associations and consumer advocacy groups.

True Tales

The RFID controversy has attracted the attention of diverse groups who think this new technology will invade consumer privacy or put too much of a financial burden on consumers.

For instance, CASPIAN (Consumers Against Supermarket Privacy Invasion and Numbering) complains about what it calls spy chips which "can be used to secretly identify you and the things you are carrying - right through your clothes, wallet, backpack, and purse." The website of CASPIAN is www.nocards.org.

A coalition of auto-parts retailers has claimed that by requiring RFID identification on products, Wal-Mart and other large retailers gain a discriminatory discount on goods.

The courts and the public will have to decide whether the advantages of RFID identification outweigh and possible problems with new technology.

Not Using the Information

If you are considering starting a customer-loyalty marketing program, it might be hard to believe that there are many companies that don't use the information they collect. But it's true. Companies often have the best of intentions when they start a loyalty-marketing program, but they somehow "forget" what a wealth of information they are amassing from the program. They often treat their programs as strictly "rewards" for the customer, which is only one aspect of a true loyalty program. It's fine for customers to receive $10 off their next purchase after they have accumulated sales totaling $1,000. But that is not a loyalty program. That is simply a rewards mechanism.

As we've discussed before, many supermarkets that began loyalty-marketing programs and invested heavily in hardware and software have not taken advantage of the marketing opportunities that such a program allows. Instead, the electronic-card programs have become simply a way to get coupon-like savings without clipping coupons.

Reward systems are part of a loyalty program. It is important to reward your customers when they present their cards to you when they purchase. But that does not make an entire program. You waste your money if you don't use the information that accrues when your customers' shopping information is tracked.

Here's a simple example to describe the difference between a rewards program and a true loyalty program:

- Baker Number One offers a card that is punched once for every loaf of bread purchased by the customer. After the card is punched a dozen times, the thirteenth loaf is free.

- Baker Number Two has a loyalty card that is scanned each time a customer buys a loaf of bread. After the customer has bought a dozen loaves, the thirteenth loaf is free.

What is the difference between these two programs?

In Baker Number One's punch-card system, there is no customer data being collected. The bakery doesn't know the customer's name, what town he lives in, how many family members he has, what kind of bread he buys, and so on. All the Baker knows is that this customer has bought 12 loaves of bread.

In a true loyalty program, Baker Number Two knows the customer's name, which appears on the cash register screen as soon as the card is scanned.

The shop's employee can say, "Thank you, Mrs. Smith," when he rings up the sale.

The bakery knows what kinds of bread this customer prefers and can pool that information with the data from all their customers to manage their baking schedule and to create new products. The bakery also knows how long it took for the customer to buy her 12 loaves. They can track customers who buy 12 loaves in 3 months as compared to customers who buy 12 loaves over the course of 3 years.

They can reward those customers differently—perhaps the bakery would like to thank the more frequent buyers by presenting them with a jar of jam to go with the free loaf of bread, or encourage the less-frequent shoppers to return more often by offering a breadboard as a gift if they purchase 12 loaves in 6 months. Since they have customer names and addresses, they can send direct-mail offers to their customer list, birthday greetings to their customers with a special offer during their birthday month, and offers for customers' favorite products.

This small example shows that the value of a loyalty program to your business is great when you gather customer-purchase information and then evaluate it to determine customers' buying patterns. But if you don't use the data you collect, you might as well have the punch-card system—you'll be getting no more from your loyalty program than Baker Number One.

The "Keep It Fresh" Dilemma

Whenever you construct a loyalty program, you want to keep the reward structure simple and consistent. For example, customers can get a $10 gift certificate once they have earned 1,000 points. Everyone's happy—customers are rewarded for their purchases and you've encouraged customers to spend more with you. The problem is that consumers quickly become tired of the same reward structure. You have to offer different and new incentives and rewards in order to keep the program fresh.

Remember that it is a *marketing* program first and foremost, and attention must be paid to the creative aspects of the program or it will wither away. You wouldn't keep marketing the same offers year in and year out—you couldn't attract all the customers you wanted if your offers never changed. Plus, your regular customers would soon tire of the same ads and would move to your competition for new products or services that better met their needs. In the same vein, once you have committed to a customer-loyalty program for your business, you will only continue to get a strong return on your investment if you find new and creative ways to keep your customers interested in the program.

Use your website to enhance your loyalty program. Your site is a great opportunity to communicate directly to customers, to explain how your program works and what its benefits are to the customer. You can develop programs that encourage your customers to visit and revisit your website, prompting them to purchase via the Web or to come to the store location.

Be sure all your materials that relate to your loyalty program match the "look" of your business. You have probably invested a great deal of time and money developing an image for your business. (If not, go back immediately to Chapter 14 on branding!) Put the same effort into establishing the look and feel of your loyalty program. It should reflect your business. This is especially important if you are purchasing a loyalty program that has been developed for your industry, but not specifically for your business.

Employee Issues

The installation of customer-loyalty programs is almost always a "top-down" process. A buy-in from the head of the organization is the first step before any kind of loyalty program can be started.

But equally key to the success of your program is how your front-line employees understand it, accept it, explain it to your customers, and work with it. This requires a good deal of attention and training before the program is instituted.

How to Engender Employee Enthusiasm

Once you have decided on a loyalty program for your business, you must begin the process of training your employees about the program. Explain the goals of the program first, and how they dovetail with your overall business strategy. Then explain how the program will work, starting with generalities and moving to all the details of the program. The amount of time such training will take depends on the complexities of your program.

Be careful that every employee who interacts with customers is well versed on the program details. All too often I encounter a staff member in a company who cannot explain the value of the program to the customer. And be sure that the employees can explain the program in terms of *benefits to the customer*—not the benefits to the business. Your customer isn't interested in how the loyalty-marketing program helps *you*.

Remember the "keep it simple" rule—if your employees can't understand the benefits of the program, neither will your customers. Don't make the explanation of the program take so long that customers are turned off. This may seem elementary, but it has happened over and over in the implementation of new loyalty programs. Roll out new additions to the programs over time, so that both employees and customers are able to digest the new facets of the program.

People Power

Brian Woolf, in his book *Loyalty Marketing: The Second Act* (Teal Books, 2001), offers a suggestion to gauge the "keep it simple" factor of your program. He says, "An easy litmus test of your program's simplicity is to ask a new employee to describe how your program works and what benefits it offers a customer. His response will quickly tell you whether it's simple or complicated."

At the same time, make sure employees tell the whole story. If there is a time frame to using points, for example, explain that up front. Nothing will lose your customer's loyalty faster than if she feels she's been lied to.

When marketing materials are being prepared for the program, show them to your staff and use their feedback to help you craft the most effective message for customers (as you already do with other marketing materials—see Chapter 5). Make sure all employees who interact with customers are familiar with new marketing materials and any new offers, sweepstakes, or other promotions that are part of the loyalty-marketing program.

Training Employees on the Program Mechanics

Now, for the back-office staff. Their contribution to the success of your loyalty program is as great as your customer sales and service employees.

Data collection and entry is a function that tends to be overlooked in the maintenance of a customer-loyalty program. You've spent thousands, perhaps hundreds of thousands of dollars, on computer software and hardware to analyze your customers' shopping behavior. But then you rely on your already-overburdened back-office staff to get the enrollment information from the customers and enter it into your expensive computer system when they aren't busy with anything else (whenever THAT is).

Do yourself and your business a favor and assign staff specifically for customer enrollment and data entry. Employees who help customers complete the enrollment information can then look it over quickly before the customer leaves to ensure that all the necessary information is complete and readable. This can be your sales staff, your cashiers, your customer-service staff—whoever is appropriate to help the customer complete the forms. Those employees will know what to look for and can make sure customers give all the information required. This will eliminate the need to go back to the customer to correct data, and will also help you have a much "cleaner" database (that is, one with correct and up-to-date information).

If possible, use as few data-entry personnel as possible. Your database will be 100 times better if the same person or people do all of the actual data entry. Like the staff who help customers complete the sign-up forms, the data-entry staff will quickly learn what to look for on the forms and will keep the information in your database consistent. While this may seem like a fine point, it is not. The information in computer databases is quite specific and must be kept correctly. Even something as trivial as typing extra returns after an address can be enough to make a mailing printed from the database wrong and cost extra for you in terms of time to correct it and perhaps re-mailing costs.

Other Things to Watch Out For

Loyalty programs have a lot going for them. It is advantageous to your business to have a handle on the buying habits of your best customers. However, there are some bumps in the road to success:

- ◆ Program expenses
- ◆ Aspects of competition
- ◆ The value of your loyalty program

The sections that follow describe a few.

The Expense of the Program

If you are going to capture information on your customers' buying habits at the point of sale, you will have to invest in hardware and software to capture and analyze the results. This can be expensive. However, keep in mind that computer and software costs have been decreasing for a long time. Although it is still expensive, installing a program today costs a lot less than it did five years ago. A key variable is training time. How long will it take to have employees trained to understand and implement the program you choose?

It is also important to know what the cost of the program itself is to your business. Programs that are run on a discounting system must keep in mind the cost of giving discounts to customers. Programs must generate additional sales, in the long or short run, to make up for the lost income from selling products at a lower price.

Points-based programs also have a real cost to the business, since points can be redeemed for merchandise that has a cost. Understanding these costs will help you to set your offers carefully and to keep the loyalty program a valuable contributor to your bottom line.

There is a hidden cost to a database that people rarely consider. "Staleness" of the data, which means that the data collected is more than two years old, will cost you in several ways.

1. You will waste money by sending mailings to people who are no longer at their previous address.

2. You will waste money by sending more than one mailing to people for whom you have more than one address (how many catalogues do you get from the same company?)

3. You will waste money by marketing programs based on incorrect data (for example, marketing a baby club to a family whose children are in high school).

As we have mentioned previously, keeping the database clean and current requires attention to detail from your data-entry people, as well as periodic review of the database to ensure that your addresses are up-to-date. You can do this by sending a first-class mailing to your database, with your return address on the mailing. Undeliverable returns will be returned to you by the post office. You can then correct addresses and remove unknowns in your database. I recommend doing this every 12 months to clean your database.

Competitive Aspects

If you are the only store in a market area that has a loyalty program, then you are at a strong competitive advantage. You can trumpet the benefits and rewards of your program with the implied comparison that your rivals have no similar program. But the landscape is constantly changing. If you have good results with a program, you can be sure that within a year your competitors will tout a new program with even better rewards.

The challenge then becomes upgrading your program quickly and responding to a new competitive landscape. When many of your competitors come up with programs, the consumer starts suffering from "loyalty fatigue" and may not be able to differentiate between the programs.

Be aware of the real and hidden costs of staying competitive in a market with other loyalty programs. Stay true to the goals for your program. Don't start matching low prices just because a competitor has lowered its prices. I know of supermarkets with well-developed loyalty programs that start engaging in a BOGO (Buy One, Get One Free) war with their competitor, rather than using the data they are collecting in their loyalty programs to weed out their worst customers, encourage their best customers, and create marketing campaigns for products that their best customers want.

As with other marketing programs, you can't just knee-jerk react to your competitors' loyalty scheme. Evaluate first how their competitive thrust impacts your business, and use your loyalty data to help you determine your best strategy to compete effectively.

Loyalty Programs Are Not Everything

Don't be complacent about the value of your loyalty program. A business with a loyalty program can be beaten by other marketing models.

A good business with great products, services, and an exciting ambiance can easily outperform one that relies solely on a loyalty program and neglects other essential needs of the business such as product mix, cleanliness, customer service, etc. A loyalty program is only one tactic in a business' arsenal to attract and keep a strong customer base.

On the other end of the spectrum, a good business that is the low-price leader in its category can beat a business that also relies too heavily on its loyalty program. In industries where price is the most important feature (for example, some supermarkets, discount stores, and certain discount-level service providers), a loyalty-marketing program may not be what is called for. After all, the basis of a loyalty program is to capture information about your customers. If your business is not built on satisfying the needs of specific customer groups, then you do not need to collect information about your customers.

The Least You Need to Know

- ◆ Loyalty programs are costly if you don't use the information gathered.
- ◆ Employees must be trained on communication and mechanics of the program.
- ◆ The database developed from the loyalty program is a valuable asset for your marketing efforts.
- ◆ Customers expect their loyalty information to be kept private.
- ◆ A loyalty program is only one piece of a total marketing and business strategy.

Chapter 21

Ideas from Other Businesses

In This Chapter

- Competing with the giants by having a niche
- Using customer information to give customers more choices
- Customer loyalty in a small business
- Establishing customer loyalty by being different
- Using a customer-loyalty program to enter new businesses
- Transactional vs. emotional loyalty

Winning customer loyalty is both an art and science.

The science is fairly cut and dried:

- You gather information about your customers including their address, age, gender, and income levels.
- You check out their buying patterns and you offer them programs and rewards based on their demographics and spending habits.

The art comes in when you attempt to make your enterprise a cut above the competition.

Building a loyal clientele will take all your talent and energy. You have to forge your own path, but you should also look at and learn the lessons of other companies that have succeeded in developing a following.

To get you started down that road, this chapter spotlights several companies that have done an especially good job of building loyal customers. These are big companies and small companies, Internet and bricks and mortar, old and new companies. What binds these companies together is their ability to keep customers coming back year after year, visit after visit.

Kenny's Books in Ireland: Competing With the Giants

How does an independent bookstore compete against superstores and chains such as Barnes and Noble, Books-A-Million, Borders, and Crown, which control nearly half of all book sales? These megastores offer 40 percent off bestsellers and 25 percent off paperbacks. They also offer fast and low-cost shipping.

> **People Power**
>
> It was Napoleon Hill, the motivator, speaker, and writer, who said, "If you want to be successful in business, all you have to do is find a niche and fill it."

An independent *can* compete with these giants if the store develops its own brand and makes its customers loyal to that brand.

Kenny's Books Shops and Art Galleries in Galway, Ireland, has a niche. It has the world's largest collection of Irish literature. It stocks more than 150,000 books, hundreds of antiquarian maps and prints, and does more than $3 million in business a year.

One day an American librarian visited the shops, made a purchase, and asked if Kenny's had a catalog. Kenny's did not, but decided to develop one. They printed the first ones in their bedrooms, stapled and hand-addressed them in their dining room, and mailed them to 100 libraries. Today, 140 U.S. libraries receive books from Kenny's.

One day an American customer bought several books. Since he lived in the United States, he couldn't visit Kenny's regularly. Would Kenny's send him packages of books each month in his special area of interest?

Sure. That began Kenny's mail-order business called, "Irish Book Parcels" with their "Personal Approval Plan." You sign up with Kenny's, and give your credit-card number and a list of topics of personal interest: Irish history, politics, art. Every few months you receive a selection of materials based on your interest.

Customers can return or exchange anything. Today, Kenny's has nearly 1,500 clients around world enrolled in this unique program. James F. Clarity of *The New York Times* called their program, "A kind of Irish literary piñata."

The Internet was their next stop (they were the second book store in the world to appear there.) Today, half of their Internet business is from repeat customers in 44 states, Guam, New Zealand, South Africa, and the Philippines. (Contact them at www.kennys.ic.)

Are they worried about big discounters as competition? "Won't affect us," said Mrs. Kenny, founder of the business with her husband in the 1940s, "You see, we're different. We have our own brand."

True Tales

In order for bookstores to succeed today, they have to sell more than books. They have to sell a comfortable ambiance for their customers. I know bookstores that have succeeded by some innovative combinations with book sales.

One bookstore near us has a full-service restaurant in the center of their space. Another has a full basement filled with books and toys for kids. Another store I know runs chess tournaments inside the bookstore.

Additional activities make each of these independent bookstores a gathering place in their towns.

Amazon.com: Building Customer Loyalty Through the Internet

One of the first companies to build an Internet-only business was Amazon.com. As Kenny's of Ireland found out, it is possible to build a book business with the Internet as one of many ways a customer could interact with a business. What Amazon.com found out is that it was possible to parlay an Internet book business into a huge supplier of consumer and business products.

Many of Amazon.com's business practices fly in the face of conventional wisdom. It doesn't have brick and mortar stores. It doesn't have salespeople. But, interestingly, without stores and salespeople, it manages to attract a loyal customer base through many innovative customer-loyalty practices:

- ◆ Amazon.com has a huge inventory of available products. Need electronic equipment or pet supplies, something for your kitchen or a new CD? Amazon.com has it all. In its core book business, it has millions of titles available, far more than any brick-and-mortar store.

- ◆ Customer selections and preferences are stored in Amazon's database. Amazon.com knows what you have bought and is able to offer you relevant suggestions for future purchases.

- ◆ Amazon.com is always price-competitive and is often the price leader. It has helped lead to discounting of the most popular books. It offers free shipping for many purchases, and it also offers used books and equipment if that's what you want.

> **True Tales**
>
> Retail customers are not the only people to benefit from Amazon.com's selection and prices. Amazon.com has given book publishers a new ability to reach millions of book browsers. Small publishers can now achieve distribution to a wide range of customers even if they cannot convince large brick-and-mortar bookstore chains to stock their books.

Amazon.com is one example of how the Internet is changing how customers interact with sellers. In the old days (about 10 years ago), if you wanted to buy a tennis racquet, a calculator, or a car, you visited a sporting-goods store or an electronics store or an auto dealership.

Today, you can check out pricing and selection with a few mouse clicks. You can visit specialty sites and purchase goods without leaving your chair.

There are many implications of the growth of the Internet for businesses with actual physical locales:

- ◆ Think about developing your own website. It's an effective way to communicate with your customers and to sell your goods to this whole new generation of Web buyers.

- ◆ Shop your competition. Visit websites offering products and services similar to your own. It will help you decide issues such as prices, guarantees, and new products you might want to offer.

◆ Develop programs and services that Internet providers cannot offer. You may want to offer fast delivery, service guarantees, letting customers take home and test products, and other benefits that Internet providers cannot match.

As the Internet continues to grow, it becomes more imperative for even small businesses to have a presence on the Internet. Your customers expect it, and you can profit from increased sales because people will find your business as they look for products and services they need.

Optical Expressions: Customer Loyalty in a Small Town

A small business is often in a better position to instill customer loyalty than a huge corporation. A small business owner will have at most a few locations and a small number of employees. In that kind of atmosphere, the owner can stress the importance of customer service, customer tracking, store appearance, consistent advertising, and the other factors that go into winning customer loyalty.

For instance, Pete Boyle is the owner of two optical shops in northeastern Vermont. Together with his optometrist partners, Pete has put together a specialized program that has succeeded in developing many loyal customers.

In the eyecare industry, there are hundreds of discount programs available to consumers. It is difficult for any business to keep up with and join all the programs. And when the businesses do join, the paperwork is endless.

Pete decided that he wanted to do something for any customer who had signed up for an insurance or discount program. However, he didn't want to deal with the paperwork and restrictions of the various programs. He needed an alternative. So he created one himself!

Optical Expression's Vision Choice program is open to any customer who presents vision insurance that Optical Expressions does not accept. For those customers, Optical Expression gives customers a Vision Choice card that offers them 40 percent off any frames in the Vision Choice collection and 20 percent off any lenses fitted in those frames.

Pete has come up with a way to satisfy consumers who want low cost but quality lenses. He bought a special line of frames that meets his needs of good quality but low cost. Consumers feel that they are getting a bargain, and Pete does not have the administrative nightmares of endless insurance and discount programs.

Pete's Vision Choice program has proven so popular that Pete has extended it to customers of a local bank and some unions. Other retailers have put in the same program (under a different name).

Because Pete's cost structure is lower in the Vision Choice frames than many of the popular branded frames, he is able to make a decent mark-up on those frames. His Vision Choice program enables him to service the needs of a lower-middle-income population while still providing high standards of care and customer service. Pete makes sure that the staff he hires is courteous and efficient. Pete himself works long hours to make sure every customer has his or her needs met.

While many optical businesses are hurting because of the big-box stores that have permeated the industry, Optical Expressions has a booming business. Pete attributes this success to his Vision Choice program and friendly staff, but also to his ubiquitous advertising. He is a strong advocate of direct mail, and he also spends money in newspaper and event advertising. Pete is very active in the local community and coaches a high school basketball team. He seems to know every customer who comes into the store and is able to talk with that customer about something of interest.

Being involved in the community. Great service. A low-cost product. A clean, professional environment. Is it any wonder that Optical Expressions succeeds while many of its competitors are going out of business?

Ben & Jerry's: Succeed by Being Different

Here's the recipe for making a successful ice-cream company:

♦ Start with some market research. Find out what your customers want. Find out how much ice cream they buy in a week.

♦ Flavor your ice cream similarly to that of your successful competitors. Price your ice cream competitively.

♦ Package your ice cream in half-gallon and gallon containers because the more ice cream your customers buy, the more money you will make.

When it comes to Ben & Jerry's, one of the more successful ice-cream companies in America, that recipe is …

Wrong.

Wrong.

Wrong.

Ben & Jerry's succeeded because they made interesting ice cream that co-founder Ben Cohen liked, with strong flavors and big chunks of nuts and cookies and candy in the ice cream. Add some cute names, hippie-type advertising, and a company that cared about social issues, and you have an improbable success.

According to co-founder Jerry Greenfield, Ben & Jerry's niche is the super premium end of the ice-cream market. The company sells pints only, in contrast to many of its competitors who sell quarts and half-gallons. Jerry believed that customers are not entirely price-driven, and that bigger quantities do not appeal to many customers. "We believe people are flavor-driven," Jerry said. "And if you are out of stock with their favorite flavor, they won't purchase or will purchase somewhere else."

The company responds to their customers' changing tastes. When customers wanted frozen yogurt, the company came out with a line of yogurt. The company lets customers help to name its products, and at one point opened the job of president of the company to the public.

> **Significant Stats**
>
> The Vermont-based company was built on a philosophy of giving back to the community. A percentage of pretax profits are put in the nonprofit Ben & Jerry's Foundation, which has given money to many charitable causes.

With a distinctive product and appealing advertising, Ben & Jerry's has presented itself as a fun company with a soul. That message has made it popular with kids of all ages and is a lesson in how you can develop customer loyalty by having a distinctive brand.

Tesco: Evolving into an Information Company

Tesco has long been a leading supermarket in Great Britain. But the company really hit its stride when it invested heavily in its loyalty-marketing program.

Today, 85 percent of Tesco sales are captured on its Clubcard. Tesco gives shoppers one point for every pound spent and a 1 percent voucher when a shopper earns 250 points. Additionally, bonus points are offered on selected items around the store.

Tesco has used the resulting data from customer purchases as a tool to understand its customers, as well as a way of deciding how and when to communicate with customers. Tesco augmented its offerings by adding a debit-card feature to its loyalty card, enabling customers to pay for transactions as well as earn points toward future rewards.

Tesco now offers its customers a wide range of financial services including savings programs, insurance, and pension programs. Because it was able to capture customer information, and because its customers were well aware of Tesco's first-class reputation, Tesco was able to spend less than half of what it costs a bank to acquire a customer.

True Tales

Authors Clive Humby and Terry Hunt have identified how Tesco examines customers by rating them on three dimensions:

♦ Contribution: Current customer profitability.

♦ Commitment: Future customer profitability. This is measured by how likely the customer will remain a customer and the customer's ability to increase purchases.

♦ Championing: The potential of a customer to mentor future customers.

Where a customer fits on this analysis will determine how Tesco markets to the customer and what types of offers the customer will receive.

Today, when you go to Tesco's website, you are able to buy groceries. But you are also able to buy books, computer games, mobile phones, and to plan vacations. Believe it or not, you can even shop for an electricity provider at Tesco's website.

The factor that originally drove customers to supermarkets was convenience. Supermarkets quickly became popular with the public, because shoppers wanted a quick and easy way to accomplish their food-buying in one trip.

Now, Tesco is taking convenience to a whole other level. You can order groceries with a few quick choices on a computer and have those groceries delivered directly to your door. While you are at it, you can also order a movie you want to watch, some flowers for a loved one, and finance a new loan. Tesco can simplify a wide range of consumer transactions because it is a technology leader and has data-collection methods that enable it to give customers satisfaction quickly.

For a company like Tesco, winning customer loyalty means providing customers with as many valuable programs as possible to achieve what its marketing director Tim Mason calls the "lifetime loyalty" of its customers.

True Tales

Tesco is offering shoppers in some London stores a free ride home after shopping. All consumers have to do is show a receipt from that day's shopping at Tesco to a taxi from one of several companies, and they will be driven home within a limited distance. The program is being tested for the next month or so before being rolled out nationally. The initiative is part of the ongoing battle for market share taking place between Tesco and the Wal-Mart-owned Asda Group, in which both sides are sparing no expense in fighting for an advantage.

Hampton Inn: 100 Percent Satisfaction Guarantee

Can a guarantee of customer satisfaction transform a company? In the case of Hampton Inn and Suites, it did.

Hampton Inn and Suites introduced its "100 Percent Satisfaction Guarantee" in 1989. Here is the guarantee: "Friendly service, clean rooms, comfortable surroundings, every time. That's our commitment and your guarantee. That's 100 percent Hampton."

The way the guarantee works is that every Hampton employee is empowered to make good on the guarantee. Every employee from front desk clerk to housekeeper to maintenance engineer to hotel manager has the power to do whatever it takes to make a guest happy, including giving a complimentary night's stay. The guest decides if the service or product doesn't measure up. There are no negotiated discounts. The guest receives a free night if he or she is unhappy.

The Hampton Inn guarantee is separate and apart from another loyalty system at Hampton Inn. Since Hampton Inn is owned by Hilton Hotels, it participates in the Hilton Honors loyalty system, which gives points for every night that a customer stays at a Hilton Hotel.

Jim Hartigan, Senior Vice President of Guest Services for Hilton Hotels, distinguishes between the two different types of loyalty programs. The Hilton Honors program is an example of "transactional loyalty." Transactional programs are based on rational thought. Small business owners have been operating these types of programs for many years. An example is this: Buy 10 haircuts, and get the eleventh one free. Customers come back because eventually they will win a prize. Hartigan says that having a transactional program is a must-do in the hotel business. You need one to be in the game.

The Hampton Inn's 100 percent Hampton guarantee is an example of emotional loyalty. Emotional loyalty lasts longer than the attitudinal loyalty. A customer buys from you because you fulfill her emotional needs. She feels pride in doing business with you. She feels connected to you.

Hartigan says emotional loyalty is the basis of the Hampton guarantee. It is based in trust and makes going to the hotel a risk-free purchase. Hampton had its guarantee program for many years before it was acquired by Hilton and embraced Hilton's points program.

Hampton's research shows that for a guarantee to work it has to be easily understood and has to relate the value of the item purchased. Hampton's guarantee is friendly service, clean rooms, and comfortable surroundings *every time*.

Significant Stats

Despite being a very liberal guarantee, Hampton Inns does not lose money on the guarantee. Its studies have found that for every $1 spent in reimbursing a guest, $7 is gained by Hampton in return business. Hampton estimates that 99.95 percent of its customers are honest. It has software that helps it track the small number of people who Hampton thinks are abusing the system. Those guests are urged to choose another hotel.

Other features of the Hampton Guarantee program include the following:

♦ Video-based training to new employees, which explains the guarantee and how employees can work with the program.

♦ The guarantee has improved employee morale and employee performance. Employees all realize their importance to the company. If they don't perform their job properly, they know that the customer will stay for free. It makes each employee's job important and gives each employee the authority to implement the Hampton Guarantee.

According to Hampton's Hartigan, "The 100 percent guarantee is not about giving back the money. It's the safety valve. It's used when all else fails. Our team members tell us that they enjoy their jobs more and feel more connected to the organization, and are more loyal and proud to work for the brand, because the hotel is willing to give back the money if the customer is not satisfied. This gives you pride in where you work."

The Least You Need to Know

- ◆ You must carve a special niche for your business when you compete with much larger firms.

- ◆ The Internet can increase customer loyalty by personalizing sales.

- ◆ Small business owners can grow customer loyalty with personal attention.

- ◆ Customers who have successful experiences with a business will be likely to continue to patronize that business.

- ◆ Emotional loyalty can attach a customer to a business for many years.

Chapter 22

Networking and Partnering

In This Chapter

- ◆ Creating a network of helpers
- ◆ Starting an entrepreneur's club
- ◆ Developing business partners
- ◆ The value of being likable

You don't have to do it all alone. You can enlist help in your attempt to increase your customers' loyalty.

Two ways you can involve other people and businesses in your quest to encourage loyalty to your business are as follows:

- ◆ Networking. This is using the contacts you've developed in your personal and business life to advance the cause of your business. No business is able to advance without the help of outsiders such as suppliers, consultants, family, and friends.

- ◆ Partnerships. Consider developing partnerships or business relationships with noncompeting businesses. If you are a small business owner, you can meet with other small businesses to discuss marketing strategies and also which types of promotions worked best to attract customers.

Noncompeting businesses can also be partners. These types of partnerships can range from sharing of information to sharing of mailing lists to joint advertising projects. These types of arrangements often work well when the noncompeting businesses are in the same shopping mall or neighborhood.

Networking for Fun and Profit

Do you have a Rolodex with the names of personal and business acquaintances? If so, you are probably already networking in your business.

Every business needs a "network" to succeed—using contacts, connections, or creativity to increase your sales.

People Power

"Networking is one of the new directions to transform our lives where everyone is a resource for everyone else."—John Naisbitt

How many names do you have in your network?

Lady Astor had 400.

It was the turn of the twentieth century. She just completed building her new home in Manhattan and planned a housewarming party for her friends. The problem was that there wasn't enough room to hold everyone in her palatial ballroom.

Her architects told her that the room could comfortably hold 400. No more. Or the fire department might close her down because of overcrowding.

She condensed her list to a select 400. This number came to mean the cream of society (and a great networking opportunity for each elite guest.)

What if your business had their own "list of 400"?

Networking could fill your "ballroom" for an entire week. Or month. Or longer.

Let's listen in on a conversation you might make to a local business without mentioning a Mr. O'Connor, one of your customers.

You: Good morning. May I please talk to Mr. Smith?

Secretary: Who shall I say is calling?

You: Well, he doesn't know me, but my name is Michael Whitcomb and I have Whitcomb's Products, and was wondering if Mr. Smith would like to know about a special widget we have for his business because …"

The next sound you hear is the hanging up of the phone.

But, if, instead, your conversation included Mr. O'Connor's name ...

You: Good morning. Is Mr. Smith in?

Secretary: Who shall I say is calling?

You: My name is Michael Whitcomb and William O'Connor said I should call Mr. Smith about something Bill said he'd like to know about ....

The secretary knows William O'Connor. She doesn't want to abruptly close the door. O'Connor is a friend of her boss. More often than not, the next voice you'll hear is Mr. Smith's.

You want to make contact with someone. But you don't know this someone. But you know someone who can put you in touch with someone who will tell you about someone who knows the someone you want.

I often tell friends, "The person you want is only four phone calls away."

"Really?" said one, "How about if I want to call the President of the United States?"

"Call your U.S. Senator," I said. "If you don't know him, call your Congressman. Or a local politician who knows one of them ..."

True Tales

When Neil opened his bookstore soon after college, he wanted to do something exciting, different, and unusual. His budget, like the size of his shop, was limited and small.

Publishers who supply writers to bookstores for signings would not return his phone calls. He was new, small, and obviously unimportant.

I had a neighbor who was friendly with award-winning writer James Michener who had just written *Centennial*, one of his record-selling books. My neighbor said, "I'll ask him if he'll come."

Michener agreed. He liked to help someone starting a small bookstore, and besides, Neil had graduated from the same college as Michener (another great source of networking).

Neil ran a large newspaper ad (his advertising allotment for the year). He ordered a few hundred books instead of the normal few dozen and held his breath ...

Crowds started lining up around the block two hours before Michener appeared. Michener remained, signing every book till the last customer left.

The bookstore was an instant success. Months later, if someone was asked for the best place to buy books, the answer was, "The book store where James Michener was when he came to town ..."

Here's how to start:

♦ List everyone you know on your Rolodex file and include the person's name, address, business, telephone number, fax number, e-mail, and website, for starters. Make sure that you put in a note explaining how you know the person and what the person does.

♦ Assemble a list of a few hundred and you're in the networking business.

♦ Don't stop. Keep adding names as you meet someone new—the person you sat next to on that recent four-hour flight or at the local Chamber of Commerce meeting. Now, when you need to contact a company, person, or institution, there's a starting point somewhere in your file.

♦ Names are people, and people die or lose contact with you. They need to be replaced. Review your file every year. Is there someone you haven't heard from or contacted within a year? They may be ready to be replaced by someone new. Or, if they were valuable in the recent past, they are worth a "thinking of you" phone call or note. Most will appreciate that you took the time to say "hello."

♦ Say "thank you." After someone gives you the information you need, remember to call back and say, "Thanks. And if there's anything in the future I can help you with …"

The more attention you give to your business acquaintances, the more these acquaintances will help your business grow. Everyone wants to help their friends succeed.

Learning from Other Businesses

Stew Leonard started the Stew Leonard's supermarket chain. But even though his name is on his stores, Stew believed in taking the best ideas he saw in other businesses and adapting them so that they worked in his stores.

When Stew visits another country, he takes notes about products and shelf designs he could incorporate in his own operation. When he visited Disney World in Florida, he decided he wanted to capture the fun and excitement of Disney by having singing milk cartons and "moo"ing cows in his stores.

Stew encourages his employees to take the best ideas they found in other businesses by sponsoring "one-idea trips." Several Stew Leonard employees pile into a van and drive a couple of hours to a retail store they heard had innovative designs or pricing or products. Each of the employees has to come back to Stew Leonard's with one idea that the retailer could put into action.

The concept behind the "one-idea trips" was thinking outside the box. In order to find ideas for their supermarkets, Stew Leonard's employees might drive to another supermarket. But, just as likely, they would visit IBM and see how that company treated their employees. Or they would visit a catalog company to see how gift baskets were put together. Stew's employees eventually started a mail-order business during the holiday seasons that resulted in tremendous sales.

The Entrepreneur's Club

You probably remember that I've mentioned my friend Stan Golomb in previous chapters. Stan was a successful marketing consultant who started a company called the Golomb Group to help dry cleaners and other small business owners market their products.

Stan Golomb believed that it was important for small business owners to get together and share marketing and sales ideas. He visualized Entrepreneur Clubs springing up around the country and wrote a book about the idea.

These clubs would have small, noncompeting business owners as members. The small business owners would share marketing ideas and results. They would talk about how they handled suppliers and customers. They would visit each other's stores and give suggestions for improvement. They would act as sounding boards for each others' businesses. Entrepreneur Clubs would be formalized networks, giving small business owners the idea to help each other out.

Stan's book has inspired hundreds of retailers around the country to share their ideas and has helped them network successfully.

True Tales

Many small business owners do meet in various settings and accomplish much of what Stan Golomb championed in his dream of Entrepreneur's Clubs.

For years when I had a retail clothing store, I met regularly with the Retail Merchants' Association. This group of downtown merchants would hold regular sessions to discuss joint marketing programs, tree-planting programs, and to develop parking for customers.

We knew that by uniting with other merchants to make our city convenient for shoppers, we could compete successfully with other towns that did not address issues such as parking, beautification, and uniform shopping hours.

Here are some other ways small business owners can profit from the exchange of ideas:

- ◆ Trade shows and conventions
- ◆ Seminars
- ◆ Trade magazines
- ◆ Internet discussion groups
- ◆ Chamber of Commerce and SBA groups
- ◆ Kiwanis, Rotary, and other civic groups

Each is described in the following sections.

Trade Shows and Conventions

At these locales you can see the latest products for your industry and listen to speeches on industry trends and innovations. It is also a great place to take advantage of networking opportunities.

Seminars

Attending seminars is a great way to pick up new ideas and meet new people. It helps every once in a while to leave your working environment and to see what other people are thinking about. By taking a seminar in, for instance, "Motivating Sales Employees," you will come back with new ideas you can use in your business. The other advantage of a seminar is that it gives you a chance to think about new ideas. When you talk to new people and see how other people handle situations you face, you are bound to come back to your job energized.

Trade Magazines

Every major industry in this country has at least one and sometimes several magazine(s) that have articles about the best practices in that industry. New products and equipment are spotlighted and advertised in the trade magazines, along with the industry's lobbying efforts in Washington D.C. Trade magazines try to highlight industry trends, so you can see what's new in your industry by reading the trade magazines.

Internet Discussion Groups

The Internet has become one of the best ways for individuals to share knowledge and experiences with other people. There are discussion groups in many industries in which business people trade opinions and also offer help for newcomers. The Internet can also be used as a pricing mechanism for small business people. If you want to check your pricing, just type in the name of the product you sell into a search engine. You can very easily find out where and how other entrepreneurs are selling your products.

Chamber of Commerce and SBA Groups

Most towns have local sources of business knowledge. The SBA (Small Business Administration) and local Chambers of Commerce usually have individuals who are more than willing to help small business owners with any problems they may be facing in their businesses.

Civic Groups

Meetings of business owners and employees at Kiwanis, Rotary, and other civic groups are a great way to meet people and exchange business ideas. They usually have guest speakers with interesting information. Also, you can volunteer to give a speech about your company which could interest other people in your business.

Partnering With Suppliers

Suppliers can be your ally on the road to increasing your business's customer loyalty. Suppliers can help you by …

- ◆ Providing you with sales and product-usage information gained from their experience with other retailers.

- ◆ Providing selling opportunities for your products. Suppliers can be an active source of sales leads and opportunities.

- ◆ Providing valuable information on competitive products and services. By letting you know the possible weaknesses of competitive products, suppliers can help you make better decisions as to which products your customers will want.

There may also be the possibility of an actual business arrangement with a supplier.

True Tales

I always try to imagine ways in which I can work more closely with my suppliers. Sometimes this leads to new business opportunities.

For instance, I have used several local printing companies for years in my marketing business. When I decided to expand my business and offer mailing services, I talked with my suppliers and they were willing to help me obtain new mailing customers. I agreed on my end to refer printing business to the printers who cooperated with me.

Because I was confident in my printers' abilities, I was happy to refer additional business to them.

Amazon.com has an interesting business relationship with its suppliers. It rewards publishers and other businesses that send customers to Amazon by giving those businesses a percentage of the goods sold. This makes customers a partner in increasing sales. Both the business and the customer benefit.

Small businesses can do the same type of thing with a "member gets a member" approach. A lot of businesses reward their customers for bringing in new customers. For instance, a salon may give a customer a free haircut when she brings a friend in to try the salon.

Another way businesses can profit from working with suppliers is to have the suppliers create a special product or service for that business. Wal-Mart, the nation's largest company, has the financial muscle to require suppliers to change products and lower pricing so that Wal-Mart consumers will benefit. Wal-Mart also helps its suppliers by giving them up-to-the-minute sales information and offering suggestions as to what sort of packaging and pricing will appeal to Wal-Mart customers.

Try to think of suppliers as purveyors of information as well as salespeople. You should try to take time to listen to sales people from supplier companies, even if they are making a cold call. Such salespeople have a good feel for what is selling in the industry. They also have superior knowledge about their products. Even if I am not interested in buying their products today, listening to their sales pitches gives me information that I can store and use when I purchase items in the future.

Working With Suppliers on Advertising Campaigns

In some businesses, the relationship between suppliers and business owners can be quite extensive.

For example, IGA is an alliance of over 4,000 supermarkets worldwide. IGA has for years had its Red Oval Club in which selected suppliers worked closely with IGA to promote specific products.

When IGA decided to launch a nationwide television campaign on cable television, it turned to several of its larger Red Oval partners (including Coca-Cola, Kraft, and Nabisco) to help fund the television advertising. In return, IGA stores in America designed end-cap displays featuring the products of the Red Oval Partners involved in the television advertising. Sales of these products at IGA stores increased dramatically during the weeks following the TV advertising.

The advertising on TV focused on the Hometown Proud theme that IGA has developed in which it showed typical American families celebrating holidays such as Thanksgiving.

This advertising campaign helped to increase customer loyalty to both IGA stores and the supplier products in several ways:

♦ The advertising focused on IGA's commitment to be a "hometown" supermarket supporting traditional American values.

♦ It positioned IGA stores as offering bargains on consumer brands that consumers value.

♦ It tied the brand name of IGA together with well-established national product brands such as Coca-Cola.

The juxtaposition of a supplier's brand name with a business's brand name is often very helpful in growing a business. Supplier companies have spent millions of dollars in advertising their products' virtues to consumers. By telling consumers that you carry and support those highly recognized products, you are tying your business's brand image into the brand images already created by your suppliers.

Partnering With Other Businesses

By working with other businesses, you can increase your customer's loyalty to your business. Here are some examples of how this can work:

◆ My friend, Tony Ingleton, developed a discount entertainment-card business in Australia. Customers pay an annual fee for the card, and when it is presented at member restaurants, theaters, sports arenas, etc., a substantial discount is given.

For many years, Tony sold the memberships to individuals only. Then he realized he could leverage his business tremendously if he partnered with groups who already had members. He offered the card to groups such as unions and football clubs with high numbers of members at a low individual cost. This was a win-win-win situation—Tony added hundreds of thousands of people to his card-membership roles, the groups had a great benefit to offer their members, and the restaurants and theaters had huge increases in their business.

◆ Hiltons Honors Club has partnerships with 60 noncompeting businesses. Want something from Sharper Image? You are able to use Hilton Honors points to help with the purchase. Making its points program into a sort of a currency encourages customers to keep coming back to the Hilton hotels.

◆ Supermarkets have combined resources with travel companies to offer low-cost trips to its best customers. Supermarkets also offer baseball and other sporting-event tickets to customers at reduced costs. Supermarkets attract a lot of attention from other businesses because the traffic count at a typical supermarket can be over 10,000 customers per week. With this many people coming through a supermarket, the advertising potentials for noncompeting businesses is exciting.

Partnerships between businesses work best when certain conditions are met:

◆ The businesses must be noncompeting.

◆ The businesses should have overlapping client bases. A business appealing to high-end customers will want to search out other businesses with matching clientele.

◆ In most cases, the businesses should be located fairly close to each other. It is usually a better fit if a consumer can go to both businesses in one shopping trip.

One of the biggest pluses for partnering with other businesses is decreased advertising expenses. Suppose you run a restaurant on a downtown street. By joining together with other businesses, you can develop advertising programs that accomplish several goals:

- You can increase the customer's sense of convenience. The customer will realize that she can do a variety of shopping in one trip.

- You can run simultaneous sales events, which further encourage shoppers to come. The more bargains and the more excitement, the more shoppers will come visit.

- You and your fellow merchants can share expenses such as the cost of mailing pieces and other advertising, as well as the cost of entertainment for customers.

- All businesses can contribute their customer mailing lists to make sure any mail advertising is seen by the greatest number of current customers.

Other ways that a group of unrelated businesses can increase customer loyalty are as follows:

- Have similar shopping hours, especially during the holiday season. When a group of businesses all agree to be open during the night or Sunday during a peak shopping season, consumers will have many more reasons to visit.

- Arrange with the local town authorities to provide free parking (this can be done with a stamping system) to customers. The businesses pay a small amount to make sure that their customers can park for free on municipal lots.

Often, businesses will go as far as adopting a joint name for the purpose of marketing. The Main Street Merchants' Association, for example, will tell potential customers where the merchants are and that there are a group of merchants who have banded together to provide services for consumers.

Now you have learned most of what you need to know to win your customers' loyalty. The final chapter of the book will show you how to apply these lessons to your business.

The Least You Need to Know

- Networking helps you build your business by using contacts that you establish everyday.

- Visit other businesses (even businesses not in your industry) to come up with new ideas for your business.

◆ Think about joining with other merchants in your community to develop joint marketing ideas and other mutually beneficial programs.

◆ Business partnerships are effective when the customer bases of the two businesses have a lot in common.

Chapter 23

Now It's Your Turn

In This Chapter

- ◆ Developing your customer-loyalty strategy
- ◆ Getting the customer on your side
- ◆ A small-business loyalty plan
- ◆ The future of loyalty marketing

Throughout this book, you've read many examples of what companies throughout the world are doing to win customer loyalty in their businesses. You've seen how your customers progress from being prospects with no knowledge of your business to being advocates who tell everyone they meet about how good your business is.

You've learned how to gather information about customers and put that information into a database. If you start a customer-loyalty program, you can offer special opportunities for your best customers. By rewarding your best customers, you will make those customers more loyal to your business.

Now it is time for you to plan a loyalty strategy for your business. In this chapter, you will see what steps you have to take to make this work in your business.

Your business is unique. You offer a special blend of products and services. Let's see how you can make some changes in your business to win customer loyalty.

Your Customer Loyalty Checklist

Customers love being rewarded for doing business with you. Many businesses have launched loyalty programs with specific rewards for customers who purchase products or services. However, the road to winning customer loyalty is different depending on what sort of business you are running.

Here are four of the most important -issues you should consider before launching a customer-loyalty program:

1. Are you primarily a service business or a retail business?

2. Do you currently have a customer list?

3. What is your competition doing?

4. Do you have enough well-trained help to run your loyalty program?

The sections that follow describe each of these issues.

Service or Retail

If you are running a retail business, you are a very good candidate to start a loyalty program. All sorts of retail enterprises, from supermarkets to airlines to casinos to flower shops to jewelry stores to dry cleaners (the list goes on and on) have started loyalty programs.

However, if your business is primarily professional services, it may not be a good idea to have a loyalty program based on quantity of purchases. For instance, a doctor or lawyer or accountant may not want to offer rewards based upon amount of services purchased. This does not stop these professionals from making sure that their staff knows which customers are spending more money and are especially important to the business.

Some professional-service businesses may want to offer rewards based upon customer purchases. For example, an optometrist may sell glasses in addition to giving eye exams. His customers may receive discounts on eyewear based upon their purchases and not receive any discount on the eye exam. But I do know of several optometric practices that give new move-ins a free eye exam to help these new arrivals choose an eyecare practice.

Your Customer List

The primary requirement of running a customer-loyalty program is information about your customers. The more information you have, the better your program is going to be.

Businesses that have databases on current customers are in a prime position to launch a new loyalty program. They can start off by offering a benefit to their current customers. They can track that benefit and see how advertising to their current customers can be cost effective. Eventually they can decide to run a full-fledged loyalty program with benefits to customers that vary depending on the value of the customer to the business.

Businesses without information on their customers should, at the very least, start to collect names and addresses of customers. This can be done in several ways. The simplest is to just ask for the information at checkout. Tell your customers that you are staring a mailing list to offer special rewards to your customers. Have a sign-up card that asks for information. Make it easy to fill out. A good way to begin is to ask for the following:

- Customer's first and last name
- Customer's address
- Customer's city, state, and zip
- Customer's e-mail address (optional)
- Customer's birthday (day and month only!)

If you do ask for your customers' e-mail addresses, make sure you also receive permission to send them occasional offers by e-mail (give them a right to opt out to e-mail promotional communications). Also, assure your customers that their e-mail addresses will be held in confidence, and not ever given out to third parties.

True Tales

Another way to encourage sign-ups is to start a birthday club. Tell customers that they will receive a special present on their birthday.

Customers are very unlikely to pass up a birthday gift. They feel they are cheating themselves if they don't take advantage of your generosity.

Everybody's favorite holiday is their own birthday! Take advantage of people's favorite day by offering them a reason to shop with you during their birthday month.

The Competition

You can't view a loyalty program in isolation. You have to understand what your competition is doing to develop a strategic plan to succeed.

If none of your competitors has a loyalty-marketing program, then you are in the driver's seat. The first company to develop a program will set the agenda. If you come out with an attractive program, your sign-ups will soar and you will be one step ahead of your competitors. You can use the information you develop to understand your customers' shopping habits, and you can also try to give your best customers sufficient rewards and incentives to stay with you that they won't even think about switching companies.

If you are late into the game, if some or many of your competitors have already developed a loyalty program, then you must study their plans. You should endeavor to put a new wrinkle in your program to distinguish it from your competition. When you enter late in the game, you have to make sure that your customers don't think that all loyalty programs are the same and why bother to sign up for yet another dull program?

When loyalty programs are very similar, customers tend to lump them in one group. I once did a survey of consumers in a suburban town. Many of the supermarkets in and near the town had loyalty cards. The cards all gave discounts on certain products, but none of the programs had any unique, exciting features.

When I asked the shoppers which was their favorite card, a majority replied, "Our 'Super G' card." The interesting aspect of this was that the local Super G supermarket was the only supermarket without a loyalty card! It did, however, have a check-

cashing card, and most shoppers had confused the two types of cards. This probably
would not have happened if the supermarkets
had loyalty programs that really appealed to
consumers.

The important point to remember in this is
differentiation. You have to make sure that your
plan is sufficiently unique so that customers will
be able to associate good values and good feelings with your program.

Loyalty Lingo

Differentiation is something that separates one person,
product, or service from another.
Customers differentiate stores on
the basis of their products, services, and rewards for customers.
Businesses differentiate customers
on the basis of how valuable that
customer is for the business.

Enough Help

Perhaps the most important consideration in deciding whether your business should
implement a loyalty program is whether you have the right personnel to effectively
administer the program. There are at least three types of employees who you will
need to make a program work well:

- Front-line employees. These employees will help sign people up to the program. Once the program is implemented, these employees will be responsible
  for making the sure the program runs smoothly from day to day.

- Technical employees. These employees will be able to make sure the data that
  comes in from the program is useful to management. They will prepare reports
  that aggregate data to show which groups of customers spend more money and
  react well to incentives. The technical employees will make sure that the proper
  customers are credited with points in a points program. These technical employees will make sure that the front-end system records data from customers
  at checkout.

- Marketing employees. These employees are responsible for developing offers to
  top customers identified in the loyalty program. They have to design a program
  that will appeal to customers and make them want to come back and do more
  business.

I once visited a 200-store retail chain that had a loyalty program that had been operating for more than five years. I presented some marketing ideas to the woman in
charge of the loyalty program and she said, "I'd love to implement these programs,
but I just don't have the time."

"What do you mean?" we said.

"Well," she replied, "I'm the only person in charge of the loyalty program and I can barely keep up with the data, let alone do innovative-marketing programs."

I've seen this type of mentality in operation in many large companies. They want to operate a loyalty program because their competitors have one. However, they do not allocate enough manpower or financial resources to the program to make it an integral part of their organization.

The result is a feeble loyalty program that does not match the competitors and provides no additional reason for customers to come to the store.

Creating "Fans" out of Customers

The biggest challenge for any business is to develop the proper relationship with customers. Ask yourself these questions:

- Do your customers enjoy shopping at your business?

- Do they feel an emotional connection with your business?

- Do they recommend other customers to your business?

How can you know what your customers feel about your business? On an ongoing basis, you should do customer surveys. You should have focus groups. You can solicit customer suggestions. You should follow up on any customer complaints and see if the complaints were satisfied.

Best of all, you can begin *customer-category management.*

Loyalty Lingo

Customer-category management means dividing your customers into categories based upon their value to your business and then treating the different categories differently.

For years, businesses have been engaged in category management. They divide their stores into categories (for instance, a men's clothing store may carry shirts, pants, ties, sport jackets, shoes, coats, etc.) They look at each category as a separate profit center and try to determine which brands and price points produce the most profitable mix.

In a similar way, some businesses are starting to look at customer categories. These businesses give the best customers the best rewards. They examine the buying habits of the best customers, and give buying priority to the goods that the best customers want.

Some businesses have institutionalized customer-category management into an integral part of their everyday treatment of customers.

Casinos have segmented customers based on spending habits and profitability. In order to please high rollers, casinos go all out to treat these profitable customers differently. They are given amenities (based on their play) that can include V.I.P. check-in, room upgrades, free meals, free saunas, free transportation, gifts, free entertainment, etc.

Customer-category managers (called "hosts" in the casino industry) develop a profile of each of the casino's high rollers and try to meet their individual needs.

Because competition for high rollers in the casino industry is so intense, casinos need to develop programs to meet their biggest gamblers' wishes.

Such a strategy is expensive. Therefore some casinos have opted out of the competition for high rollers. They have determined that their best bet is to cater to the everyday gambler, the type of person with a budget of a few hundred dollars or less to play on slot machines. These casinos also practice customer-category management, but they do it on a different scale. They have rewards for customers based on play, but the rewards are far more pedestrian than the rewards for big-money high rollers.

The benefits for extended play at a slot machine could be a free entrée or even a free meal at a deli. Casinos also routinely give away free drinks to all their customers, with the expectation that alcohol will loosen the purses of their customers.

The key to casino customer management is to know which customers make your casino profitable. If you cater to high rollers, then you have to make those players feel comfortable. If your high rollers are slot-machine players, then you have to devise incentives to keep those kind of players eager to pump more quarters and dollars into the slot machines.

A Plan for You!

Most small businesses do not have a loyalty-marketing program in place. However, with a little effort and a little investment, you can develop a loyalty-marketing plan that can make your business more profitable. The sections that follow give you ideas of what you should do.

Start by Defining Your Market Area

This is the area where your customers come from. If you already have a customer file with names and addresses, then this is easy. Just make a list of customers sorted by zip codes.

If you do not currently have information on where your customers live, then ask the next 100 customers who shop with you where they live. Then put them on a map of your area. One hundred random customers will give you a good idea of where most of your customers come from.

Advertise to the Areas Where Your Customers Come From

The advertisements can go in local papers, on cable TV, or you can send out a post-card or letter mailing to your customers. When the customers come in to respond to your offer, make sure that you write down their names and addresses. You have just taken the first step to establishing a database of your customers!

Some of your customers will respond more frequently to your offers than others. Those customers should be sent offers more frequently.

True Tales

I have several clients who have established a customer database through postcard mailings. Once or twice a year they send postcards to every household in a radius around their business. They do this to make sure that they are maintaining contact with new move-ins and people who may be interested in shopping their business for the first time.

In the other 10 months of the year, my clients sent out promotional mailings to customers who have responded to previous mailings. This is the core of their customer list. Customers who respond should be contacted more often.

When a customer comes in, these businesses record how much the customers have spent. That way they have an inexpensive way of determining who their best customers are.

The best customers receive additional awards, such as free tickets to cultural and sporting events. With a small amount of investment, my clients have achieved knowledge of their customer base that is similar to much more sophisticated loyalty programs.

Watch Out for Your Competition

Ultimately, the test of the success of any loyalty program is how customers react to it. You can have a very simple loyalty program, with no bells and whistles, and have a very positive customer reaction, especially if you have the first loyalty program in your town or in your industry.

But when your competitors are offering loyalty programs with lots of benefits, as a late arrival to the game you have to try to have a loyalty program that will really have special rewards and mean something to your customers. Otherwise, you may be better served by ignoring the loyalty competition entirely and just sticking with providing the best products and services to your customers. You can still collect and use some customer information without having the burden of maintaining a full loyalty program.

The key is to stand out from your competitors. Whether that requires a loyalty program or better pricing or better selection or better service will depend on your particular industry.

Advertise Using Direct-Marketing Techniques

One of the best ways you can grow your business is to advertise in a tested, measurable way. Whether you advertise to your top customers only or you advertise in a more general fashion, try to devise an advertising campaign that is measurable.

One way to measure advertising is to have a coupon or gift certificate or some other way of discerning whether a customer is responding to your advertising message. Advertising that can be measured is called direct marketing.

The advantage to direct marketing is that you can test different offers. Suppose, for example, that you have 20,000 households you want to advertise to. You can send each of 1,000 households offers that vary by pricing or type of merchandise or have a different creative tone.

If one of the 1,000 test mailings does significantly better than the others, you can roll out that mailing to all the 20,000 households. One of the greatest benefits of direct mail is the ability to test on a small population and use the results to market to a much larger population.

The Future Is Now

It is always dangerous to forecast the future of business events. Twenty years ago, no one would have forecast the dominance of Wal-Mart, the rise of the iPod, or the bankruptcies of so many airline companies.

But there are certain trends that appear likely to dominate loyalty marketing in the next few years. Keep your eye out for new trends, but make sure you are paying attention to these keys to loyalty marketing:

- The Internet
- Information collection
- Loyalty to your customers

The Internet

The Internet has become such an everyday part of commerce and social exchanges that it is hard to remember how little we thought about the Internet 20 years ago.

High bandwidth, the proliferation of new buying and selling opportunities, and the information boom, together with remarkable search engines such as Google, have made the Internet a useful part of most people's lives.

Internet sales and commerce are going to continue to boom, so you should think about the Internet seriously if you want to grow your business. Here is what you should be doing today:

- Develop or expand your website. Consumers are becoming more and more comfortable about shopping on the Internet or using the Internet to find out information about businesses they might shop at.

- Begin collecting e-mail addresses of your customers. E-mail is a cost-effective means of marketing, but make sure that your customers approve of your sending e-mail messages to them. These messages can have a marketing message, but you will want to use e-mail to answer any questions your customers may have, or you can use e-mail to handle customer complaints.

- Use the Internet to see what your competitors are up to. As more information becomes available on the Internet, you should track what your competitors charge for products or services similar to what you sell. Even if you don't, your customers will.

Information Collection

The future is now when it comes to information collection. The relative low cost of computing power and the willingness of consumers to trade information about themselves for rewards makes the collection of information on customers important for every business.

Future information-collection possibilities include the following:

♦ Offering true one-to-one marketing. This already occurs in the computer industry, where Dell Computer only builds a computer system after hearing what each particular customer wants. Other examples could include supermarkets that could send you a personalized shopping list or personal specials over the Internet or by mail or at in-store kiosks (this has been done by a small chain in Wisconsin).

♦ On the Internet, businesses can create stores within stores for each customer, based upon her shopping preferences. Amazon.com already does this to an amazing degree by suggesting books for you and offering specials to you based on previous buying patterns.

♦ Businesses can band together and offer special rewards to consumers who shop in any of their noncompeting stores. The SuperCard in Ireland has benefits tied to shopping at scores of retailers.

Loyalty to Your Customers

Regardless of any technological improvements in the future, the bottom line to winning customer loyalty will always be your loyalty to your customers.

Fashions will change. Products will change. The kinds of services that people will want *will* change. The one constant in loyalty marketing is that businesses who put satisfying the customer first will come out ahead.

Start today by making sure your customers are happy, and you will be well on your way to winning customer loyalty.

The Least You Need to Know

♦ Develop a customer-loyalty checklist to see how you can improve your customers' loyalty.

♦ Practice customer-loyalty management and treat different groups of customers differently.

♦ Plan a step-by-step loyalty program for your business.

♦ Show loyalty to your customers by adapting to their changing needs.

Glossary

added value   The gift given to the customer as a "thank you" after the sale is completed. Unexpected, unadvertised, and unasked for … but often remembered longer than the purchase of the original item.

advocates   Loyal customers who tell anyone who will listen how great your business is.

affinity card   A card that has a tie to a specific charity or organization. For example, a card that pays a percentage of the amount charged on the card to a charity.

big-box store   This is a large discount store built in a non-descript rectangular building which resembles a big box.

bounce-back program   Incentives created by a business to entice customers to come back to shop again and again.

brand   This is something that exists in the minds and actions of customers. A relationship between a customer and a product or firm.

category killer   A store that specializes in one type of product and has a huge selection of that product. Examples include Borders for books, Toys "R" Us for toys, and Circuit City for electronics.

cherry picker   Someone who shops only to take advantage of sales and specials. This type of shopper shops at many different stores and usually has very little loyalty to any one store.

comp   Reward issued by a casino to a customer (short for "complimentary"). A comp can be a meal, hotel room, cash, gifts, etc. Comps are usually based on the amount that a customer bets. The more dollars bet, the greater the value of the comp.

customer-category management   This means dividing your customers into categories based upon their value to your business and then treating the different categories differently.

customer management   A method of making decisions based on the buying habits of customers.

customer segmentation   A way of treating some customers differently from the rest of your customers. Usually customer segmentation is done on the basis of purchases, although segmentation can be done on other factors such as age, geography, or type of item purchased.

database   Information about your customers and their shopping habits that you collect and store. You can use the information in your database for many purposes, including marketing.

data mining   Methods to examine the information gathered from customers. Data mining can show how customers change their buying habits based on incentives. It can also show how often new customers come back after their initial shopping trip, as well as which customers are buying which items in the store.

demographics   The study of information about people including race, births, marriages, mortality, etc.

differentiation   Something that separates one person, product, or service from another. Customers differentiate stores on the basis of their products, services, and rewards for customers. Businesses differentiate customers on the basis of how valuable each customer is for the business.

direct marketing   Selling goods and services directly to consumers on an individual basis as opposed to mass-media advertising. Direct marketing usually has a response mechanism, some device with which the consumer can directly communicate with the seller of goods.

empathy   To be empathetic is "to feel or find one's way into another's state of mind."

empowerment   Giving your employees the authority to make decisions on behalf of your business to help a customer with a question, concern, or problem, without having to consult higher management.

focus group   A focus group is a meeting to bring together a cross-section of your customers to discuss your business. This definition is from *Forbes Magazine*—"Six people around a table eating pizza is a party. Six people around a table *talking about* eating pizza is a focus group."

frequency   How often a customer comes to your place of business.

horizontal leveraging   This is using customer information gathered in one business to offer other business services to customers.

intelligent loss of business   This is achieved by only meeting the needs of customers who agree with the goals of your business. For example, if you sell high end jewelry you may decide not to carry imitation diamonds for people who cannot afford your products. On the other hand, by opening a store that only sells items for less than one dollar, you are turning away people who want higher priced brand-name merchandise.

limited edition   A guarantee from a business that only a limited number of items will be produced. In the art world, a limited-edition print is often signed by the artist and numbered (e.g., Number 1 of 100). The plate used to make the prints is destroyed when the last one of the limited edition is created.

list broker   Someone who sells lists of consumers based on criteria such as location, age, gender, income, and home value.

market area   The geographic region that most of your customers come from. For some businesses, this is very small (for example, most convenience-store customers live within one mile of the store—that's why it's "convenient.") The average market area for the average single-location small business is within a five-mile radius of the store's location.

monetary   How much a particular customer has spent in your business.

niche marketing   Advertising to specific audiences, rather than to the general public. When you know what niche, or segment of the general population, your business appeals to, then you can focus your marketing efforts to that group.

pull advertising   Tries to have consumers buy your particular version of a product.

push advertising   Tries to increase consumer demand for a product.

recency   When a customer last spent money in your business.

spam   Unsolicited e-mail, usually advertising, sent to consumers and businesses without their consent. Spam is the electronic equivalent of junk mail. Today more than half of all e-mail is considered spam.

Appendix B

Further Readings

George, Richard J. and John L. Stanton. *Delight Me ... The Ten Commandments of Customer Service.* Raphel Marketing, 1997.

Golomb, Stan. *How to Find, Capture, and Keep Customers.* Raphel Marketing, 1993.

Gross, T. Scott. *Positively Outrageous Service.* Warner Books, 1991.

Hawkins, Gary E. *Building the Customer Specific Retail Enterprise.* Breezy Heights Publishing, 1999.

Jenkinson, Angus. *Valuing Your Customers.* McGraw–Hill International (U.K.) Limited, 1995

LeBoeuf Michael. *How to Win Customers and Keep them For Life.* Berkley Publishing Group, 1989

Peppers, Don and Martha Rogers. *The One-to-One Future.* Doubleday, 1993.

Quinn, Feargal. *Crowning the Customer.* Raphel Marketing, 1992.

Raphel, Murray and Neil Raphel. *Up the Loyalty Ladder.* Harper Business, 1995.

Raphel, Neil and Janis Raye. *Loyalty Marketing Resource Book*. Raphel Marketing, 1998.

Rosenspan, Alan. *Confessions of a Control Freak*. CyberClassics, Inc., 2002.

Stone, Bob. *Successful Direct Marketing Methods*. NTC Business Books, 1988.

Sugarman, Joseph. *Marketing Secrets of a Mail-Order Maverick*. DelStar Books, 1988.

———. *Success Forces*. Contemporary Books, Inc., 1980.

Woolf, Brian. *Customer Specific Marketing*. Teal Books, 1996.

———. *Loyalty Marketing: The Second Act*. Teal Books, 2002.

Samples of Direct Mail Promotions

The advertising examples in this appendix are intended to spur your imagination. Be creative with your own marketing. Once you have developed advertising images, use them multiple times for maximum effect. Your direct mail piece can also be the basis of your radio or television ad. An idea you develop for your Internet site can also be used in your newspaper advertising.

Direct Mail Letter Promotion

When you start a new business, your first step toward winning loyal customers is to entice people to try your services. This direct mail letter (see Chapter 6) was used to announce the opening of a new restaurant and to attract new customers.

The letter uses many of the principles of writing good copy, but in particular it shows the value of the "headline." The concept of the "Free Lunch" is carried throughout the letter to reinforce the benefit offered, and the business type itself (a restaurant).

The three tenets of any direct mail piece are always:

- The offer
- The creative
- The list

For this letter, the offer is clear: the free lunch, no strings attached.

The creative is the style in which the letter is written: breezy and casual, as if the owner of the restaurant is speaking directly to the recipient. This is a deliberate choice on the part of the copywriter. The idea is to give the letter the "feeling" of the restaurant itself: comfortable, warm, and welcoming.

The list was very specific: 200 highly placed people who worked in the vicinity of the restaurant (lawyers, elected officials, businesspersons, etc.). In this case, the list was compiled simply by a few people who knew who the "movers and shakers" in the community were.

This announcement and promotion for the restaurant gave it a tremendous "jump start" to build a loyal customer base. Most of the people who tried this offer became regular lunchtime clients, and because they were influential members of the community, brought along many other customers who became regular patrons as well.

For a new business with a limited advertising budget, a direct mail letter with a creative offer and copy, sent to a targeted list of potential customers, can be a winning combination.

the alley deli

Gordon's Alley, Atlantic City, NJ
Proprietor: Norman Gordon
Take out & delivery: 345-1060

Richard Thomas
County Executive
817 Atlantic Avenue
Atlantic City, NJ 08401

WHOEVER SAID
"THERE'S NO SUCH THING AS A FREE LUNCH"
DIDN'T KNOW ABOUT THIS LETTER.

Good morning Richard,

Let me introduce myself.

My name is Norman Gordon. I own the just-opened Alley Deli in Gordon's Alley.

And if you're wondering whatever happened to the good old fashioned (and delicious) deli sandwich.. . it's back. Right here!

I've enclosed a copy of our menu. I'm so proud of the excellent quality and superb taste of everything we have, I would like you to become a charter member of our TASTER'S CLUB.

It's a great organization. No dues. No meetings. All you have to do is eat and enjoy.

Your only requirement is to accept one free lunch from me.

Whoever said there's no such thing as a free lunch?

There is.

For you.

I'll call you in a few days. Pick and choose what you want from the enclosed menu and I'll have it delivered to you a short time after you call.

Enjoy!

Norman Gordon

Direct Mail Brochure

This direct mail promotion is an example of a larger, more complicated mailing piece (see Chapter 6). When you want to promote an event that is really important to your business, you can give the event more impact by creating a promotional mailing that emphasizes how special it is.

The creative: this mailing was created as a large fold-out brochure, printed on heavy stock. It was designed in the style of an overnight mailing (although it was mailed via bulk mail to reduce postage costs). It was printed only in red and black, to make the word "urgent" stand out, so recipients would be attracted to it.

The offer: the most exciting offers were printed up front, right on the cover of the brochure (free trip, merchandise give-aways, dollars off your purchase). Within the body of the brochure, sale prices of many specific items were highlighted.

The list: this brochure was sent only to the store's customer list. The mailer itself noted that this was a private sale, for customers of the store only. This further enhanced the "urgent" theme of the mailer: this sale wasn't being advertised to the general public.

Every year, the store had its biggest sale of the year on New Year's Day, and for every New Year's sale, created a unique direct mail brochure to let only its loyal customer base know about the sale. It was by far its most profitable promotion for many years.

the shops in . . .

Gordon's

gordon's alley, atlantic city, n.j. 08401

*Bulk Rate
U.S. Postage
Paid
Permit No. 63
Linwood, N.J.
08221*

URGENT
DELIVER IMMEDIATELY

The New Year's Day Sale in Gordon's Alley!

JANUARY 1, 1986. From noon to 4 PM

Free: *a trip for two to Disney World!*
Free: *$1,000.00 in merchandise given away.*
Free: *You've already won dollars toward whatever you buy with your enclosed lucky number.*

A private sale for our customers only!

Address Correction Requested

FOUR **URGENT** REASONS TO SHOP EARLY!

URGENT! | URGENT! | URGENT! | URGENT!

THE GREAT MEN'S $39.99 SWEATER SALE!

You know how proud we are of our sweaters! Great designers and bought from around the world. Not all colors in all sizes but a good selection for the finest wools. Sizes small to extra-large. They sell to $100. each! **Sale: $39.99**

THE MEN'S SHOP IN GORDON'S

WOULD YOU BUY A $70.00 PERRY ELLIS FINE COTTON LISLE TURTLENECK BLOUSE ON SALE FOR $9.99?

You read it right! It looks like silk, feels like silk and has a very dressy look and style. Black or berry. We sold them for $70.00. (Well, we didn't sell them.) Now, while they last: $9.99.

THE WOMEN'S SHOP IN GORDON'S.

HOSIERY SALE $1.99
(values to $12.00)

Socks, knee-highs, panty hose, tights. Good selection but not all colors in all styles but, wow . . . . **$1.99!**

THE ACCESSORY SHOP IN GORDON'S.

ON SALE FOR THE FIRST TEN PEOPLE TO CALL.

A $75.00 grooming package for men or women for only $39.99! Here's how it works:
1. We will accept ONLY ten appointments for New Year's Day, January 1, 1986.
2. You receive a complete grooming package including a manicure, pedicure, facial, wash and set (or haircut). This is a basic grooming package we sell for $75.00.
You can have this **whole** package for only $39.99. Only to the first ten people who call the Nail Salon at 347-8251.

THE NAIL SALON.

URGENT LETTER

Direct Mail Sweepstakes

These coupons came with a promotional mailing similar to the one on the previous pages. There are several important elements to consider when you develop a sweepstakes promotion for your business.

Try to personalize them. People always respond better to something with their name on it. Since these were sent to the store's own customer list, it was not difficult to print the name and address of the recipient right on the coupon. Then, when they are redeemed, the store has an automatic record of everyone who brought in the coupon. That's a great way to keep track of the effectiveness of your mailing.

There are three levels of prizes/gifts on these coupons. Only one person will win the biggest prize (the trip for two), but more people (twenty-one) have a chance to win smaller prizes. Everyone wins something in this sweepstakes, even if only $2.00 off a purchase (see Chapter 5). This way, everyone is a winner when bring in your coupons!

Spell out all the particulars in a contest. For example, there are travel time restrictions with the free trip. Include them on the sweepstakes coupon, so there are no surprises or unhappy winners later. Leaving out critical information makes you look like you're trying to hide something.

Don't forget to publicize the winners! If you have sent this promotion to your own customer list, the general public doesn't even know about it. Let them know by featuring the winners in your next newspaper ad. You'll encourage new customers to visit to see when another sweepstakes might be available.

Here's YOUR lucky coupons!

EACH ONE HAS YOUR NAME!

- **FREE** dollars (**You** already have won with **your** lucky number!)
- **FREE** merchandise (Bring in **your** certificate for drawing)
- **FREE** New Orleans trip for two (Bring in **your** certificate for drawing

---

Here's your lucky number: № 2297

You have already won dollars on New Year's Day. Bring this coupon with your name to Gordon's on New Year's Day. Look for the big signs at the front and rear wrapping counters. Match your lucky number above to the ones posted. You WILL win from $2.00 to $250.00 in merchandise!

Mrs. Shirley Gordon
118 S. Newton Ave.
Atlantic City, N.J. 08401

Here's your entry for the $1,000 in merchandise

Simply deposit this certificate in the big box on the counter in Gordon's on New Year's Day. twenty one winners will be drawn at the end of the business day,.

Mrs. Shirley Gordon
118 S. Newton Ave.
Atlantic City, N.J. 08401

1st prize: $ 250.00 in merchandise.   2nd prize: $ 100 in merchandise
3rd to 10th: $ 50 in merchandise   11th to 21st: $ 20 in merchandise.

Win a trip for two to New Orleans!

This is your entry for the free trip for two to New Orleans. Bring to Gordon's New Year's Day. Winner drawn at end of day.
Adults only. Employees of family members of Gordon's not eligible.

Mrs. Shirley Gordon
118 S. Newton Ave.
Atlantic City, N.J. 08401

IMPORTANT: New Orleans weekend trip NOT exchangeable for any other award. Must be used Friday to Sunday. Reservations when confirmed are not changeable. Trip includes round trip air Philadelphia-New Orleans, two nights at hotel. Reservations must be made by Gordon's Alley Travel a minimum of 30 days before departure. Not available during Holidays. Restrictions apply. Must be used on or before July 1, 1989.

Direct Mail Postcard Mailing (Birthday Promotion)

Birthday promotions serve several purposes for a business. They acknowledge a special day for each of your customers—their birthday! They offer a gift to your customer, and they give your customers a reason to come back and shop with you (see Chapter 3).

The creative: the oversized postcard format (5-½" × 8-½") creates a strong visual impact at half the cost of a letter-envelope mailing. The eye-catching four-color art attracts the attention of the recipient. Almost everyone who receives this type of postcard will at least read the offer, since it doesn't require even opening an envelope.

The offer: birthday cards should have a free gift for the customer for coming into the business anytime during his or her birthday month. The gift can be actual merchandise or dollars off a purchase.

The list: the best birthday lists are those compiled by the individual business. Ask for your customer's birthday month and day but not the year. You can routinely collect birthday information, or start by asking your customers to sign up for a Birthday Club. Birthday lists can also be rented from a list broker. Only adult birthdays are available and about 50 percent of the adult names in a community are available on a rented birthday list.

If you send birthday cards to your current customer list with a great offer, you will have a successful mailing. Some businesses achieve returns as high as 60 to 70 percent from their best customers. Realistically, returns of 20 to 30 percent are typical from your own customers and 5 to 20 percent from a rented list.

Direct Mail Reminder Postcards

This card was used by an optical practice to remind patients that it's time to come in for a checkup. This is very important for certain service businesses, such as opticians, dentists, physicians, veterinarians, beauty salons, etc. Any business that sees its customers on a fairly regular basis can institute a practice of sending reminder notices according to an appropriate schedule (see Chapter 3).

This is a great way to communicate with your customers on a regular basis. The notice provides a service to your clients, so that they remember to make appointments on a timely basis. It also helps the business maintain a steady flow of client visits by contacting them according to an established schedule. The mailings also serve, as all direct mailings do, to remind your customers that you are still in business at your location, ready, willing and able to do business with them. You may sell merchandise that doesn't require a regular visit, so a reminder to your customers may encourage them to come in for sunglasses, dog food, or their favorite shampoo.

The key to reminder mailings is that they be sent on a regular basis. Many businesses leave this job to someone who has a lot of other chores, and the reminder mailings can be neglected for many months. If that happens, you will lose a great deal of potential business. When several months of reminders are sent out all at once, the calls start coming in, and there are only so many hours in the day to see clients. Therefore, people will have to be scheduled for visits far into the future, which many customers will not accept.

The postcard format of this reminder card is sufficient for this type of mailing. It is the most economical for the business, and the cards can be sent via bulk mail if they are sent according to a regular schedule.

Direct Mail Postcard Mailing (New Move-In Promotion)

New Move-In mailings are used primarily by retailers to encourage new residents to try their business (see Chapter 2). You can send mailings through a marketing firm who purchases nationwide lists of new movers and creates the mailings for the individual businesses. In a very limited area, you might be able to work with a local real estate firm who could supply you with names and addresses of new homeowners, and you can create the mailings yourself.

Virtually any business can use New Move-In cards effectively. Businesses that consumers visit frequently and have many local competitors often use New Move-In programs to show new residents the benefits of their particular retail operation. The card shown here has worked well for a variety of businesses, including supermarkets, convenience stores, dry cleaners, art galleries and restaurants.

When a New Move-In comes to your business with an offer from a card he or she has received, one of your employees should give the new customer a tour of your business. This is a great opportunity to start winning the customer's loyalty by helping the New Move-In feel comfortable. A follow-up mailing to that customer, with another special offer, will encourage the customer to return to the business a second time. Most retailers feel that once someone has shopped at a business three times, he or she will be a regular customer.

Some communities have "Welcome Wagon" programs which actually bring food and special offers to New Move-Ins. Other businesses band together to send multiple offers for different products and services to new residents. Some businesses prefer to send solo mailings to highlight their business alone.

Direct Mail Holiday Mailings

Holiday mailings are appropriate for almost every business. Holidays are a great excuse to have a celebration, sale, entertainment, or other special event. Often, people don't work on holidays, which gives them an excuse to go shopping.

The best response to holiday mailings, as with all mailings, will be from your own customer list. If you don't have a customer mailing list, start one today. Your response from mailing to your own customer list will usually be 5 to 10 times greater than your response from mailing to the general public. Most customers will be happy to sign up when you tell them they will be receiving special offers not available to the general public.

When you have your own customer list, you should mail to that list, ideally, once a month. This is where holidays come in—they give you a great excuse to contact your customers. There are holidays to celebrate every month of the year. What about August? Well, that's the month you have your anniversary sale!

If you have a retail location, once or twice a year you should send a mailing to everyone who lives near your business, not just your own customer list. Then, the people who respond to this mailing can be added to your own customer list. A marketing firm or even your local post office can help you send a "saturation" mailing to all the households in your area.

Saturation mailings may cover the same ground as your newspaper advertising or radio spots. But as direct mail, they do something other types of advertising can't—they are delivered directly to the home so you know people are receiving your message. And like all direct mail, you can measure the response you get to the program, simply by counting up all the people who bring in your mailer to redeem the offer.

Summary

We do not believe you should confine yourself to one type of advertising. But we do think you should confine your advertising to one type of branding. Tell your customers what your business stands for and why they should buy from you. Reach out to your current customers as often as possible, since they are the source of most of your sales and profits.

By developing a thoughtful marketing campaign and by keeping track of your customers, you can dramatically increase your chances of winning customer loyalty.

Index

Check Out These
Best-Selling
COMPLETE IDIOT'S GUIDES®

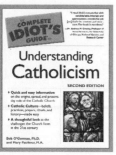

Understanding **Catholicism**
SECOND EDITION

Bob O'Gorman, Ph.D. and Mary Faulkner, M.A.

1-59257-085-2
$18.95

Learning **Spanish**
THIRD EDITION

Gail Stein

0-02-864451-4
$18.95

The **Bible**
SECOND EDITION

James S. Bell Jr. and Stan Campbell

0-02-864382-8
$18.95

Being a **Groom**
SECOND EDITION

Jennifer Lata Rung and Mark Rung

0-02-864456-5
$9.95

Grammar and Style
SECOND EDITION

Laurie E. Rozakis, Ph.D.

1-59257-115-8
$16.95

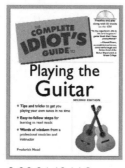

Playing the **Guitar**
SECOND EDITION

Frederick Noad

0-02-864244-9
$21.95 w/CD

Personal Finance in Your **20s & 30s**
SECOND EDITION

Sarah Young Fisher and Susan Shelly

0-02-864374-7
$19.95

Knitting and Crocheting
SECOND EDITION
Illustrated

Barbara Breiter and Gail Diven

1-59257-089-5
$16.95

The **Perfect Resume**
THIRD EDITION

Susan Ireland

0-02-864440-9
$14.95

Buying and Selling a Home
FOURTH EDITION

Shelley O'Hara and Nancy D. Lewis

1-59257-120-4
$18.95

Low-Carb Meals

Lucy Beale and Sandy G. Couvillon, M.S., L.D.N., R.D.

1-59257-180-8
$18.95

Calculus

W. Michael Kelley

0-02-864365-8
$18.95

More than *450 titles* in *30 different categories*
Available at booksellers everywhere

ALPHA